MORAL ISSUES IN MENTAL RETARDATION

Moral Issues in Mental Retardation

Edited by Ronald S. Laura
and Adrian F. Ashman

CROOM HELM
London • Sydney • Dover, New Hampshire

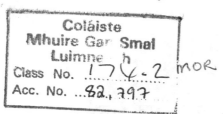
© 1985 Ronald S. Laura and Adrian F. Ashman
Croom Helm Ltd, Provident House, Burrell Row,
Beckenham, Kent BR3 1AT
Croom Helm Australia Pty Ltd, First Floor,
139 King Street, Sydney, NSW 2001, Australia

British Library Cataloguing in Publication Data

Moral issues in mental retardation.
1. Mentally handicapped
I. Laura, R.S.   II. Ashman, Adrian F.
362.3   HV3004
ISBN 0-7099-1692-2

Croom Helm, 51 Washington Street, Dover,
New Hampshire 03820, USA

Library of Congress Cataloging in Publication Data
Main entry under title:

Moral Issues in Mental Retardation.

1. Mental Retardation—Moral and Ethical Aspects—
Addresses, Essays, Lectures. I. Laura, R.S. (Ronald S.)
II. Ashman, A.F. (Adrian F.)
RC570.M57   1985   362.3'8   84-29329
ISBN 0-7099-1692-2

Printed and bound in Great Britain by
Biddles Ltd, Guildford and King's Lynn

CONTENTS

Acknowledgements
Preface
Contributors

ACKNOWLEDGEMENTS

To the many people who have assisted, encouraged, and contributed to this volume, we express our gratitude. Without the secretarial assistance of Ms. Pam Kristenson, Ms. Mary Stroud, Ms. Gai Gardner, and Mrs. Margaret Dicker, it is difficult to see how the preparation of the manuscript could otherwise have been brought to fruition. We express also our thanks to our friends at Croom Helm for their confidence in undertaking to publish this volume and for their patience in awaiting its completion. Finally, we owe a great debt to our wives. They have been constantly supportive and understanding of the intellectual indulgences which led to the production of the book, and it is they who in consequence deserve a portion of whatever praise those indulgences may yield.

PREFACE

It has been our intention in producing this book to
provide the opportunity for philosophical reflection
on the much neglected topic of moral issues in
mental retardation. The material included in this
anthology will be of value not only to those
students and professionals who work in the area, but
to all individuals concerned with the evaluative
problems of technology and medicine which currently
confront our culture. We do not pretend to have
exhausted the important questions or to have treated
them with the thoroughness they deserve. If our
pedagogical efforts have served to foster an
increased awareness of the moral dimensions of the
decisions made in the service of mental retardation,
however, we shall with pleasure regard the book as
tolerably successful.

R.S.L. and A.F.A.

In memory of our beloved fathers who would so have delighted in the delight we have taken in the production of this volume. In appreciation of their profound influence and love.

CONTRIBUTORS

Adrian F. Ashman is a Lecturer in Education and in Psychology at the Univerity of Newcastle, Australia. Dr. Ashman's current research interests concern the cognitive skills of retarded persons, notably in the area of planning and decision-making, and in issues relating to the normalisation of handicapped people. He has published widely in the area of individual differences in cognition and is the co-editor of <u>Mental Retardation: Facts and Issues</u> (1978), and <u>The Education and Training of the Mentally Retarded: Recent Advances</u> (1984).

Michael Bayles is Director of the Westminister Institute for Ethics and Human Values, Westminister College, and Professor of Philosophy at the University of Western Ontario, London, Canada. Previously, he taught at the University of Idaho, Brooklyn College of the City University of New York, and at the University of Kentucky. He is the author of numerous articles on ethics, bioethics and political and legal philosophy, including "Sterilization of the Retarded: The Legal Precedents", <u>Hastings Centre Report</u> (1978). Professor Bayles' books include <u>Principles of Legislation</u> (1978), <u>Morality and Population Policy</u> (1980), <u>Professional Ethics</u> (1981), and <u>Reproductive Ethics</u> (1983).

R.S. Downie was educated at the Universities of Glasgow and Oxford and has been Professor of Moral Philosophy at Glasgow University since 1969. Particularly interested in the Philosophy of Medicine and the Philosophy of Social Work, his book publications include <u>Roles and Values</u> (1971) and <u>Caring and Curing: Philosophy of Medicine and Social Work</u> (1980).

Susan C. Hayes is a Senior Lecturer in Behavioural
Sciences in Medicine at Sydney University,
Australia and Honorary Psychologist in the
Department of Paediatrics at Westmead Centre,
New South Wales, Australia. Her specific
interests include legal and ethical issues in
medical practice; and mental retardation and
the law. She is senior author of "Mental
Retardation: Law, Policy and Administration"
and "Simply Criminal". She is active in
programmes to establish group homes for
mentally retarded adults.

Dr R.F. Khan read Philosophy at St. Xavier's
College, Bombay, and King's College, London.
He taught Philosophy at the University of
Singapore until 1965 and is currently a Senior
Lecturer at Monash University.

Jacquelyn Ann K. Kegley received her M.A. Summa Cum
Laude from Rice University in 1964 and her
Ph.D. from Columbia University in 1971. She is
Professor of Philosophy and Chair of the NEXA
Sciences and Humanities Convergence Program,
The California State University and Colleges,
at the Bakersfield campus. She is co-author of
Introduction to Logic and editor of and
contributor to A New Challenge to the
Educational Dream: The Handicapped and the
Humanistic Delivery of Services to Families in
a Changing and Technological Age. She
delivered an invited lecture to the Royal
Institute of Philosophy in January, 1982.

John Kleinig M.A., Ph.D., B.D. is Senior Lecturer in
Philosophy at Macquarie University, New South
Wales, Australia. He was educated at the
University of Western Australia and Australian
National University. He has held several
visiting appointments at other institutions,
including the University of Arizona and
Westminster Institute for Ethics and Human
Values (Canada), and is currently (from
September, 1984) a Fulbright Scholar at the
John Jay College of Criminal Justice (CUNY), as
Visiting Professor of Criminal Justice Ethics.
Among his publications are four books,
Punishment and Desert (1973), Philosophical
Issues in Education (1982), Paternalism (1984),
and Ethical Issues in Psychosurgery (forth-
coming), and some fifty articles. His next
major project is a monograph on The Value of
Life.

Ronald S. Laura was educated at the Universities of

Harvard, Cambridge, and Oxford and has taught at the Massachusetss Institute of Technology and Harvard University. Since 1979, he has been Professor of Philosophy of Education at the University of Newcastle, Australia, where he teaches in the Faculties of Education and Medicine. His specific interests include Bioethics and the Philosophy of Special Education. His publications include Children's Rights (1978), Ethical Issues in Undertaking Research (1979), Problems of Handicap (1980) and The Impossible Takes a Little Longer (1982).

Peter Singer was born in Melbourne in 1946 and studied Philosophy at the University of Melbourne and Oxford University. His first teaching appointment was at University College, Oxford. Since then, he has taught at New York University, La Trove University, and in his current position as Professor of Philosophy at Monash University. In addition to his position in the Philosophy Department, he was appointed recently Director of the Centre for Human Bioethics at Monash University.

George P. Smith, III is an international authority in the field of Bio-Medicine and was the Fulbright Visiting Professor of Law and Medical Jurisprudence at The University of New South Wale's Law Faculty during 1984. He has been a Professor of Law at The Catholic University Law School in Washington, D.C. since 1977 and, additionally served as an Occasional Lecturer at The School of Medicine of The Uniformed Services University of The Health Sciences in Maryland and The Catholic University School of Nursing. A former Distinguished Visiting Scholar at The Institute of Ethics, Georgetown University, Washington, D.C., and a Senior Commonwealth Fellow in Law, Science and Medicine at the Yale University Law School, and University Fellow at Columbia University as well as Visiting Fellow at Cambridge University, England, Professor Smith is currently a Special Consulting Counsel to the House Committee on Science and Technology of The United States Congress and a Consultant to The New South Wales Law Reform Commission.

Bonnie Steinbock is Assistant Professor of Philosophy at the State University of New York at Albany. Her edited volume Killing and Letting Die (1980) has provoked debate and has stimulated further philosophical exploration of difficult issues in medical ethics. She is also the author of a number of articles in ethics and bioethics in various philosophical journals.

INTRODUCTION: THE PHILOSOPHY OF SPECIAL EDUCATION

Ronald S. Laura and Adrian F. Ashman

In recent decades considerable interest has been expressed in the wide range of moral issues provoked by the practice of medicine and the biomedical research underpinning it. Prodded by a seemingly endless chain of technological innovations in medicine, philosophical contributions to the area have served to ensure a lively and extensive debate. Despite the accumulation of an increasingly influential literature in bioethics, it is surprising that so little work has been done on the bioethical and associated philosophical problems in the discipline of Special Education. As far as we are aware, the first attempt to establish the Philosophy of Special Education as a distinct and legitimate area within the discipline of Special Education was represented by Professor R.S. Laura's Problems of Handicap, published in 1980. In this anthology professional philosophers were gathered for the first time to reflect upon and to examine systematically the panoply of issues arising out of Special Education and in respect of the individuals of which it treats. The present volume is concerned to advance the Philosophy of Special Education one step further by continuing the tradition set by Problems of Handicap. In order to keep the anthology within manageable bounds, however, we have confined the scope of the discussions to philosophical issues of mental retardation. The topics within this volume are nonetheless various, as is the nature of the preferred philosophical treatments of them.

For those who may be unfamiliar with the philosophical orientation, it may be instructive to note at the outset a few of the idiosyncrasies that characterize much of philosophical thinking. There is first the traditional distinction between 'descriptive ethics' and 'philosophical ethics'. Descriptive ethics views morality essentially as a kind of socio-cultural data in need of explanation. The objective of descriptive ethics is to ascertain, for example, what moral views people actually hold or claim to hold, and to provide causal accounts of the origins of the actually existing morality of those people in relation to their sub-community or larger culture. A sociologist, for instance, would be inclined to regard one's religious background as a factor relevant to the explanation of one's anti-abortionist stance.

In contrast to descriptive ethics, philosophical ethics is not concerned primarily to determine whether this or that moral belief is accepted or universal, but to determine whether this or that moral belief should be accepted or can be justified. The emphasis is not upon what ethical beliefs we hold, but upon whether it is ethical or right to hold them and to act in accordance with them. There was a time in the history of our race, for example, when slavery was held to be right by vast numbers of people, perhaps even by the majority, but from the fact that vast numbers of people held that slavery was acceptable, it did not follow that they were justified in their belief or that they were ethical in its social implementation.

Students of philosophy are sometimes confused in undertaking discussions of philosophical ethics, because philosophers tend to conflate matters of applied or normative ethics, matters of what people ought to do, that is, with the analysis of the concepts and reasoning processes which figure in such decisions. The reason for this confusion is that the philosophical discussion of ethics often involves doing two things at once. On the one hand, philosophical ethics makes recommendations on the justifiability or acceptability of a course of action, while on the other engaging in a technical discussion of basic moral principles and their appropriate analysis. One way of viewing these proceedings is to see that what appear to be two different activities are really just two different aspects of the same activity. Normative judgements about the ethical views we should hold and in terms of which we should act are parasitic or dependent upon the reliability of the basic moral principles by appeal to which we decide which course of action is preferable. Once this point is appreciated, it is easier for those approaching the subject for the first time to grasp the point of the philosopher's

use of analogy and hypothetical test cases.
Conjecture is the way in which the philosopher
explores the scope and limits of moral concepts and
moral reasoning; it also reflects one way in which
our moral intuition and our moral sensibilities can
be enhanced and informed in the very course of
discussion.

Concerned to emancipate our moral reasoning
from an unyielding commitment to the principle of
equal rights for all, Professor M.D. Bayles argues
that the equal rights principle, if applied
consistently, may actually impede rather than
facilitate justice. Cognizance of this asymmetry is
particularly important in the case of persons with
mental handicaps, as they or their advocates argue
that it is the principle of equal rights to which
society should adhere in the formulation of
legislation, etc. on their behalf. Mentally
handicapped persons, in other words, should be
entitled to the same rights as persons without
mental handicaps. Without questioning the
presumption that retarded persons are entitled to
equal rights, Bayles argues that the equal rights
principle does not provide a morally satisfactory
basis for the determination of society's
responsibilities to the mentally handicapped. He
tries to show that in addition to the assurance of
equal rights with so-called normal persons, persons
with mental handicap are entitled to special
considerations which flow from the special duties
and obligations which society has to them.

In the first section of his chapter Bayles is
concerned to determine the extent to which the equal
rights argument can be coherently articulated
without discriminating unjustly against mentally
handicapped persons. In the second section of the
chapter he illustrates the practical difficulties of
trying to apply the equal rights principle on behalf
of mentally handicapped persons in the context of
employment without discriminating against them. In
his third and final section he sketches a
justification for the implementation of a social
policy to ensure 'a life of basic satisfaction' for
all people who through no fault of their own would
otherwise be unable to do so.

In Chapter Two, Professor R.S. Downie tries to
make explicit the ambivalence implicit in the
attitude we adopt towards the mentally retarded. On
his view it is the principle of 'respect for
persons' that motivates and guides the care provided
to mentally handicapped people. There are

3

difficulties both of a practical and theoretical kind, however, in the application of this principle, since individuals with mental handicaps possess some but lack other of the attributes logically associated with the concept of 'person'. The attendant ambivalence is manifest not only in our moral attitudes towards the mentally retarded, but also in the way in which we understand and proffer explanations of their behavior.

This being so, Downie argues that sympathetic insights drawn from our understanding of so-called 'normal persons' are often misleading in their extensions to the mentally retarded. The basic reason for this 'failure of fit' results first from the fact that the behavior patterns of normal persons are simply not the same as those of the mentally retarded and second, from the inability of otherwise normal persons to project themselves empathetically inside the behavior patterns displayed by the mentally retarded. Downie attempts to show also that the causal model of understanding fares equally badly in the scenario.

In his concluding section Downie urges that it is literature which can assist in the education and guidance of those responsible for the care of mentally retarded persons. It does so, he suggests by encouraging sympathies of the 'empathetic kind', capable of perceiving real needs, by helping those who care for the retarded to understand their own emotional conflicts, and by stimulating moral questions appropriate to the task in which they are engaged.

The perils of de-institutionalisation is the theme taken up in Chapter Three by Dr Susan Hayes. Nowithstanding society's current justification of de-institutionalisation on economic and philosophical grounds, the move away from institutional living is essentially a negative goal, a move away from what is believed to be an uneconomical and inhumane situation. The difficulty, Hayes points out, is that the negative goal motivation away from institutions does not in itself secure in the community the positive provision of the essential services and continued assistance appropriate to the care of persons with mental handicaps. Without adequate support facilities in the community, de-institutionalisation collapses into re-institutionalisation. Retarded persons thus confront the situation in which their transition to the community is ephemeral. Their community sojourn is sandwiched between the move from one type of institution to another, from health services, for example, to corrective services. Hayes explores the perils of de-institutionalisation and the ethical issues surrounding it.

In his chapter "Mental Retardation and Paternalist Control" Dr Russi Kahn considers the problem (or whole tangle of problems) attendant upon the paternalist exercise of control over the mentally retarded. The justification of paternalism in the case of the mentally retarded has often been couched in terms of its necessity for the prevention of harm to themselves. Although Kahn concedes that paternalistic restraints in these terms may be justified in regard to the severely retarded, it is not at all clear that the same argument can be legitimately extended to the case of the mildly mentally retarded. While it is to be admitted that without paternalist control even the mildly retarded would face more hazards than their so-called 'normal counterparts', it does not follow that paternalism provides the most effective way of promoting their interests. By overriding and suppressing the autonomy of retarded persons, paternalism is by its very nature inimical to their good in any essential sense. The alternative to paternalistic tutelage is, Kahn urges, counselling coupled with compensatory provisions, and it is to the elaboration of these matters that he turns his attention in the last section of his chapter.

Chapter Five takes up the question of psychosurgery, and Dr John Kleinig skillfully explores the relevant issues. Although psychosurgery is an organic therapy designed to alleviate certain chronic psychiatrically defined disorders, its varied applications raise a number of important ethical concerns that can easily escape our notice. Contrary to popular belief, the use of psychosurgery is not confined to medical efforts to ameliorate chronic psychiatric disorders. Recent studies have shown that a significant proportion of psychosurgical operations have been performed on mentally retarded persons. Kleining also reports that psychosurgery is sometimes employed as a substitute for more standard forms of care for the retarded, not readily available in certain countries or places. The situation is complicated by the fact that in certain circumstances mentally retarded persons exhibit behavioral disturbances of such a radical kind that without psychosurgery, or so it is alleged, they would otherwise be rejected by their family, thus removing the only source of care available to them. In this chapter Kleining considers the question of the extent to which psychosurgery can legitimately be employed as a technique for behavioral management.

The next chapter in the anthology is by Professor Peter Singer who takes up the question of whether we can compare the value of one human life against another. To assume, for example, that the life of a severely and irreparably mentally retarded human being is of comparable value to the life of an otherwise normal human being, is, on Singer's view, misguided and gives rise to serious ethical dilemmas. One such dilemma with which he is here concerned is the case of the child born with gross mental defects who is kept alive despite the wishes of the parents to the contary. According to Singer, the value of a life, human or otherwise, depends upon the characteristics it possesses, not the species to which it belongs. That a child is a member of the species homo sapiens is not in itself morally relevant to the decision whether it is to be kept alive. Singer urges the systematic development of a system of ethics sufficient to afford discrimination on the basis of the quality of life enjoyed by a being rather than on its alleged sanctity.

A contrasting position to that put by Singer is proposed in Chapter Seven by Professor Bonnie Steinbock who challenges the view that there would be no ethical impropriety in a society which, in accordance with the wishes of parents, failed to provide life-saving medical treatment to a child born severely defective mentally. Steinbock finds the distinction between 'human beings' and 'persons' unacceptable as a basis for adjudicating the value of lives. In order to establish the conceptual domain of her own position in contrast to Singer and other philosophers of similar intellectual persuasion, she uses the recent and controversial case of Baby Jane Doe to explore a range of engaging legal and ethical issues. In the end she does not deny that infanticide is never permissible. Her main point is that although an infant cannot, in the required sense, be regarded as a 'person', it is nonetheless ethically encumbant upon us to treat it as if it were a person. The issue of whether the severely and irreparably retarded should live or die thus reduces on her view to the question of whether life or death is in their best interest.

Chapter Eight, Professor George P. Smith, III follows up the question of life/death decisions concerning infants born with severe mental defects. On his view recent posturing by the United States government in an effort to protect the lives of defective newborns has served only to complicate hopelessly the relevant decision-making processes. The question whether to maintain the life of an infant born with severe mental handicaps depends upon a complex melange of interests, not simply upon the interests of the infant. Relying heavily upon a decision-making model which emerged from the Sheffield Children's Hospital Study in England in the 1970s, he uses the classical doctrine of triage to construct a practicable framework of deliberation for the medical maintenance of defective infants. Triage obliges he claims, recognition of the complex web of factors which have to be weighed in cases such as that of Baby Jane Doe, amongst which fundamental economic principles (e.g., cost benefit analysis) figure prominently. The criteria for resolution ultimately proportion two elements on the scale of justice. On the one side is the economic cost or disutility of maintaining 'aggressive modalities of treament', while on the other is the degree of good or social utility that results from their being thus maintained.

In Chapter Nine, Professor Jacquelyn Ann Kegley is concerned to examine the impact of genetics on our understanding of mental retardation and to highlight some of the ethical issues arising therein. The chapter begins with an instructive review of the biochemical bases of the genetic diseases which cause mental retardation, discussing also some of the available genetic techniques for its treatment and prevention. Consideration is given to the ongoing debate about the extent to which genetic constitution or environmental factors determine the life-forms on this planet. The complexity of decision-making with which we are confronted stems from this debate, she suggests, in combination with the conjectural nature of current biomedical research in the area.

Kegley observes that the essentially 'private' character of reproductive decisions has been transformed by technological developments which are themselves social, not private, in character. Conflicts emerge between the rights of individuals and the rights of communities in respect of personal autonomy and social obligation. How does society allocate its scarce health resources when the allocation involves a conflict between individual and community interests? She opts for the broadest possible educational opportunities on matters of genetic disease and the ethical complexities to which it gives rise.

In Chapter Ten, Professor Ronald Laura begins by rehearsing recent developments in genetics that have transformed biology into molecular biology and the science fiction of control over human evolution into a reality, both wondrous and frightening. Citing the discovery of recombinatory D.N.A. as a revolution in the history of science, he argues that our newly discovered capacity to manipulate the evolutionary future of every life-form on this planet gives rise to a panoply of philosophical issues of staggering complexity. Indeed, it has been suggested by some of the most eminent scientists that genetic manipulation of foetal babies would serve to guarantee a healthy and genetically more desirable population. So why not pre-program our species to screen out genetic abnormality? This is the question mainly addressed in this chapter.

The question of the scope and limits of these alterations and the reason for them are among the most pressing issues of our time. Concerned to show that we can only accept the challenge of our times if we know what that challenge entails, Professor Laura argues that we have unwittingly technologized our ethics in a way that begs the question in favour of technology. We have accepted the possibility of genetic manipulation at the expense of social reconstruction. The time has come, he believes, to redress that balance. He is convinced that this will not happen unless the issues are set in the context of the public forum where informed and ongoing reflection is possible.

In the concluding chapter Laura and Ashman emphasize the importance of the continued development of Philosophy of Special Education as an area of study within Special Education itself. Without an awareness of the philosophical assumptions underpinning our educational theories, we unwittingly deprive ourselves of the opportunity to reflect critically upon the implications of their development, use, and ethical significance. In our understandable haste to grapple with the urgent problems confronting special education, we must not lose sight of the ethical concerns that inspire and result from our grapplings. The authors are concerned to remind the reader of the work yet to be done in this area, and conclude by synthasizing certain of the ethical considerations brought to relief in the contributions to the volume.

Chapter One

EQUAL HUMAN RIGHTS AND EMPLOYMENT FOR
MENTALLY RETARDED PERSONS

Michael D. Bayles

Many handicapped persons and their advocates
argue simply for equal rights with nonhandicapped
persons. After years of having fewer rights than
others, they believe that equal rights will provide
a sufficient basis for social policies. But are
equal rights enough? Or do handicapped people also
need special rights which nonhandicapped people do
not have? If so, is a claim to special rights
compatible with the claim to equal rights? After
presenting a strong argument for equal rights, this
paper discusses the limitations of basing all policy
on equal rights, and suggests a supplemental basis
of duties.

As an important example of the difficulties of
basing policy solely on equal rights, this paper
focuses on equal human rights of persons living with
the handicap of mental retardation and their
implications for employment. Mental retardation is
here understood to be a complex characteristic
consisting of: (1) significantly subaverage general
intellectual functioning; and, (2) deficits in
adaptive behaviour which are; (3) manifested during
the developmental period.[1]

Many mentally handicapped persons are not
retarded, because they have normal intelligence.
Similarly, persons with subnormal intelligence who
do not manifest it during the developmental period
are not classified as retarded. Subnormal
intelligence can, for example, result from disease
or injury later in life. In North America, it is
estimated that about three percent of the population
is mentally retarded. However, the adaptive aspect
of its definition makes mental retardation at least
partly relative to society. As society becomes more
complex, more people of lower intelligence have
difficulty adapting. Thus, mental retardation might

become a more significant problem as society becomes more technologically and socially complex.

One must be clear about the definition of human rights. They are a subset of moral rights. As such, they must be distinguished from legal and social rights which must be legislated or recognized. To exist, human rights do not have to be legally or socially recognized. Indeed, one reason for asserting human and other moral rights is to gain legal or social acceptance. This is, however, not to say that all legal and social rights correspond to moral rights. Some are simply created as a matter of policy or efficiency, such as the right in the United States but not Canada for persons to deduct mortgage interest from their taxable income.

Human rights are those moral rights which all, or almost all, persons have, independent of their previous conduct or social position. Moreover, human rights are inalienable in that one cannot lose them or sell them to others. While inalienable, human rights are not absolute; that is, they do not necessarily always override other considerations.

Like all rights, the force or cutting edge of human rights lies in their imposing obligations on others. If human rights did not impose obligations on others, recognizing them would not be important. The right to life, for example, is important because it imposes an obligation on others not to kill. Sometimes it is unclear who has the obligations corresponding to human rights, but usually it is governments, everyone, or both.

These features of human rights make their advocacy desirable for those who speak on behalf of retarded persons. As human rights do not depend on previous conduct or social position, retarded persons do not have to show that they have earned them. As they are inalienable, retarded persons will not lose them. They are thus rights mentally retarded persons have equally with others. Since human rights impose obligations on others, they provide a strong basis for claims by retarded persons. Consequently, equal human rights appear to provide a strong basis for policy toward mentally retarded persons. The question is whether this basis is morally sufficient in such areas as employment.

The potential difficulties can be seen in the United Nations Declaration on The Rights of Mentally Retarded Persons. It first invokes faith in human rights. It then goes on to declare that mentally retarded persons have "the same rights as other human beings".[2] Thus, mentally retarded persons are entitled to equal rights with nonretarded persons, but not to more rights than nonretarded persons, that is, to special rights. The U.N. Declaration specifies six sets of rights of mentally retarded persons. These rights must be rights all human beings have or derivable from them, or else the claim to the same or equal rights must be abandoned.

Yet, because mentally retarded persons are especially disabled, morally adequate policies for them seem to require special considerations and rights. But if mentally retarded persons are granted special rights which nonretarded persons do not have, then they do not have the same rights. Equal rights are then not enough. Two people do not have the same or equal rights if one person has all those the other has and some additional rights. Moreover, as will be discussed, the force of the claim to equal rights undercuts the basis for claiming special rights for mentally retarded persons in areas like employment. Before discussing this point, however, it is important to see the force of an equal rights approach and why arguments of other groups, such as women and blacks, to special considerations are not plausible for mentally retarded persons.

NONDISCRIMINATION

To see the power of the equal rights approach, one must consider it as a counter to the history of discrimination against mentally retarded persons. Mentally retarded persons have been denied the rights to work, to procreate, to marry, to attend schools, and to live in the community. The assertion of equal rights forcefully denies that mental retardation itself is a reason to discriminate against people. Mental retardation is not a characteristic which reflects on the moral worth of a person, as does, say, being vicious. The view that mentally retarded persons are disposed to immorality and crime, popular at the turn of the century, is mistaken. Moreover, not all mentally retarded persons are alike; they vary from mildly retarded persons who are a bit slow to profoundly retarded persons, some of whom are unable to feed or dress themselves or even to speak. To treat all mentally retarded persons the same and to assume

13

that all lack the capacities for jobs or any of the activities mentioned is unfair and unjust. It is comparable to denying all women certain jobs simply because most women lack the physical strength to perform them. Thus, equal rights of mentally retarded persons implies that they must be considered individually and not discriminated against simply because they are retarded.

These contentions must not be misunderstood. They do not imply that one can never deny mentally retarded persons certain social advantages, meaning legal rights and privileges, social benefits and positions. If such social advantages are denied, however, it must not be simply because an individual is mentally retarded. Instead, one must show that the individual lacks abilities necessary for exercising particular social advantages or engaging in particular activities. Furthermore, these abilities must be shown to be relevant to the specific tasks involved. If mentally retarded persons are denied consideration for employment, it should be because they lack some ability required for the positions, just as nonretarded persons are denied consideration if they lack such an ability.

In the past, requirements have often been set for positions even though they were not necessary for performing the tasks of the jobs. Because intellectual and adaptive abilities are not relevant to many rights people have, such as the right not to be tortured, mentally retarded persons ought not be denied such rights on any ground. The burden is always on those who wish to exclude a person from a social advantage such as a job, to show both that an ability is necessary for it and that an individual lacks that ability.

Many people believe that if mental retardation is not itself a justifiable ground for discrimination, then one cannot consistently try to avoid and prevent mental retardation. If mental retardation is not a basis for discrimination, how can it be an undesirable characteristic? As one author has written, "It takes considerable rhetorical agility to urge the public to support screening programs so as to prevent the conception of handicapped individuals while at the same time insisting that full respect be paid to such developmentally disabled adults as are already among us".[3] However, this problem is not as difficult as alleged.

An analogy with physical disabilities is appropriate. First, few if any people today believe

that a physical disability, such as loss of a limb,
is a reason for discriminating against a person.
Second, due to physical disabilities, some people
lack abilities necessary for certain social
advantages, such as specific jobs. Third, even
though physically disabled persons have equal rights
with nondisabled persons, physical disabilities are
undesirable. Fourth, society takes serious measures
to prevent physical disabilities due to accidents or
other causes. Parallel considerations apply to
mentally retarded persons. For instance, first,
mental retardation is not a reason for
discriminating against a person. Second, due to
mental retardation, some people lack abilities
necessary for certain social advantages, especially
many jobs. Third, mental retardation is
undesirable; no one wants to be mentally retarded.
Fourth, society takes measures to prevent mental
retardation due to drugs taken by pregnant women,
physical injury in childbirth, and gene-based
disorders such as phenylketonuria.
    Consider the problem of whether to abort
fetuses determined to have mental defects. The same
problem exists for physical as for mental defects,
but no one believes it suggests physical defects are
not undesirable. Indeed, were mental retardation
not considered undesirable, the question of aborting
affected fetuses would not arise. However, this
problem is one of the ethics of abortion rather than
mental retardation. How one resolves this issue
depends on one's view of abortion[4], not one's view
of the desirability of mental retardation.
    Thus far, the argument for the equal rights of
mentally retarded persons is impressive and sound.
However, it has a disturbing implication. The
argument has been that denying persons social
advantages because they are mentally retarded
violates their equal rights. But if the claim to
equal rights implies that it is wrong to
discriminate against persons because they are
mentally retarded, it also seems to imply that it is
wrong to discriminate in their favour (give
preferential treatment) in employment and other
areas because they are mentally retarded. Mental
retardation itself should be morally irrelevant, a
basis for neither unfavourable nor favourable
treatment. How can one say that mental retardation
is irrelevant when people are denied social
advantages, but relevant for awarding social
advantages? Thus, the claim to equal rights
undercuts claims to additional special rights

15

because people are mentally retarded.

A similar and much discussed problem has arisen with respect to preferential treatment of women and blacks in employment and education. However, the reasons often offered for preferential treatment of women and blacks are not applicable to mentally retarded persons. One argument for preferential treatment of women and blacks is that it compensates for past discrimination. An underlying premise is that one day all the handicaps due to previous discrimination will be gone, and then special social advantages will no longer be justified. Any job related handicaps they suffer are due to inadequate education and employment experience; remove these and they will be equally capable. Unfortunately, one cannot foresee the day when the handicaps of persons who are mentally retarded will disappear, for that simply amounts to eliminating mental retardation.

A second argument has been that discriminating on the basis of a characteristic (for example, being female, black, or mentally retarded) is wrong only if the discrimination indicates people are second-class citizens, stigmatizes them as inferior, or denies them significant participation in social life.[5] The crucial difficulty in applying this principle to mentally retarded persons is that any program which singles them out, even for preferential treatment as in sheltered workshops, is almost certain to stigmatize them as inferior. Many persons have suggested that selecting blacks and women for preferential treatment indicates they are inferior or they would not need special advantages, and labelling theory makes this claim even more likely to be true for mentally retarded persons.

A further consideration is that preferential treatment for mentally retarded persons is unfair to nonretarded persons who might equally benefit from special programs. For example, persons whose general intellectual functioning is not low enough to qualify them as mentally retarded might benefit from special job training or other employment advantages as much as those who are mentally retarded. Other people with sufficiently sub-average intelligence are not mentally retarded because their deficit was not manifest during the developmental period. In short, mental retardation is not a characteristic which determines a unique class of persons who can benefit from special social advantages, so its use as a basis for awarding them is unfair.

The appeal of the equal rights approach is the strong argument it provides against discriminating against people because they are mentally retarded. But on the equal rights approach, just as mental retardation is not a morally relevant basis for denying people social advantages, it cannot be a morally relevant basis for awarding them. Yet, to develop their potential, mentally retarded persons need special social advantages, advantages others do not need. If the equal rights approach is to support special considerations for mentally retarded persons, it must be on the basis of what is involved in the rights themselves.

RIGHTS AND SPECIAL EMPLOYMENT ADVANTAGES

To determine whether equal rights can justify special social advantages for mentally retarded persons, as in employment, the nature of rights must be more precisely considered. To have a right is to have a valid claim or entitlement against one or more persons to some condition. To be precise about rights, one must specify who has the right, against whom it is held, and to what condition. There is no problem in specifying who has the rights: all retarded persons. Those against whom the rights are held are those people who have corresponding obligations.. As noted earlier, for human rights these obligations are either everyone or governments. For present purposes, the most important consideration is precisely specifying to what the rights entitle one.

Rights can be to either of two types of conditions. One can either have a right to some desirable condition or state of affairs, or to have an opportunity to bring about such a condition or state of affairs. Rights to the existence of some states of affairs can be called 'outcome rights', and rights to bring about those states of affairs can be called 'opportunity rights'. For example, a right to adequate housing is a right actually to have adequate housing. In contrast, a right to sexual freedom is to an opportunity to have sexual intercourse, not actually to have it.

The distinction between outcome and opportunity rights is not the same as that between positive and negative rights. The latter are usually distinguished by whether others are obligated actually to perform an action or only to refrain from action. There are significant difficulties in

17

distinguishing rights on this basis.[6] The distinction above is based on what the rightholder obtains, not on what others must do. Thus, others might have to act to provide persons opportunities and might only need to refrain from actions for persons to have outcomes.

One might think that because all rights depend on being exercised, they are really all opportunity rights. They provide the opportunity to bring about a state of affairs by exercising a right. However, the difference between outcome and opportunity rights exists even when the rights are exercised. To exercise a right is to call for the fulfillment of the corresponding obligations. Many rights, such as that not to be physically struck, are assumed to be continually exercised unless explicitly waived by consenting to be touched. Both outcome and opportunity rights can be exercised or waived. However, when they are exercised, they are still different. A right to adequate housing is to having that housing, not to an opportunity to buy or rent it; and an exercised right to sexual intercourse is still only to an opportunity for it.

If rights are to outcomes, then equal rights can justify special social advantages for mentally retarded persons. For example, the equal right of mentally retarded persons not to be defrauded might require programs, such as those providing special guardians, to assist them in protecting their interests.[7] To provide equal protection against fraud to mentally retarded persons requires special efforts. The provision of health care, especially mental health, provides an additional example. Programs to train psychiatrists specially for work with mentally retarded persons and to ensure that they are available through regular mental health facilities might be required to provide mentally retarded persons the same mental health care as nonretarded persons. In these cases, the special social advantages are required to fulfill equal rights to the same outcome. They are not based on people being mentally retarded, but on the ground that special effort is needed to provide the same outcome. Others, such as children, who also need special assistance to achieve the outcome, are also entitled to it. Thus, equal rights can provide a basis for some special social advantages for mentally retarded persons.

However, if rights are to opportunities, then equal rights of mentally retarded and nonretarded persons cannot justify special social advantages for retarded persons. Opportunity rights are only to chances to try to bring about desirable conditions. For example, an equal right to live in a neighbourhood does not guarantee that one can live there. If an individual lacks the money to purchase a house or to pay the rent in that neighbourhood, the person is not entitled to extra income to be able to afford to live there. Thus, since the right to live in a neighbourhod is simply an opportunity right, equal opportunity rights will not justify special modifications of zoning laws for mentally retarded persons. Mentally retarded persons obtain opportunities which others do not have if zoning for single family dwellings contains an exception allowing multiple dwelling units for mentally retarded persons. To justify such exceptions, one must assert that mentally retarded persons have an outcome right to live in a neighbourhood, while other persons have only an opportunity right. These are not the same rights; they are unequal rights.

This difference between outcome and opportunity rights is especially important with respect to employment. Principle 3 of the U.N. Declaration on the Rights of Mentally Retarded Persons states that a mentally retarded person "has a right to perform productive work or to engage in any other meaningful occupation to the fullest possible extent of his capabilities".[8] This does not mean that mentally retarded persons have rights to jobs for which they lack relevant capabilities. Does it, however, mean (1) that they have an opportunity right to jobs, or (2) that they have an outcome right to jobs using their capacities to their fullest? If the latter interpretation is taken, then retarded persons have a right which nonretarded persons lack. "Normal" people do not have a right to a job making full use of their capacities. Indeed, it is unclear whether they even have a human right to a job, for the article of the U.N. Declaration of Human Rights which specifies a right to work[9], also asserts a right to protection against unemployment.[10] As another right guarantees security in the event of unemployment[11] it is doubtful the protection is from unemployment but rather from the hardships consequent to it. Consequently, on this interpretation, mentally retarded persons are not receiving equal rights, but special rights and social advantages which others lack.

Moreover, if one interprets the right to work as an outcome right, one must carefully specify the outcome. The U.N. Declaration suggests that it

BAYLES

would be to a job using one's capacities to the fullest, which is certainly a right others lack. However, one could simply specify it as to a job. Perhaps other people also have such a right[12], but on this interpretation the right is fulfilled no matter the nature of the job. Thus, a sheltered workshop or a janitorial job in one's own residence for ten cents an hour would fulfill the right. Finally, one might specify the job as requiring certain minimal levels of skills and wages, but any plausible level would mean that some nonretarded persons do not have that right.

If one interprets the right to work as an opportunity right, then mentally retarded persons are not likely to get jobs. Given the supply of unemployed nonretarded persons, retarded persons will usually fail to secure jobs because more qualified applicants will usually be hired. Of course, there are some jobs mentally retarded persons can perform as well as or better than nonretarded persons, but they are rather few. Increasing automation and computerization are likely to make them a decreasing proportion of those available.[13] In the future, most jobs will require increasing intelligence and education. Consequently, if mentally retarded persons have only an equal opportunity right to compete for jobs, the vast majority of them are probably condemned to unemployment.

One might respond that in order to enjoy an opportunity right for a job, mentally retarded persons should be provided special training so that they can compete successfully with nonretarded persons. This argument, however, faces serious problems. First, the distinction between having and enjoying rights does not help. Enjoying a right can mean either taking joy in the fact that one has the right or enjoying that to which one has the right. [14] The former is irrelevant, and the latter does not help. Are mentally retarded persons to enjoy an opportunity to compete for jobs or actually having jobs? It depends on whether the right is to an opportunity or to an outcome. Furthermore, one must distinguish enjoying a right from its value. Mentally retarded persons can enjoy an opportunity right to a job, but it might not have much value to them. Similarly, both a plumber and a journalist can enjoy a right to freedom of speech, but it will usually be more valuable to the journalist.

Second, nonretarded persons can argue that they too should receive training to develop their

20

capacities, for otherwise they are being denied equal rights. One can avoid this problem by recognizing that all persons who lack specific job related skills are entitled to special training. But if nonretarded persons also receive such training, they are again likely to be hired over mentally retarded persons. Moreover, this approach assumes that lack of ability for a job justifies special advantages to help a person acquire that ability; and that assumes that the right is to an outcome, a job, not merely to an opportunity to compete for one.

In short, there are two alternatives. Mentally retarded persons have an outcome right to a job using their capacities to the fullest, in which case they have a right nonretarded persons do not have, more than equal rights, or the job may not be meaningful. Or the right is to an opportunity to compete for a job, in which case mentally retarded persons in competition with nonretarded persons are unlikely to obtain positions often.

The question of job training is essentially one about education, and similar concerns arise about education in general. Equal rights imply that mentally retarded persons should not be denied education in regular classes simply because they are mentally retarded. Some mentally retarded persons, however, do not do well in regular school programs. Does the assertion of equal rights justify special programs such as learning disability classes and early infant stimulation programs for mentally retarded persons? The decision depends on whether a right to education is to an outcome or to an opportunity. It is not clear whether the human right to education is to an outcome or to an opportunity. The U.N. Universal Declaration clearly makes the right to higher education an opportunity right dependent upon ability, but it is not clear about the right to primary education.[15] If the right to primary education is an opportunity right, then special education programs for mentally retarded persons cannot be justified on the basis of equal rights.

If the right to primary education is an outcome right, then again one must carefully specify the outcome. If it is to the full development of a person's intellectual capacities, specially gifted persons have as much a right as mentally retarded persons to special programs. If one specifies the right as one to a certain level of intellectual ability, then retarded persons have an argument for

21

special education which gifted persons do not (except perhaps for those who are so bored with standard classes that they do not learn). Though not all retarded persons can attain a level of intellectual ability which might plausibly be established for accomplishment in primary education, this is not a major difficulty, because the corresponding obligations are nullified to the extent they cannot be fulfilled.

One might think that all these difficulties about special social advantages for mentally retarded persons could be avoided by basing rights on needs. For example, one could claim that all people who need special job training have rights to it. Unfortunately, a needs theory merely hides the problem of outcomes versus opportunities; it does not avoid it. A person always needs one thing for something else; one needs special training for a job. All the problems one hopes to avoid reappear when one specifies for what something is needed. If, for example, the ultimate goal is merely an opportunity to compete for a job, then mentally retarded persons do not need special training. If the goal is a job using capacities to the fullest, then mentally retarded persons are being accorded outcome rights which nonretarded persons do not have.

Assertions of equal rights for mentally retarded persons provide a significant base for moral policy. However, an equal rights approach fails to justify special programs for mentally retarded persons in important areas such as employment. Moreover, the equal rights argument for nondiscrimination undercuts granting mentally retarded persons special rights because they are mentally retarded. Mental retardation itself is not a morally relevant basis for denying or granting rights, and the arguments for preferential treatment of other minorities do not work for mentally retarded persons. Either equal rights are not enough, or mentally retarded persons do not have a moral basis for special social advantages such as job training which currently exist or are being advocated by mentally retarded persons and organizations concerned with their well-being. The equal rights approach promises a satisfactory life for mentally retarded persons, but it fails to justify the special programs necessary for this. Its promise is false. To provide a satisfactory life for mentally retarded persons, one must go beyond the false promise of equal rights.

BEYOND EQUAL RIGHTS

The difficulty with using equal rights alone as the moral basis for policy towards mentally retarded persons provides one specific instance of the inadequacy of basing ethics on rights alone. Another is a society in which all citizens always insist upon exercising their moral and legal rights. Such a society would be morally deficient. For example, it would be morally worse if creditors always insisted upon foreclosing on delinquent debtors. On the other hand, a society in which all citizens only respected the rights of others would also be morally deficient.[16] It would lack the kindness and helpfulness morally appropriate towards others but not required by their rights.

At least two other moral categories are necessary to supplement rights. (1) Some duties are not based on rights. For example, the duties to aid people in need and to prevent avoidable suffering (even of animals) do not necessarily correspond to rights of those in need or suffering. (2) Conduct can be morally desirable but not ethically required by a duty or right. A person has no duty to be kind to others, but it is clearly desirable that one act kindly.

Rights theory is an individualistic basis for obligations because rights provide individuals with a basis for demanding outcomes or opportunities. Moral duties can also be founded on collective social policies. There is a moral duty to pursue morally justified policies. The choices of programs for fulfilling the policies are discretionary; choices must be made in the priority of policies and methods of fulfilling them. Once programs are adopted, then specific legal and social rights are created. However, these rights are not founded on moral rights but on the programs which promote the policies. For example, the policy of economic development does not dictate grants to high technology companies or a twenty percent capital gains tax, but once these programs are adopted, qualifying companies and individuals have rights to grants or lower taxes.

Moral principles are those which almost all rational persons would accept for governing people's conduct in a society in which they expect to live. [17] People must be rational in determining both what they desire and what principles imply. It is not irrational for people to have a concern for other people, even if it is limited benevolence and

23

not as great as their concern for themselves. Indeed, a failure to have any benevolent concern for others is often a sign of mental disorder.

On this basis, one can justify a moral principle which supports many special social advantages for mentally retarded persons. The difficulties and problems that mentally retarded persons confront in society are not restricted to them. As pointed out above, persons can have intellectual or adaptive deficits without being mentally retarded. It is not safe to assume that one will never confront these problems because one is not mentally retarded. Illness or injury can put one in a similar condition. Thus, a rational person has good reasons for both self-interest and limited benevolence to accept the following principle: There is a moral duty to pursue a policy of assisting all persons to achieve a life of basic satisfaction if, through no fault of their own, they cannot achieve such an existence without assistance. [18]

This principle provides a basis for special social advantages for all handicapped persons, including mentally retarded ones. It does not, however, specify the means for doing so or which people should be assisted first. Thus, it does not indicate whether priority should go to structurally unemployed, mentally ill, physically handicapped, elderly, or mentally retarded persons. Moreover, the questions of specific programs (for instance, sheltered workshops, housing facilities, and so on) are a matter of choice. They cannot be claimed as a matter of moral right. They certainly cannot be claimed as a matter of equal rights, because the principle applies only to persons handicapped through no fault of their own. Moreover, pursuit of this moral policy must compete with pursuit of other moral policies.

Nevertheless, the principle of assisting persons to achieve a life of basic satisfaction can support a special program of employment for mentally retarded persons and others similarly handicapped. Employment is a fundamental ingredient of a life of basic satisfaction. It is not merely or even primarily for the income it brings, but for its importance in a person's self-conception. People often identify themselves as teachers, plumbers, janitors, clerks, and so forth. Moreover, the belief that one is doing something worthwhile, contributing in some way to society, whether by making automobiles or by directing a corporation, adds meaning to life, although some jobs seem much more meaningful than others.

This importance of meaningful work to a life of basic satisfaction makes employment advantages more important for handicapped persons than other disadvantaged persons. The elderly, mentally ill, and temporarily unemployed, for example, usually either have worked or are likely to work again when their illness or economic conditions improve. But mentally retarded persons are not likely ever to work unless given special employment considerations. A program employing mentally retarded persons, perhaps by subsidizing special jobs for them, would probably not cost more than simply providing them income support without employment. Consequently, an argument can be made for special employment advantages for mentally retarded persons. It does not rest on an equal right to work; rather, it argues from a collective policy to a special program which would then confer special rights or advantages.

This general approach goes beyond claims of equal rights, because it provides a basis for assistance to some persons which need not be provided to other people. It does not dissolve into mere charity, with its connotations of paternalism and superiority of the donor, for it is based on a social duty which almost all rational persons have good reasons to accept. However, because this social duty does not specify priority of persons or the means to fulfill the policy, which special social advantages should be provided, to whom, and how, are not determined. Some of these special advantages can be provided through the government, and advocates for mentally retarded persons must pursue programs for them in competition with programs for other disadvantaged persons and other policies. Other special social advantages can be provided by voluntary organizations of people who have chosen to fulfill this duty by aiding specific groups of disadvantaged persons, such as mentally retarded ones. Some people aid elderly persons, others mentally ill persons, and so on. Individuals and groups cannot be faulted for not aiding all disadvantaged persons.

In going beyond equal rights for mentally retarded persons, the moral duty to pursue a policy of assuring a life of basic satisfaction for disadvantaged persons provides a basis for more rewarding lives for mentally retarded persons and a morally better society for everyone. Equal human

25

rights are not enough. Society can do better, and
there is a moral basis for doing so. Employment for
mentally retarded persons would be an element of
such a society.

NOTES

1.   See Maloney, M.P. & Ward, M.P. Mental
Retardation and Modern Society, New York: Oxford
University Press, 1979.
2.   Friedman, P.R. The Rights of Mentally
Retarded Persons, New York: Avon Books, 1976,
p.176.
3.   Wikler, D. "Ethical Issues in Programming
for Developmentally Disabled Adults, "Central
Conference for University Training Programs in
Developmental Disabilities, 1980, p.2.
4.   See Bayles, M.D. Reproductive Ethics
Englewood Cliffs, N.J.:   Prentice-Hall, 1984.
5.   See Fullinwider, R.K. The Reverse
Discrimination Controversy: A Moral and Legal
Analysis, Totowa, N.J.:   Rowman & Littlefield, 1980.
6.   See Shue, H. Basic Rights: Subsistence,
Affluence, and U.S. Foreign Policy, Princeton, N.J.:
Princeton   University   Press,   1980,   particularly
Chapter 2.
7.   For an elaboration of this point see
Friedman, The Rights of Mentally Retarded Persons.
8.   Ibid, p.177.
9.   See United Nations Declaration of Human
Rights, Article 23 (1) in D. D. Raphael (Ed.)
Political Theory and the Rights of Man, Bloomington,
Indiana: University Press, 1967.
10.   Ibid,
11.   Ibid, Article 25 (1).
12.   See De George, R. "The Right to Work",
Valparaiso University Law Review, 1984, 19.
13.   See Maloney & Ward, Mental Retardation and
Modern Society.
14.   See Shue, Basic Rights: Subsistence,
Affluence, and U.S. Foreign Policy.
15.   Universal Declaration of Human Rights,
Article 26.
16.   See Ladd, J. Legalism and Medical Ethics,
in J. W. Davis et al. (Ed.) Contemporary Issues in
Biomedical Ethics, Clifton, N.J.:   Humana Press,
1978.
17.   See Bayles, M.D. Principles of
Legislation, Detroit: Wayne State University Press,
1978; and Brandt, R.B. A Theory of the Good and the

Right, Oxford: Clarendon Press, 1979.
    18. See Bayles, M.D. Morality and Population Policy, University of Alabama: University of Alabama Press, 1980.

Chapter Two

AMBIVALENCE OF ATTITUDE TO THE MENTALLY RETARDED

R.S. Downie

The attitude we adopt towards mentally retarded persons is in many respects ambivalent. This paper will examine two connected aspects of this ambivalence: as it is expressed in moral attitudes, and as it affects our explanation and understanding of the behaviour of mentally retarded persons. The strategy will be to describe the moral attitude which it is thought appropriate to adopt toward people of normal intelligence, and then, to examine the ambiguities in the manner in which that attitude is directed towards mentally retarded persons. A similar plan will be adopted in the analysis of the concept of understanding. In the final section, I shall make some brief practical suggestions as to how literature can be used in training those who have to deal with the mentally retarded.

RESPECT AND THE MENTALLY RETARDED

The caring professions generally acknowledge that the fundamental moral notion governing their activities is that of respect for the individual. However, this notion is vague in many ways, and I shall therefore begin by elucidating some aspects of its logical structure and moral content. .
It should be noted that philosophers sometimes speak of 'respect for persons' as a principle, and sometimes as an attitude. The two are connected, however, and the connections are both logical and causal. If a person has a certain attitude towards something, he will necessarily adopt certain principles of action towards it, and the general nature of the principles can be inferred from knowledge of the attitude. This illustrates the logical connection. For example, if you have an

attitude of disapproval towards smoking you will necessarily not smoke on principle, will sit in non-smoking compartments, and so on. There is also a causal connection between a principle and an attitude. To act as if one has an attitude may require the establishment of a principle, which may be the necessary first step in acquiring the attitude.

If we apply this analysis to 'respect for persons as ends', we find that the expression can refer both to an attitude and to a principle of action. The attitude is <u>logically</u> basic. The principle has to be explained in terms of it; it is the principle which logically must be adopted by someone who has the attitude of respect. But, it is also <u>morally</u> basic as it includes in its scope, modes of feeling and thinking as well as of acting. That which is morally fundamental is a total quality of life rather than a principle of action in the narrow sense. Our primary task, therefore, is to attempt to characterize the attitude of respect for persons.

The most important point about an attitude (for present purposes) may be brought out if we say that an attitude is two-sided. In the first place, it must be an attitude <u>of</u> something, where 'something' is always a disposition of some sort, such as hope, fear, distrust, forbearance or the like. In the second place, attitudes must be <u>to</u> something; it is conceptually impossible for an attitude to lack an object. It will be possible to describe this object in various ways, but for any particular attitude there will be one description under which the object of the attitude must by definition fall. For example, an attitude cannot logically be one of hope unless it is to an object which is believed to be in some sense a good to the hoper.

The connexion between hope and an imagined good is thus a necessary one, and we might go as far as to say that a person could not understand the meaning of 'hope' unless he knew what it was to imagine a good, and that to imagine a good is to lay the foundation for acquiring the concept of hope. A similar analysis applies to all attitudes; they can be identified by means of the characteristics which their object is believed to possess, and thus, a belief is at the root of all attitudes. The object under the description which is implied by the attitude-name may be called the <u>formal object</u> of that attitude. For example, the <u>formal object</u> of hope is an imagined good, which may come about, and the formal object of fear is a believed danger, and so on.

What is the formal object of the attitude of respect? Of the several relevant senses of 'to respect' the one basic to 'respect for persons' is that of 'to value' or 'to esteem'. To respect persons is to value them as persons. It seems, then, that the formal object of the attitude under investigation is something like 'that which is thought valuable or estimable'; respecting something implies thinking it valuable or estimable. Thus, to understand in more detail what it means to respect persons we must find out why persons are regarded as valuable.

Why, then, do we respect or value persons? The answer must lie in those aspects of human beings which importantly distinguish them from the rest of creation. Now, there can be considerable discussion as to what these are, but they certainly include important ingredients, such as, a capacity for self-determination and a capacity for forming and pursuing ideal values. By 'self-determination' I mean adopting ends and forming policies of action to bring them about; self-determination thus goes beyond the mere having of likes and dislikes (which we may call 'liking values'), though these will form its basis. In the capacity for forming and pursuing ideals, I include of course the capacity for morality, which for Kant was the essence of uniquely human value. This Kantian doctrine is really a secularized version of the Christian conception of man alone as made in God's image and possessing a soul capable of salvation, but the realm of ideals extends beyond the scope of the moral.

It will be noted that I have not mentioned either the exercise of theoretical reason or the possession of emotions. This is so because these features, in so far as they are characteristically human, are already included in self-determination. The working out of problems, however abstract, is done at the behest of the practical reason - there is an aim involved, even if it is only the satisfaction of curiosity. That which can work out theoretical problems without a purpose of its own is not a man but a computer. Again, emotions either involve purposes and plans - for example, fear involves plans to escape or to defend oneself - or they are at the instinctive level of an animal.

One problem which arises from any attempt to isolate the common features which constitute the unique worth of human beings (what may be called

their 'distinctive endowment') is that the very
attempt seems to undermine the stress on
individuality which prompted it. If there is some
feature or features of human beings which make them
worthwhile, does it not follow that what we value is
not individual human beings but humanity in the
abstract, which can be exemplified equally well
whoever the exemplar is? Kant has sometimes written
as though humanity in the abstract is what is
valuable. However, the very nature of
self-determination and the formation of ideals
guarantees the centrality of the individual, since
the capacity for choice and commitment is in a sense
a capacity for individuality, for making one's own
decisions and plans, ungoverned by anything else.
All the same, this apparent difficulty does make it
clear that what is valuable in human beings is not
merely their possessing this capacity, which is in a
sense common property, but their individual exercise
of it.

Now I have spoken of respect for human beings,
and then gave an account of what we respect in human
beings in terms of self-determination and the
formation of ideals. However, not all human beings
possess these attributes. For instance, it is not
meaningful to attribute capacities for
self-determination and the formation of ideals to
those in terminal coma, to the senile, to the
severely mentally ill, to the mentally retarded and
to infants. Does it follow, then, that human beings
in these categories are not proper objects of the
attitude of respect or agape?

To answer this question we must consider what
is involved in exercising the attitude of respect in
the normal case.[1] First, it involves active
sympathy with their projects, the objects of their
self-determination. Sometimes this requires us to
give positive assistance, to make another person's
ends our own ends, and sometimes it means standing
back and allowing them to do what they want.
Secondly, respecting a person requires us to
recognise that an individual has values or ideals
which may differ from ours, and that in any case,
there are inter-personal moral standards which apply
to all alike, and restrict our self-determination in
the interests of all members of a harmonious and
co-operative society.

If we try to apply this analysis to the
mentally retarded (and the other difficult cases
mentioned above), we run into difficulties. For
example, we do not feel we should necessarily accede

to the wishes of a mentally retarded person, far less assist him to attain his objectives, if we believe that what the person intends is likely to harm him. It might be said that the same is true of the mentally normal. However, we can consult with the mentally normal and draw attention to the risks or drawbacks of a given project, whereas we cannot always be sure that the mentally retarded person (or the senile, or young child) understands his situation. It follows, therefore, that we ought not to allow the mentally retarded person an entirely free hand in deciding his future. This restriction is of course, a matter of degree, but it is reasonable to say that in extreme cases those without a full measure of the 'distinctive endowment' of a human being <u>ought</u> not to be given the same sort of respect accorded to a normal human being.

There is another side to this. I have claimed that active sympathy with someone's projects is an essential component of the attitude of respect in the normal case. I have pointed out also that active sympathy in the normal case sometimes requires us to stand aside and to <u>allow</u> someone to pursue his aims in his own way; it can sometimes be officious, patronising, interfering, or possessive to be 'helpful' in every instance. In the case of the mentally retarded, however, the temptation to 'help' can be overpowering. This is particularly the case within families, where there can be strong identification with the mentally retarded person and where 'pity' can become a morally inferior substitute for 'active sympathy'. Indeed, the desire to 'help' can overpower the legitimate claims of other members of the family and work to their detriment as well as to that of the mentally retarded person. Again, we are dealing with matters of degree, and there is no way of drawing a clear theoretical line between the 'active sympathy', which is a proper component in the attitude of respect, and the 'pity' which may become its pathological substitute and destroy it.

This ambivalence in the attitude of respect is a logical reflection of the ambivalence in the status of its object. Sometimes the word 'person' is used - in ordinary speech as much as in philosophical literature - to mark off those human beings who have the full complement of mental capacities. Consequently, it is not used of those who lack some or all of these capacities.[2] The word 'person' is used in this evaluative way, for example, when we say of a senile old man that he is no longer a person: "There isn't a person there any more", or we say of someone severely mentally ill, "You can't at present regard him as a person at all", or we say of an infant, "He's not really a person yet".

On the other hand, sometimes we object to this and believe intuitively that the old or the mentally handicapped are being denigrated by this terminology, that is, they are being regarded as lacking something of <u>moral</u> value because they lack some <u>natural</u> capacities. This reaction is often based simply on over-emotional response to a misunderstanding. Because a human being is not a 'person' in the semi-technical sense and is, therefore, not entitled to full 'respect' in the correlative technical sense, no one is saying that he should be treated badly, or disregarded, or in any avoidable way made to suffer. Yet, there may be something more than emotional reaction behind the resistance that some people - perhaps those especially who are involved in caring for the mentally retarded - experience when they are told that the mentally retarded are not fully persons and are, therefore, not entitled to respect in the full sense.

One way of identifying the legitimate source of this resistance is to compare our moral attitudes to animals. A great deal of our moral attitude to animals is to be stated in the principle that it is wrong to cause needless suffering. But our moral attitudes to animals cannot wholly be accounted for by referring to animal sentience; there is another important factor. Consider, for example, the repugnance that some people feel at the spectacle of the caged lion, or the over-fed poodle trimmed into a fashionable shape. Contrast such repugnance with the approval some people feel at the well-trained sheep-dog. The point is not that the caged or pampered animal is necessarily suffering - in many cases it may well be much better off than in the wild state and show no tendency to return to the wild state. It is rather that its animal nature is not being respected; it is being subjected to purposes foreign to it. In a similar way, a slave may well prefer to remain such, but we still feel that there is something morally wrong with the state of affairs which leads him to concur in his slavery. And so too, many people's moral attitude to the higher animals is moulded by their awareness that animals can have a dignity which must be respected,

even though the animals are used as means to further
human ends. This factor, along with their
sentience, seems to constitute our moral attitude to
animals. It is therefore possible to maintain that
we have moral duties to animals (duties which, as in
the cases of children and so on, are made easier to
perform by the existence of non-moral attitudes such
as affection and pity) and that these are to be
explained by means of the idea of respect for the
type of personality in question.

Applying the same idea to the mentally retarded
we can say that they retain a certain dignity, and
the morally appropriate attitude to them cannot
therefore on all occasions be simply a regard for
their sentience. But sometimes it is, and there is
therefore ambivalence in our moral attitude.

UNDERSTANDING THE MENTALLY RETARDED

Turning now to the normal case of explaining
and understanding behaviour, let us suppose that a
person says, 'I did A because I chose to do it.'
Clearly, this does not amount to an explanation so
much as a claim: 'I am responsible for this action'
or 'This action is mine'. If such a claim is made,
we can go on to ask, 'Why did you choose to do it?'
To this question a typical answer would be 'because
I wanted such-and-such', and this reply seems to
explain the action in a way in which the bare
mention of choice does not - it is informative. But
what kind of information does such explanation
provide?

To mention a desire is to show the point of a
choice or to make sense of it. For example, if we
ask why a man decided to tidy his garden and are
told that he wants to sell his house, we see the
point of his decision. The explanation sets the
chosen action in a framework: sometimes, as here, a
framework of familiar human purposes which may
itself require illumination by reference to a
further want. And this is the kind of explanation
which we are ordinarily looking for when we ask why
someone does something. I am maintaining, then,
that the only informative explanation of responsible
action is of the 'because he wanted' type, to be
construed as giving the sense or point of an action,
where 'sense' or 'point' may be understood as
referring to necessary, but not sufficient
conditions.

The task of social science in explaining

35

behaviour is that of tracing the patterns or systems of influence which shape human purposes. Some of these patterns are economic, some political, some legal, some religious or ideological, and so on. Knowledge of these frameworks is of great assistance in understanding human behaviour. In tracing the patterns into which human behaviour tends to fall, social scientists frequently use the term 'social role'. While there is no unambiguous use of the concept, far less a definition of it, it is a useful tool of social science because it can act as a bridge concept to explain the influence of society on the conduct of the individual. Thus, individuals act in society as labourers, builders, musicians, farmers, teachers, doctors, probation officers, fathers, and so on, where these terms indicate a social function.

However, while individuals act in these various roles, thus contributing to the maintenance of society, the roles in turn shape and influence the whole personality of the persons who act in them. For this reason, a knowledge of the social sciences is essential for any adequate understanding of individual action, because the influence of society is present in every individual action. Of course, while people act in social roles, they do not act just in one, and the difficulty in applying social science to human behaviour is that of knowing the relevance of the different frames of reference of the different social sciences. Nothing brings the social sciences into a greater disrepute than the pretentions of one social scientist - a Freudian psychologist, or a Marxian economist, say - to explain all human behaviour in terms of a few simplistic concepts. This can be said without at all decrying the great explanatory power of both Freudian psychology and Marxian economics. To explain or understand action then is to see it as part of a pattern of human purposes.

But a person is not just the sum total of his roles; he is a person who has these roles, who entertains various purposes. To have anything like a full understanding of action it is therefore necessary to gain some imaginative insight into how a person sees his roles, what he feels about his purposes. In other words, there is an important personal dimension to action which is not caught by the concept of a social role, and there is correspondingly an element of personal intuition in the understanding of action. Some social scientists have used the term verstehen here. It is not entirely clear what is meant by the term, but it has become the received expression for the kind of understanding of action we aim at when we try to put ourselves on the inside of actions and capture their meaning. Social work theory sometimes uses the (equally unclear) expression empathy in attempting to describe the process of understanding an action from the inside.

The difficulty with this, however, is not that these processes of verstehen or empathy do not take place, but that it is doubtful whether the sort of understanding coming out of them is properly to be called scientific. Scientific understanding is a matter of fitting events into a pattern, of tracing systematic connections. Moreover, scientific understanding is concerned with things in their generality, with the common or universal properties of things or events. The same is true of the understanding which the social sciences give of action. They are concerned with what a soldier, an entrepreneur, a dentist, might do, or they are concerned with 'people in stress situations', or the 'one-parent family'. Understanding of this kind, however important, is not the same as the sort involved when we suddenly see, or slowly come to realize, what it is for a specific individual standing in front of us, to be a soldier, or to be in a specific situation of stress. Understanding of the latter sort is concerned with actions in their particularity, with the uniqueness of situations. We might put the point differently by saying that whereas science, including social science, gives us horizontal understanding, we must in concrete situations supplement this by what we could call vertical understanding. This understanding comes from insight into a personal history. (This point is important for my claim in the final section that a study of literature is important for the education of those dealing with the mentally retarded.)

If we apply this analysis of explanation and understanding to the case of the mentally retarded person, we find uncertainties and ambiguities. First of all, the behaviour patterns are not of the same kinds as those of the mentally normal person. Secondly, it is harder in the case of the mentally retarded for the normal person to have the sympathetic insight, the verstehen, into what it is like to be on the inside of such behaviour patterns. The problems and uncertainties which thus arise in applying this model of understanding to the behaviour of the mentally retarded encourage the use of a totally different model (and one which is incompatible with the attitude of respect as I have described it) - the causal model of understanding.

The causal model of understanding incorporates the assumption that what people do is not, despite appearances, freely chosen by them but is governed by forces and factors over which they have no control. Thus, one may say to oneself 'She can't help lashing out at me like that, she's experiencing the change of life' or 'He obviously would marry very young, he's from a broken home', appealing not to any rational thought on the agent's part but to underlying causal factors seen as explaining the action. Instead of reacting spontaneously with hostility, disapproval, and so on, as would be appropriate towards a person who is responsible for his actions, a stance of detachment is taken up based on the idea 'Of course, he can't help it'. We are tempted in ordinary life to do this to avoid the strain of fully 'reactive' encounters with other people.[3]

Medical and social workers are particularly prone to the temptation to adopt this latter kind of 'objective' attitude. For example, some social workers are apt to construe everything done by a client as manifesting the workings of subconscious complexes of one kind or another. Others, of a different persuasion, see what he does as manifestations of alienation, of the class struggle. Again, medical workers tend to say 'You only want to do that, you only see things in that way, because you're ill. When you're well, you'll see things quite differently'. In both cases the effect is to undercut the reasons the agent himself would give for his action or thought and replace them by mechanisms on which the caring worker is an expert. The motivation for doing this may be, as in private life, the wish to avoid reactive encounters. But the caring worker may have no ulterior motive and may simply believe that he knows more about why his client acts as he does than the client himself. In either case, the implication is that the client is not to be regarded as a self-determining being who acts in pursuance of his own purposes.

It could be argued that to assume that such attitudes are wrong, I am begging the question against determinism, which is after all a widely held position. But this is not the case, for many determinists also would wish to reject an analysis of human action which made no reference to the wishes and purposes of the individual agent, and depicted him, not just as determined, but also as governed by forces outside his conscious control. Even those determinists who think that some forms of determinism can be reconciled with moral responsibility would have to admit that this form cannot be so reconciled.

All this may seem unreasonable to some members of the caring professions. After all, they will say, we are talking about people who are retarded and who are, therefore, governed to a more than average extent by non-rational factors. In these cases at least, whatever is to be said about 'normal' cases, we are dealing with people for whom a detached, 'objective' attitude is correct, as it would be for the psychiatrist dealing with someone who is mentally disturbed. Now, it cannot be denied that there is something in this argument, but several points must be noted in qualification of it. For example, there is always a temptation to extend this kind of attitude beyond those people, or those aspects of people, which would justify it. The temptation is there because this kind of objective is often the easier option, and can indeed seem more 'professional'. But the adoption of this attitude is hurtful when it is discovered by the recipient, or vaguely 'sensed', because the person is made to feel that he is not being taken seriously as a person. In other words, this kind of attitude, correlated with the attempt to see behaviour in causal terms, is incompatible with the moral attitude of respect, although it is compatible with pity. It can also be added that the policy of treating people as rational unless proved otherwise may have the effect of fostering rationality, which is not an all-or-nothing matter.

It is indeed the phrase 'not all-or-nothing' which constitutes the whole difficulty. Were the mentally retarded person either like or unlike the mentally normal person, the theoretical difficulties would disappear. But since there are degrees of mental retardation, there are problems about the appropriate moral attitude. There are also problems about what sort of understanding is appropriate; whether to employ the sympathetic appreciation of how behaviour fits into patterns of familiar purposes, or the causal understanding we might have when there are biochemical bases for behaviour disorders. There is, therefore, an ineradicable ambivalence in our attitudes to the mentally retarded.

THE USE OF LITERATURE IN EDUCATION

The final question I wish to consider is that of the training or guidance of those who have to deal with the mentally handicapped, whether these are parents, social workers or others. When social work moved from the stage of philanthrophy, of voluntary societies, to become a profession, those concerned were anxious that it should have its own expertise matching that of other professions. The first move was to base social work practice on the model of the psycho-analyst/patient relationship, and psychology became the main knowledge base for social work. More recently social work has turned to sociology and social administration. I do not wish to suggest that these disciplines are replaceable, for I have earlier stressed how they can provide detailed knowledge of behaviour patterns. Rather, I wish to point out that they do not provide any guidance or training in making judgments of situations of the kind which crop up for those dealing with the mentally retarded. How if at all, can such training be provided?

If at all, it can be provided by a study of literature. God forbid that literature will be studied only because it is useful, but a study of literature is _educative_ because it is able to provide insight into the particularity of situations. Whereas science, including social science, proceeds by induction from specific instances to generalized (often idealised) patterns, literature explores unique situations which may include conflicts of value of the kind discussed elsewhere in this volume, and thereby enables us to acquire insights into universal human predicaments. Study of this sort is as relevant to the career of a social worker as is the study of highly abstract systematic sociology. There is a helpful bibliography in Clare Morris' pamphlet Literature and the Social Worker.[4]

There is a surprising amount of poetry and other literature dealing with mental retardation. This is perhaps the case because the creative imagination responds to the ambiguous nature of the mentally retarded person. Thus, the 'fool' who has profound insights because of his simplicity, who remains blameless in a corrupt world, who is both comic and tragic, who inspires both possessive love and repugnance, or who is a challenge to respectable values, is an obvious source of fascination to creative writers. A study of Wordsworth's The Idiot

Boy illustrates the theoretical points I have been labouring to express with the immediate impact of poetry.[5] Again, John Silkin's poem <u>Death of a Son</u> (who died in a mental hospital, aged one) expresses more clearly than any treatise the attitudes of a parent toward the life and death of a mentally retarded child.[6]

In more detail, the study of literature - poetry, novel, drama - can be helpful to those dealing with the mentally handicapped in several different ways. To begin with, it can extend the sympathetic imagination. There are two aspects to this. The first is that whereas the social sciences dealing with mental handicap must, if they are to be sciences or respectable academic disciplines, stand back from the phenomena with which they are dealing and present their accounts in the detached prose style of science. Literature, on the other hand, characteristically involves us directly and makes us vividly and emotionally aware of what it is like to be in the situation the social scientist discusses. Literature develops our sympathies and this makes us feel something of what it is like to be a relative or to be a helper of the mentally handicapped person. It may even provide some feeling as to what is means to be handicapped. Literature therefore develops sympathy of the passive or empathetic kind. Now, passive sympathy easily generates motivation to act, and active sympathy, however well-meaning, can be blind or clumsy or humiliating unless it is informed by a sensitive understanding of particular situations or relationships. Literature has this second aspect, namely, that it can sensitise sympathy or give it a cognitive shaping. In other words, imaginative literature can develop in a helper a perception of real need.

Secondly, literature can be a help in coming to terms with the emotions and conflicts which are raised in anyone caring for the mentally handicapped. The same is true of those dealing with problems of bereavement. Questions of the meaning of life, of the tragedy and tears built into human relationships, inevitably arise in such situations and require some sort of answer if the life of professional care is to seem worthwhile. Literature can deal with these issues with an immediacy lacking in the abstractions of philosophy or social science.

Thirdly, literature generates moral questions. It is a matter for literary theorists to discuss whether literature ought to set out to be didactic, but it is in fact the case that good literature inevitably gives rise to moral questions. For example, in dramatising a particular episode literature can raise questions about the attitude of society to mental handicap in general, or it can challenge our own self-perceptions on these matters. The utilitarian cost-benefit approach to the problems of mental handicap seem plausible as presented in an academic textbook, but literature can force us to look beyond the false finality of a calculus and challenge us to refashion our attitudes. It is not that literature presents us with some unrealistic ideal, but rather that it explores for us the many facets of our ambiguous attitudes toward the mentally handicapped. When this happens, we find ourselves reconsidering the quality of our care and the nature of our social attitudes.

NOTES

1. Downie, R.S., & Telfer, E. Caring and Curing. London: Methuen, 1980.
2. Silkin, J. "Death of a Son", In K. Allott (Ed.), The Penquin Book of Contemporary Verse, Harmondsworth: Penquin Books, 1962.
3. See, for example, Strawson, P.F. "Freedom and Resentment", Proceedings of the British Academy (Vol. XLVIII), 1962; and Downie, R.S., Loudfoot, E.M., & Telfer, E. Education and Personal Relationships, London: Metheun, 1974.
4. Morris, C. Literature and Social Sciences, London: The Library Association, 1975.
5. Wordsworth, W. "The Idiot Boy", In Poetical Works of Wordsworth, London: Oxford University Press, 1959.
6. Silkin, "Death of a Son".

Chapter Three

THE ETHICS OF DE-INSTITUTIONALISATION -
AND AFTERWARDS

Susan C. Hayes

The year 1744 heralded a major change in the
care of mentally abnormal persons in England. The
Poor Law Act of 1601[1] had imposed a secular
responsibility upon local parishes to aid the poor,
but the 1744 Act[2] extended this concept and
imposed a responsibility upon the parish to care for
lunatics, the cost of confinement being charged
against the Poor Rate. Although some lunatic
hospitals and private madhouses were already
established by the late 18th century[3] these tended
to cater for the poor who were acutely insane, and
frequently, limits were placed on the duration of
treatment, after which the patient was discharged
whether sane or not.[4] An interesting feature of
the law relating to the protection of the property
of idiots and lunatics was the historical Royal
Prerogative of the King as the guardian of such
persons and wardens of their estates, with his
consequent right to the income derived therefrom as
a source of revenue.

In return the King was bound in conscience to
maintain idiots and Lunatics from the Royal
Purse.[5]

The Royal maintenance of idiots is parallelled in
the modern concepts of the State's provision of
services for mentally retarded persons and the
concomitant "right" of retarded citizens to
services.
An important development in the provision of
services for the mentally abnormal was the movement,
in the mid-19th century, to construct specialised
segregated residential institutions.

Asylums for the criminal and delinquent, for

the insane and feebleminded, and for the poor
and the orphaned became the pre-eminent
response to all forms of social disorder.[6]

Whilst it was simple to recognise and segregate
some groups (for example, convicted criminals from
non-criminals; children from adults) it was a more
difficult and lengthy process in the case of other
groups. The development of mental tests in the last
decade of the 19th century culminated in the Binet
test in 1905.[7] Despite this advance and the
establishment of special-purpose institutions (for
example, in 1872 a specialised asylum for idiots and
imbeciles was established in Newcastle in New South
Wales), mentally ill and mentally retarded patients
inhabited the same institutional sites, and
sometimes the same wards, until the present time.

Ironically, the last 500 years has seen the
care of mentally retarded persons go the full
circle. Families, villages and parishes originally
cared for their mentally abnormal members in what
would now be described as "community-based
residential services". Then, legislation imposed an
obligation upon the community to care for its
"lunatics". The Royal right to income from the
estates of mentally abnormal persons further
established an obligation of care. As communities
expanded and fragmented, caring and protection was
administered in increasingly specialised asylums.
The asylum environment in turn engendered
environments epitomising segregation,
understimulation, overprotection, and abuse. Now
that Western societies have embraced a
"community-based residential" system once more -
with the catchwords of "normalisation" and
"integration" - it remains to be seen whether the
concept of responsibility to provide care has
survived.

THE MOVE TOWARDS DE-INSTITUTIONALISATION -
THE ETHICAL AND PRAGMATIC BACKGROUND

The Principle of Normalisation
     Defined first by Nirje, the principle of
normalisation "means making available to the
mentally retarded patterns and conditions of
everyday life which are as close as possible to the
norms and patterns of the mainstream of society."[8]
This principle has been developed and applied in
Scandanavian countries for decades, and has become

widely accepted since being enthusiastically adopted by North Americans during the 1970s.

Negative Aspects of Institutions

Adoption of the principle of normalisation in the United States of America arose as a response to a number of impetuses. 'First was the dramatic effect of litigation against state agencies for the purpose of improving services for mentally retarded citizens. Landmark cases include:

1. Wyatt v. Stickney[9] in which an Alabama federal court upheld the right of residents of a state institution for mentally retarded clients to habilitation, and established detailed service standards;
2. Pennsylvania Association for Retarded Children v. Commonwealth of Pennsylvania[10], in which the court permanently enjoined Pennsylvania officials from denying or postponing provision of a free public programme of education and training to mentally retarded children in that State; and
3. Suzuki v. Quisenberry[11] which reinforced the principle that placement in less restrictive settings be considered prior to institutional commitment.

A second source of impetus for the de-institutionalisation movement arose from the nature-nurture studies (beginning in the 1930's and gathering weight in the 1950's and 1960's) which emphasised the importance of environment in the development of intelligence. Some studies report beneficial effects of institutional life, which can include increased IQ, better problem-solving ability; greater language development; and more sophisticated behavioral skills.[12] The idiosyncratic nature of the institutional environment, and possible negative characteristics of the pre-institutional environment (including family dynamics, deprivation of stimulation, nutrition, health care, violence and abuse, and educational opportunity) are significant, however, in determining whether institutional life is beneficial or harmful. The preponderance of research into the effect of institutional life indicates that institutionalised retarded people are less intelligent and less developmentally advanced than comparable groups who have not been institutionalised.[13] Lack of interpersonal and physical stimulation; little opportunity for development of a stable relationship with a care-giver; large numbers of residents; institution-oriented rather than resident-oriented rules and practices; little experience with activities of daily living (such as, cooking, housekeeping and catching public transport); and few "normal" role models are some of the features of institutional life which militate against full development of the retarded resident's potential. [14]

A third reason for the widespread acceptance of de-institutionalisation was the exposure of the degrading, inhumane and cruel conditions existing in some facilities. The Willowbrook[15] scandal in the United States in 1972 is a prime example of how public outrage added weight to the de-institutionalisation movement. Examples of institutional abuse are not confined to the United States of America, nor are they "past history". In 1982, in a New South Wales Department of Health institution for retarded persons, a young man had all of his fingernails cruelly removed, possibly by a member of staff.[16] The young man suffered physically and emotionally. Following an investigation by the Ombudsman, it was recommended that compensation be paid to the victim and his parents.

Abuse of mentally retarded people is not confined to institutions. There are case histories of retarded people being sexually or physically abused, or exploited (in terms of physical labour, or financial affairs) by their families, boarding house proprietors, and strangers in the community. Nevertheless, institutional abuse is more likely to be prolonged and widespread, and to remain undetected particularly when public access to the institution is limited. Furthermore, the value system created by the institutional staff may encourage a situation where abuse not only occurs, but is condoned or even regarded as the norm.

We have taken service workers who have tended to drift into those places where devalued people are served, who themselves may be perceived deviantly. They have often identified with devalued professional models, learned to act differently with the people they serve, have been kept in image-degrading jobs

and service settings, established all their
social ties with others in similar status and
the result has been the creation of a massive
subculture of differentness and dehuman-
ization.[17]

Less dramatic examples of perversion of the
value system of institutional staff are also
indicative of the lack of humanitarianism - these
include the opening and reading of residents' mail;
lack of provision of preventive health measures;
physical punishments such as deprivation of meals or
exercise; petty examples of spite, including
destroying a resident's loved possession or refusing
a second cup of tea; bullying and threats ("you
won't be going home for Christmas if you do that
again"); administering unnecessary sedatives, for
the convenience of the staff; and having a communal
wardrobe so that it becomes impossible for residents
to take pride in their appearance.
This "subculture" is less likely to be created
and perpetuated in a community-based residential
environment.

Fiscal Reasons
Leaving aside the ethical, legal and
humanitarian factors adding impetus to
de-institutionalisation, there is no doubt that
institutional care is expensive, but precisely how
expensive in comparison with non-institutional care
it is difficult to estimate, partly because not all
patient costs would be saved if the person were not
institutionalised.[18] Other factors which make the
comparison difficult are the hidden costs of
community-based care, including loss of earning
capacity of family members (often the mother's
career is sacrificed); extra expenses incurred by
the family (for example, "baby-sitting" fees are
extended over many years; transport by private car
or taxi rather than public transport; and costs of
extra therapies, diets, medications and appliances);
extensive use of non-specialised community services
which are not included in estimates; and, finally,
the epidemiological problems of assessing and
sampling the numbers of retarded people in the
community.
Further problems in estimating relative costs
are:

1. the inability or unwillingness of families

to adopt the role of permanent care-giver,
particularly as the lifespan of retarded
people increases and parents become elderly
and incapacitated,
2. expectations of higher quality care for
   retarded people,
3. the unknown quantity of future inflation,
4. increasing salaries of care-givers, and
5. the fact that almost as soon as estimates
   are made, they become outdated. There is
   little point in quoting precise figures
   comparing institutional and
   non-institutional costs because of their
   obsolescence, and variation between nations
   and regions. It is more profitable to
   examine the relativity between different
   modes of care.

It has been estimated that about 20% of the
cost of caring for a retarded institutionalised
person would remain in the event of de-
institutionalisation. Thus, a saving of 80% of
average annual per patient costs in public
institutions could be made of the person were not
institutionalised.[19] As the life expectancy of
retarded patients increase, this per annum reduction
in costs represents a significant lowering of
expenditure from the public purse.
A recent study in South Australia compared
costs for institutional and community living units
for a defined marginal (i.e., not totally dependent)
population.[20] Total costs per occupant per day in
institutional care varied from $A17-28, whereas
community living unit costs varied from $A8-22. The
most expensive community units had fully rostered
staff and additional part-time staff at peak period.
The study concluded that "there can be little
doubt about the economic viability of utilising
community-based living units in preference to
institutional-based care"[21] and furthermore, for
totally dependent people "it does appear that
smaller more localised living units ... are feasible
from the economic viewpoint".[22]
Although the study found slight increases in
cost as total care units became smaller (for
example, from 100 to 25 beds), it argued that the
increase would be offset by the significant social
advantages (for staff, residents, and families)
which would be gained in the smaller units.

Conclusion

Whatever the basis of the argument for de-institutionalisation - whether the pragmatic economic view taken by government economic advisors, or the humanitarian position which compares standards of living within and without institutions, or the philosophical stance emphasising normalisation - when the evidence is all in, it is clear that there is no rational or moral reason for maintaining large, whole-of-life institutions for mentally retarded persons. If for no other reason than the fiscal one, sooner or later governments must implement programmes of deinstitutionalisation, but in so doing, they must not abandon their duty of care and support for retarded citizens. The following sections examine some of the difficulties faced by retarded people, their families and care-givers, as a consequence of the hiatus between the dismantling of the legal and welfare systems established for institutional care, and the establishment of systems necessary for community-based living.

LEGAL AND WELFARE SYSTEMS FOR
COMMUNITY-BASED LIVING - THE GAPS

Guardianship

(There) are, in my opinion - and, I believe, in the opinion of the close relatives of the mentally retarded, or intellectually disabled, and of other concerned members of the community - serious inadequacies in the law relating to the guardianship of such persons, and serious deficiencies in the powers of the Court to appoint guardians for such persons. [23]

The judgment quoted above concerns the case of an adult mentally retarded woman, C., who resides as an "informal patient" in an institution which is no longer gazetted as a mental hospital. The woman's parents, now separated, engaged in a dispute over visiting rights. In the past, the Superintendent of the hospital had intervened and laid down rules, for no apparent good reason, restricting the father's access to his daughter. The father objected, challenging the right of the Superintendent, and of C.'s mother, to establish such limits. When, upon degazettal of the hospital, C. was discharged as a "patient" there was no-one whom the law would recognise as having authority to make decisions affecting her welfare. Because the Court found C.'s condition to be not one of "mental illness", but of "mental informity", it was not open to the Court (under the Mental Health Act[24]) to appoint a committee of the person (to act as guardian). The Court therefore had to determine whether it had inherent jurisdiction to intervene in the matter. Following extensive historical research which examined statutes as far back as 1323[25] the Court concluded that:

> C. falls within that class of persons described in the Charter of Justice [promulgated pursuant to the provisions of the New South Wales Act (4 Geo.IV c.96)] as "natural fools" and that, accordingly, this Court has jurisdiction to appoint a committee of her person and estate.[26]

This contorted, lengthy, and expensive case serves as a prime illustration of the difficulties which are faced in the absence of appropriate guardianship legislation for mentally retarded citizens. Some of the basic flaws in the guardianship situation which exists in many jurisdictions are summed up by the American Bar Association's Commission on the Mentally Disabled:

> The criteria for establishing a guardianship are often broad and vague permitting the imposition of restrictions on persons who are "different" as well as on those who are disabled. The procedures often omit the safeguards we have come to expect when restrictions on liberty are imposed or fundamental rights threatened in other contexts. And perhaps most importantly, even today in many jurisdictions, guardianship orders and guardians have failed to recognize that individuals with disabilities are often capably of doing many things for them-selves.[27]

More than twenty years ago, the U.S. President's Panel of Mental Retardation recommended the development of limited guardianship of the adult person, with the scope of guardianship specified in the order.[28] Furthermore, it is important that the law recognise the differences between mental illness and mental retardation, and provide appropriate guardianship legislation for the latter group, separate from mental health Acts. The court procedures attendant upon applications for guardianship need to be simplified so that applicants are not faced with lengthy, expensive Supreme Court proceedings. Some Australian States (and other jurisdictions)[29] have created Guardianship Boards which have the advantages of being more readily accessible, and able to respond quickly when the need for guardianship arises, although often retaining the disadvantage of not providing for limited guardianship powers.

Finally, it is essential that legislation bearing on competency contain provisions which restrict guardianship orders to a specific length of time, or provide for periodic review.

Mentally retarded citizens residing in the community face complex decisions affecting their lives in the areas of property management, relationships with other people (family, and care-givers, for example), medical treatment, entering into contracts, legal rights and obligations, and testamentary capacity.[30] In many instances, decisions will be made by the mentally retarded person. Appropriate guardiansip legislation needs to be put in place for those occasions when responsibility for decisions affecting a mentally retarded person's life and welfare needs to be taken by a third party. In the absence of such legislation, the mentally retarded person's life can be influenced by ad hoc, conflicting, ill-informed, and illegal decisions made by a plethora of persons from various agencies. When a legal challenge to one of these decisions is mounted, either by the retarded citizen or another, a situation arises such as occurred in C.'s case [31], where a sledge-hammer is used to kill a fly.

The ambiguities in guardianship legislation should ideally be resolve before de-institutionalisation programmes take effect. Where this has not occurred, there is, nevertheless, great virtue in swift and effective law reform, after the commencement of programmes of de-institutionalisation.

Rights to Service

If de-institutionalisation is to culminate in the opportunity for achievement of greatest potential for each mentally retarded adult, there is a moral obligation upon the state to provide the

resources which will enable fulfilment of this goal.
Retarded citizens will require extra assistance at
some time during their lives, and prhaps throughout
their lifetime, in areas such as education, medical
and health care, social service benefits and
subsidies, and vocational habilitation. Within a
large institution, provision of services may not be
optimal, but hospital standards and accreditation
systems at least ensure the basics.[32] Statutory
requirements determine staffing qualifications and
allocations; structural requirements of buildings;
criteria for medical and surgical facilities; floor
areas per bed; space for waiting areas, dining
rooms, bathrooms and so forth; basic furniture,
furnishings, and equipment; cleaning and
disinfecting; sanitary arrangements; overcrowding;
and a multitude of other areas. There is no mention
of patient assessment or improvement, or of
principles of patient care which would reflect
public expectations, but at least there is
recognition of the fact that there needs to be a
certain level of plant, space, and staff numbers per
patient.

When the economic argument for de-
institutionalisation does manage to overcome
government inertia, the consequence is frequently
too much emphasis upon reducing funding. In
attempts to save public monies, governments
dismantle institutions and their inherent resource
structure without substituting a community-based
system of support services.

When de-institutionalisation occurs as a
consequence of court action, the judge may order
that the mental retardation institution be replaced
by a system of small-scale community living
arrangements supplemented with necessary community
services (as occurred in Philadelphia in 1978, when
Pennhurst was closed).[33] If the
de-institutionalisation process occurs as a
consequence of a change in government policy, orders
and plans to establish community services may be
conspicuous by their absence.[34]

Bitter experience has demonstrated that
de-institutionalisation programmes in the absence of
adequate community services are in effect
re-institutionalisation programmes. Retarded
residents are moved out of the institution,
abandoned in the community without adequate
preparation or support, and as coping abilities
disintegrate, they are gradually re-admitted to
other institutions – nursing homes, mental

52

hospitals, and gaols.

 There are disturbing signs that the momentum of
large residential institutions is surviving the
challenge of community services, and that
today's construction of nursing homes and
'small' (100-500 bed) retardation institutions
will require that yet another generation of
clients use the facilities. Part of the blame
is due to past adoption of the essentially
negative goal of 'deinstitutionalization', in
which the goal of emptying buildings took
precedence over the creation of viable
community systems."[35]

 If deinstitutionalisation is to be viable, it
needs to be based upon plans and idealogies, to
incorporate staff conversion and re-training, to
have long-term benefits for the community as well as
retarded citizens, and to be firmly entrenched by
legislation which commits the state to provision of
adequate and appropriate community-based services.

CONCLUSION

 That deinstitutionalisation is a desirable aim
is firmly established on humanitarian, ethical and
economic grounds - but it remains essentially a
negative goal, a move away from an undesirably
situation. Without provision of appropriate and
essential services, protections and rights for
retarded citizens living in the community,
community-based living will in turn engender an
"away from" movement - away from abandonment,
isolation, lack of resources and supports, and
hopeless lurching from one inappropriate community
service to another. When societies rid themselves
of institutions, they must be careful not to rid
themselves of the doctrine of parens patriae, the
state serving as the benevolent parent caring for
his or her poor, sick or wayward children. The
historical roots of caring for those who could not
care for themselves are embedded in the concept of
local communities, villages or parishes providing
support and assistance. Community-based living for
retarded citizens is merely a re-emphasis upon
principles and moral obligations which have been
recognised for centuries.

NOTES

1. 43 Eliz. c.2.
2. 12 George II c.5.
3. Scull, A.T. Museums of Madness, Penguin Education, 1982.
4. Cummins, C.J. A History of Medical Administration in New South Wales 1788-1973, Health Commission of N.S.W., Sydney, 1979, p.8ff.
5. Ibid, p.9.
6. M. Lazerson, "Educational Insitutions and Mental Subnormality: Notes on Writing a History", in M.J. Begab and S.A. Richardson (Eds), The Mentally Retarded and Society: A Social Science Perspective, Baltimore: University Park Press, 1975, pp.33-52, at p.35.
7. Wrightsman, L.S., Sigelman C.K. and Sanford, F.H. Psychology, 5th ed., California: Brooks/Cole, 1979, p.323ff.
8. Nirje, B. "The Normalization Principle and Its Human management Implications", in R.B. Kugel and W. Wolfensberger (Eds), Changing Patterns in Residential Services for the Mentally Retarded, President's Committee on Mental Retardation, Washington, 1969, p.181.
9. Wyatt v. Stickney 344 F. Supp. 373; 503 F. 2d 1305 (5th Cir. (1974)).
10. Pennsylvania Association for Retarded Children v. Commonwealth of Pennsylvania 334 F. Supp. 1257 (E.D. Pa. 1971).
11. Suzuki v. Quisenberry 411 F. Supp. 1113 (D. Hawaii 1976).
12. Zigler, E. and Balla, D. "Motivational Aspects of Mental retardation", in R. Koch and J.C. Dobson (Eds), The Mentally Retarded Child and His Family, New York: Brunner/Mazel, 1976, pp.377-399.
13. Ibid.
14. Hayes S.C. and Hayes, R. Mental Retardation: Law, Policy and Administration, Sydney: Law Book Co. Ltd., 1982, p.148ff.
15. Rivera, G. Willowbrook: A report on how it is and why it doesn't have to be that way. New York: Vintage Books, 1972.
16. Simpson, J. "The Law and Intellectually Disabled People - Some Casework Experience", Council for Intell. Disability Today, April 1964, 4(1), pp.5-9.
17. Bronston, W.G. "Concepts and Theory of Normalization", in Koch and Dobson, Op. Cit.

pp.490-516 at p.498.
18. See generally, Conley, R.W. The Economics of Mental Retardation, Baltimore: Johns Hopkins University Press, 1973.
19. Ibid, p.297ff.
20. Final Report of the Intellectually Retarded Persons Project, A New Pattern of Services for Intellectually handicapped People in South Australia, S.A. Health Commission, November 1981.
21. Ibid, p.63.
22. Ibid, p.73.
23. R.H. v. C.A.H. & ors, Supreme Court of New South Wales Protective Division, No. S.109 of 1983, per Powell J. at 1-2, date of judgement 11 July 1984.
24. Mental Health Act 1958 (NSW), s.39.
25. Statute de Prerogativa Regis 1323 17 Ed. II cc.9,10; see footnote 23 above, at 31.
26. Footnote 23 above, at 35.
27. Sales, B.D., Powell, D.M., Van Duizend, R. et al, Disabled Persons and the Law - State Legislative Issues, New York: Plenum Press, 1982, p.459.
28. Ibid, p.460.
29. Hayes and Hayes, Op. Cit. p.230ff.
30. Human Rights Commission, Ethical and Legal Issues in Guardianship Options for Intellectually Disadvantaged People, Discussion Paper No. 4, Canberra, 1983.
31. See footnote 23 above.
32. Hayes and Hayes, footnote 14 above, p.214ff.
33. Laski, F. "Right to Services in the community - Implications of the Pennhurst Case", in R.J. Flynn and K.E. Nitsch (Eds), Normalization, Social Integration, and Community Services, Baltimore: University Park Press, 1980, pp.167-176.
34. Dept. of Health, N.S.W., Inquiry into Health Services for the Psychiatrically .Ill and Developmentally Disabled (Richmond Report), NSW Govt. Printer, Sydney, 1983, Part 2, p.23ff.
35. Hogan, M.F. "Normalization and Communitization - Implementation of a Regional", Community-Integrated Service System, in Flynn and Nitsch, Op. Cit. pp.299-312 at p.311.

Chapter Four

MENTAL RETARDATION AND PATERNALISTIC CONTROL

R.F. Khan

It is widely believed that paternalistic
control needs to be exercised over the mentally
retarded in order to prevent them from harming
themselves or otherwise promote their interests.
Clearly the severely mentally retarded need such
protection and care, but the general practice is to
extend paternalistic control to all cases of
specifiable mental retardation. Consequently,
people who are classified as mildly retarded,[1] -
for example, many cases of those suffering from
Down's Syndrome, - are declared to be the proper
objects of paternalistic direction and guidance with
regard to the central areas of life and practical
affairs. Where they are to live and with whom,
whether they are to marry or have sexual relations,
whether they may have children, whether they should
engage in commercial transactions, possess money and
manage property, - these are all matters, which it
is held, the mildly retarded are incapable of
handling on their own, without putting their
interests at risk. This is not only the official
view but it is a belief that is generally, and
possibly more firmly, held in the community at
large. One has only to notice the response to the
merely physically handicapped, particularly those
whose physical handicaps affect speech and facial
expression (as in the case of some spastics), to
recognize the general community attitude where
mental deficiency is believed to exist.

Let us grant that the mildly retarded when left
on their own do incur greater risks (risk damage to
their interests to a greater degree or more
frequently) than those who are mentally more
competent. Is this fact sufficient to justify
paternalistic intervention in their lives?

57

THE CASE FOR PATERNALISM

Daniel Wikler, in a most interesting paper,[2] argues that, given the existing institutional structure of society, paternalism with regard to the mildly retarded is justified. Society sets the norms of competence with respect to institutional activities such as marriage, parenthood, making contracts, buying and selling goods, managing property etc. These standards of competence are so determined as to more or less require the manifestation of normal mental capacity. The norms society oprates with are conventional in the sense that things might have been arranged differently. We might have had a different institution with regard to contractual commercial transactions, for example, permitting the parties concerned to annul contracts simply because they proved inconvenient; or a different notion of family relationships which, for example, did not require parents to be responsible for the well-being of their children. Under these new condition, "persons whose mental powers are much weaker than the average would be competent to enter contracts, marry and make other important decisions without regularly risking serious reverses that they could not predict and understand."[3] Consequently, these people would no longer be held to be in need of paternalistic guidance.

As things are, however, the norms of competence prevailing in society suit people of normal mental capacity, and there is a reason why this is so. The reason is that such arrangements have greater social utility, either because the majority of people are 'normal' or because altering them would be, as such, less desirable (e.g. make the exchange of goods and other communal undertakings more difficult). We have a choice, then, between pursuing general social utility at the cost of declaring the mildly retarded to be incompetent and in need of protection; or abandoning the greater general good for the sake of allowing autonomy to the mildly retarded on the same basis as other people in society. Wikler holds that, in this context, "The morality of paternalism reduces to a question about distributive justice." [4]

It seems clear that, faced with such a choice, most people would not consider it unreasonable to declare the mildly retarded to be incompetent and in need of care. The judgment would be supported not only on the basis of promoting the welfare of the majority, constituted by the normal, and so of society as a whole, but also on the grounds that abandoning current standards of competence would destroy central institutions of social life. Thus, for example, relaxing the rules regulating the validity of contracts, so as to allow contracts to be declared void if and when they prove inconvenient, would hardly allow any place for contractual transactions in social life. Lifewise, in the area of morality, to allow promises to be broken on grounds of inconvenience or disinclination would in effect amount to giving up the institution of promising. No human society, it may be said, can afford to abandon such institutions; consequently, no society can afford to relax the rules governing these institutions.

Wikler seems to think that the choice before us, with regard to the issue of paternalism and the mildly retarded, is between allowing equal liberty to all and the promotion of general welfare. But it can be argued that abandoning the 'pro-normal' standards of competence with respect to many of our central institutions will not only detract from the general welfare but will also remove the conditions necessary for the possession and exercise of many rights. For example, what moral rights would survive the introduction of a standard that made it permissible for people to get out of engagements, either of a particular or of a general kind, simply on the basis of declared inconvenience? Certainly not particular rights based on transactions such as promises or other committments; nor general rights such as the right to be told the truth.

Such considerations seem to justify paternalistic control of the mildly retarded in so far as they fall below the standards of competence set by society: If, as it seems it must be, society is geared to suit people with normal mental abilities, then inevitably the mildly retarded will find (social) life to be hazardous. Humanitarian and compassionate grounds, then, would require that we manage and direct their lives in order to protect and promote their interests. Paternalism, then, becomes a matter of strict obligations, - we owe it to the mildly retarded to enforce it.

To lend weight to these considerations, the analogous case of children may be mentioned. We owe it to children, just because of their mental incapacity, to direct their lives and prevent them from harming themselves. If paternalism is justified in their case, then how can it not be

justified in the case of the mildly retarded who
are, in relevant respects, - and this is often
actually said, - very much like children?
    So stated, the case for paternalism regarding
the mildly retarded seems to be sufficiently
plausible and persuasive. Can anything be said
against it?

PROBLEMS OF PATERNALISM

    In what follows, I shall try to argue against
the exercise of paternalistic controls in the case
of the mildly retarded on a number of grounds. If
what I have to say does not overthrow the case for
paternalism it, at least, dents it considerably; and
the points I draw attention to collectively provide
a basis for an alternative policy towards the mildly
retarded.
    Firstly, clearly, there is no unequivocal duty
to exercise paternalistic control over the mildly
retarded. This is so, even when we view the matter
exclusively in terms of the interests of such
people. The mentally retarded are already marked
out from the rest of the community in terms of their
condition. The stigma brings with it undesirable
consequences in the form of humiliation, segregation
and unjustified discrimination. The paternalistic
control exercised over them by emphasizing (and
over-emphasizing) their difference from the rest of
the community may be expected to make their
treatment in this regard considerably worse.
Consequently, they may, on the whole, gain by the
lifting of paternalistic controls, the likely loss
because of absence of guidance being more than made
up by the avoidance of the additional pain and
humiliation they would otherwise have experienced.
Given this, then, we cannot owe it to the mildly
retarded to take over and direct their lives.[5]
    The second point that needs to be made is that
it is not reasonable to draw a parallel between
children and the mildly retarded in order to
determine our response to them. Even if we hold
that the mildly retarded are like children in terms
of their mental capacities, - and the comparison can
only be vague (children of what age?), - they are
clearly unlike children in other, and centrally
relevant, respects. Thus, the mildly retarded have
desires and goals which many children do not have.
These desires and goals are either the product of
their biological and social development as adults,

60

e.g., the desire for sexual relations; or they are the product of the special circumstances in which they, unlike children, find themselves, viz. classified as sub-normal and mentally defective, which is not how children are normally seen.

But apart from this, the most important relevant difference between children and the mildly retarded is that children grow out of their condition, whereas the mildly retarded essentially remain in it. This fact is surely morally relevant. it is because of this that we feel called upon to provide for the mildly retarded, but not for children, what might be called compensatory goods, seeking to make up for what they lack. We respond in this way to other cases of permanent and substantial loss. In the case of the blind, we seek to provide an environment where their lack of vision, and the loss this entails, is sought to be made up for in terms of activities related to other senses, e.g., by the provision of gardens wich emphasize the scent and not the colour of flowers or of opportunities to engage in the production of music. The mildly retarded constitute similar objects of compensatory endeavour on our part. What the compensatory goods are to be in their case is to be determined by their condition, the character of their deprivation, - or what we take this to be. What precisely these compensatory goods may be will be discussed when I outline the alternative policy to paternalism. But before I do that I want to mention my third and final ground for rejecting paternalistic intervention in the lives of the retarded.

This objection derives from certain doubts concerning the viability of paternalism expressed by John Stuart Mill in the essay On Liberty.[6] Paternalism seeks to protect and promote the good of the individual whose freedom is restricted. The question then arises: How reasonable is it to expect the individual's good to be preserved or secured by making him do what he does not want to do and by stopping him from doing what he wants to do?

Mill argues against paternalism on more than one basis.[7] I shall, however, only consider the line of objection which has relevant for our purpose. Mill maintains that it is most unlikely that paternalistic interference will benefit the individual concerned and that it is more likely that it will, on the whole, produce more harm than good. This is because estimates of the individual's interests made by the intervening agency are unavoidably unreliable. These estimates are arrived at from the outside, so to speak, and they miss out on the intimate view which the individual, actually affected by the situation, has of it. In contrast, the individual's own assessments of what constitutes his good are immeasurably superior and reliable: "... with respect to (one's) own feelings and circumstances, the most ordinary man or woman has means of knowledge immeasurably surpassing those that can be possessed by any one else."[8] The individual's knowledge is based on first-hand experience, on immediate acquaintance with what happens to and around him; whereas those who seek to direct his life from the outside can only proceed on the basis of 'general presumptions'. Such general presumptions, Mill points out, "may be altogether wrong, and even if right, are ... likely ... to be missapplied ..."[9] Consequently, attempts by others to direct a preson's life are not likely to promote his interests and the chances are that such attempts may be productive of more harm than mistakes and miscalculations committed by the individual acting on his own. ("All errors which he is likely to commit ... are far outweighed by the evil of allowing others to constrain him to what they deem his good").[10]

If we take the individual to be the better judge of his own good, then we may take his declared choice to indicate what his good consists in: "His voluntary choice is evidence that what he so chooses is desirable, or at least endurable, to him, and his good is on the whole best provided for by allowing him to take his own means of pursuing it."[11] Hence, preventing the individual from acting according to his voluntary choice will imply that we are deflecting him away from where his good lies.

It follows from this that it would not be reasonable to expect paternalistic interferences in the life of an individual to protect or promote what constituted his good. But that is supposed to be the very rationale of paternalism. Hence, it is not reasonable to support such a policy.

Mill allows exceptions to his rejection of paternalism. Thus, we are justified in forcibly preventing someone for risking his life, say, by trying to cross an unsafe bridge, if there is no way of drawing his attention to the facts. Here we act on the general presumption that normally people do not want to die, and we are justified in doing so because of our inability to use other means, such as advice and warnings, in the situation.[12] Another exception mentioned, and this has excited much comment, is the case of someone seeking to sell himself for a slave. Mill seems to think that the irrevocable character of such a transaction justifies us in preventing him from doing so.[13] However, the exceptions that are relevant to our discussion are those which would exclude, together with children, the mentally retarded. Mill makes it quite clear that his defence of the individual against paternalism is only meant to apply to "persons ... of full age and the ordinary amount of understanding",[14] to those "in the maturity of their faculties";[15] and a person's choices are to be regarded as significant indicators of his good only if he "possess (a) tolerable amount of common sense and experience."[16] On this basis, children and, with them, the mentally retarded would qualify for paternalistic direction and guidance because they are deprived of 'the ordinary amount of understanding' and sufficient 'common sense and experience' to enable them to make informed and rational choices.

It cannot be denied that there is a difference, and very possibly a considerable difference, in the quality of the choices made by children and the mentally impaired, on the one hand, and the kind of adult Mill had in mind, on the other. Nevertheless, Mill's case against paternalism, - although explicitly meant to repel attempts to coerce only those who are capable of informed and rational choice, - has significant implications for such control exercised over children and the mildly retarded. The fact that individuals in these two categories are mentally less competent does not imply that they have no interests; nor does it imply that they are not capable of intentional conduct. Given, then, that there are ends which they may voluntarily pursue, it still remains doubtful, on Mill's premisses, that we should let others determine and secure their interests. The significant difference that, according to Mill, exists between the individudal's privileged view and the estimates of value made by others on the basis of general presumptions also applies in this case. and we very commonly recognize this fact, at least with reference to children. Thus, it is often said that adults who exercise paternalistic care over children rarely, if at all, see things from the point of view of their charges; with the result that they often produce more harm than benefit. George Orwell points out that one of the great merits of

Charles Dickens (as a novelist) is his ability to
enter into the child's point of view and present the
mental atmosphere of the child's perception of the
world. Speaking of a scene involving Pip in Great
Expectations, Orwell refers to the successful
description of it in terms of the child's vision:
"All the isolation of childhood is here. And how
accurately he has recoded the mechanisms of the
child's mind, its visualizing tendency, its
sensitiveness to certain kinds of impression."[17]
Orwell picks out Dickens as special in this respect,
even amongst novelists of the first rank, - a
judgment that rightly underlines the corresponding
incapacity to see things from the child's point of
view on the part of most of us.

If this can be maintained in the case of
children, then it can be equally affirmed with
respect to the mildly retarded. William James, in a
paper whose title highlights the point I am trying
to make, refers to "the blindness with which we all
are afflicted in regard to the feelings of creatures
and people different from ourselves."[18] He too
draws the same distinction as Mill, - between how
things appear from the external stand-point and the
assessments made from the point of view of the
person concerned: "The spectator's judgment is sure
to miss the root of the matter, and to possess no
truth. The subject judged knows a part of the world
of reality which the judging spectator fails to see,
knows more while the spectator knows less ..."[19]
This accounts for "the stupidity and injustice of
our opinions, so far as they deal with the
significant of alien lives".[20] In James' view, it
seems that the greater the difference in life styles
between the 'judging spectator' and the 'subject
judged', the greater the chances of the former's
judgment being distorted, - a contingency that must
haunt all attempts to work out what is good and bad
for the mentally retarded.

Mill as well as James sometimes give the
impression that they hold it to be impossible for
any one to see and estimate things accurately enough
on behalf of another person. But it is not
necessary, even if it is possible, to hold this
extreme view. We may concede that there may be
occasions where one may understand and follow the
'mechanisms of the mind' of some individual in our
care, whether child or retarded. But we will still
be justified in doubting that this happens, or is
likely to happen, often or normally or typically.
And, on that ground, challenge the reasonableness of

a policy which seeks, in the likely absence of relevant understanding and knowledge, to manage the lives of these people in order to promote their real interests.

The objection gains support from the additional fact that the inability to see and value things from the point of view of those who are protected may lead, perhaps unwittingly, to the imposition of values and preferences of whose who carry out the protection.[21]   Paternalism, then, may collapse into an attempt to bring about conformity with a given set of values; and the good sought on behalf of the individual turn into something which is picked out for him in terms of these external norms.

WHAT IS THE ALTERNATIVE TO PATERNALISM?

I will consider this question with regard to the mildly retarded. If paternalistic control is lifted then we may expect, as Wikler points out, the mildly retarded to encounter special hazards or, at least, more hazards than their mentally normal counterparts. On the other hand, as we saw above, it may be reasonable to expect them to be either worse off, or no better off, under paternalism. Should we then leave it at that? Should we do nothing with regard to the special risks they run in a world deliberately geared to the possession of normal mental capacity?

Clearly, there is something we can do with regard to the special problems the mildly retarded encounter and the special risks they run. We can offer our services in an instrumental capacity in the form of advice, counselling, and even financial and other aid to recompense for losses they may sustain when they try to manage their own affairs. Such a response may be placed in the category of providing compensatory goods designed to alleviate the deprivation they suffer from. We try to make things easier for the physically handicapped such as the blind and those confined to wheel-chairs, and we may do likewise for the retarded. We seek to make up for the lack of physical capacity such as loss of sight and mobility; for example, by trying to make it possible for the blind and those confined to wheel-chairs to take part in sport. We may take similar and appropriate measures in the case of the retarded.

What such compensatory provision for the retarded might entail in practical terms may be

illustrated in outline. If they live on their own,
then we may help them to budget their income by
providing advice and book-keeping services but
leaving it to them to decide how they are to spend
their money. And on those occasions when, having
spent their money unwisely, they face the gas or
electricity being cut off, then we may given them
extra funds to meet the contingency. If such people
have children and find it hard to cope with the day
to day business of looking after them, then we may
help them to do so. If they are imposed upon by
predatory salesmen or other rapacious people, we may
intercede to protect their rights as consumers. In
general, then, we will consider how, and in what
form, we can help them to overcome and make up for
the special hardships their condition imposes on
them, but without engaging in any kind of coercive
direction. And if we can afford to provide such
compensatory goods and services than we <u>owe</u> it to
them, as we owe it to the physically handicapped, to
do so.

One final point needs to be made. Paternalism
regarding the mildly retarded seeks to promote their
good. One of the things that is most undesirable
about their lives is the segregation and tutelage
they suffer from. These people desire nothing more
than to be free from these restrictions and live
like other members of the community, - not in terms
of pursuing high aspirations and ambitious goals but
with respect to the affairs of ordinary life. They
crave this most intensely and their inability to
satisfy this central desire is the cause of great
unhappiness to them. Should not paternalism, then,
if it is instituted on their behalf, seek to reduce
their pain and promote their interests in this
essential respect? But how can it possibly achieve
this goal? How can paternalism, which consists in
imposing tutelage, seek to bring about its removal?

NOTES

1. The category I am referring to may be taken to
    constitute, in terms of I.Q., a class of
    individuals ranging from 31 to 89 points; with
    the likelihood of performance being improved
    through education and exposure to experience.
    There are, of course, other ways of assessing
    an individual's capacities, viz. adaptive and
    social behavior. cf. Hayes, S.C. and Hayes, R.
    <u>Mental Retardation</u>, Sydney: The Law Book

Company, 1982, p. 81-85.
2. "Paternalism and the Mildly Retarded", Philosophy & Public Affairs 8, No. 4 1979, reprinted in R. Sartorius (Ed.), Paternalism, Minnesota: University of Minnesota Press, 1983. My references are to the latter.
3. Op. Cit. p.89.
4. Op. Cit. p.92.
5. Wikler mentions this consideration as constituting a powerful argument for 'granting civil liberties to the mildly retarded' (Op. Cit. p.93, note 5). He does not consider it in the body of his paper because, as he puts it, "The argument appeals to our concern for the retarded person's welfare, rather than to any right of self-direction, and it stands (or falls) independently of the issue addressed in the paper" (Ibid). In other words, he takes the issue discussed in his paper to constitute balancing matters concerning general welfare against the acquisition of rights on the part of a minority, and the latter fact is not to be assessed in terms of consequential value. As against this, many people hold that the provision of civil liberties to the mildly retarded is justified mainly on the grounds that it contributes to their happiness, i.e. helps to make their lives less undesirable. The latter approach is more likely to achieve practical success than arguments in terms of abstract rights. It is more difficult to ignore and deny the undesirable consequences of not being given rights possessed by others in society than theoretical arguments designed to prove the irrationality of such a policy.
6. My references are to the Everyman's Library edition, Utilitarianism, Liberty, and Representative Government, London: J.M. Dent & Sons, 1954.
7. The two main lines of attack are that paternalism is unjustified on utilitarian grounds and, what Gerald Dworkin calls, 'a noncontingent argument' relying on 'the absolute value of a free choice' [see his article 'Paternalism' in The Monist 56, No. 1, 1972; reprinted in Sartorius (Ed.) Op. Cit.]. I say nothing about the 'noncontingent argument' in my discussion, largely because Mill's conception of a free choice goes further than the mere exercise of voluntary choice and involves regarding it as the outcomes of

critical scrutiny and assessment. The
stipulation disqualifies the mildly retarded,
and possibly other categories of people, from
the scope of the argument.

8.   Op. Cit., p.133.
9.   Ibid. What Mill has in mind here are beliefs
     of the form: 'Most people would or would not
     want ...' 'No one wants ...' etc.
10. Ibid.
11. Op. Cit. p.158.
12. Op. Cit. pp.151-152.
13. Op. Cit. pp.157-158.
14. Op. Cit. p.132.
15. Op. Cit. p.73.
16. Op. Cit. p.125.
17. "Charles Dickens" in George Orwell, Critical
     Essays, London: Secker and Warburg, 1954,
     pp.13-15.
18. "On a certain blindness in human beings" in
     William James, Selected Papers on Philosophy,
     London: J.M. Dent & Sons, 1961, p.1.
19. Op. Cit. p.2.
20. Op. Cit. p.1.
21. See C.L. Ten, Mill on Liberty, Oxford:
     Clarendon Press, 1980, p.112.

Chapter Five

PSYCHOSURGERY AND THE MENTALLY RETARDED

John Kleinig

Somatic therapies have a long history, but the
contemporary interest in psychosurgery is usually
associated with the work of a Portuguese
neurologist, Antonio Egas Moniz, who in 1936
reported favourably on the results of destroying
portions of white matter in the anterior part of the
frontal lobes of patients suffering from intractable
psychotic disorders. Vigorously promoted by others,
the procedure was used extensively in the treatment
of severely disturbed World War II veterans, with
sufficient apparent success for Moniz to be awarded
(along with Walter Hess) the Nobel Prize for
Physiology/Medicine in 1949. Many of the patients
treated by Moniz and those who followed him were
suffering from what was then broadly referred to as
'schizophrenia', though nowadays schizophrenia
strictly defined is not well indicated for
psychosurgery. The term 'schizophrenia' now is
generally reserved for affective rather than
cognitive disorders - for endogenous depression,
severe obsessive-compulsive neuroses and
debilitating phobias.
    In the mid-1950s, there was a significant
decline in the use of psychosurgery. Much of this
decline is attributable to the development of
antipsychotic and antidepressant drugs.
Nonetheless, there was a growing concern about the
value of psychosurgery. Although early clinical
reports had been enthusiastic, the advent of less
partisan and longer-term studies cast a somewhat
different complexion on the usefulness of the
procedure. It became clear that in many cases the
benefits of psychosurgery had been purchased at
considerable cost.
    But though the use of psychosurgery declined,
it did not cease. There were important advances in

69

brain physiology, operative technique and the siting of lesions, and these markedly decreased the likelihood of adverse sequelae. The dangers of destroying neocortical tissue began to be recognized, and the development of stereotactic instruments and pneumoencephalography enabled a much more precise location of lesions - in particular their siting in the circuits of the limbic system, which was rapidly assuming importance as the functional centre for emotion, motivation and memory. This was not the only factor which perpetuated the use of psychosurgery. Drug and other therapies did not always live up to what was expected of them, and there remained a group of patients for whom only psychosurgery (if that) seemed to offer any hope. This group was augmented by those suffering from other disorders for which less dramatic therapies had proved ineffective or insufficient. Of particular significance were patients given to episodes of uncontrollable rage and aggressive behaviour. In the late 1950s, following earlier animal studies and a modicum of human research, some of these patients began to be psychosurgically treated. [1]

All this may seem to have little relevance to the situation of mentally retarded persons. Psychosurgery, after all, is intended to treat psychiatric disorder, not mental retardation. Although there was a time when the two were confused and conflated, that time has surely passed. But the matter is not quite so simple.

In 1963, a Japanese team headed by Dr. H. Narabayashi reported on the psychosurgical treatment of sixty patients manifesting 'behaviour disturbances'. Stereotactic procedures were used in the unilateral or bilateral destruction of the amygdaloid nucleus (one of the structures involved in the limbic system). Narabayashi describes his intentions thus:

It was originally our intention to investigate the value of amygdalotomy upon patients with temporal lobe epilepsy characterized by psychomotor seizures and focal spike discharges on the electroencephalogram as well as marked behavior disturbances such as hyperexcitability, assaultive behavior, or violent aggressiveness. The indications for amygdalotomy were then extended to include patients without clinical manifestations of temporal lobe epilepsy but with EEG

abnormalities and marked behavior disturbances.
Finally, cases of behavior disorders without
epileptic manifestations, clinically and
electrically, but associated with various
degrees of feeblemindedness or with subnormal
intelligence were also included in the
series.[2]

Forty of Narabayashi's sixty patients were
under the age of fourteen, several were only five
years old, and eleven were said to suffer from
erethistic feeblemindedness (without epileptic
seizures). As well, a number of those diagnosed as
suffering from temporal lobe epilepsy or as
manifesting EEG abnormalities were also mentally
retarded. In fact, all but six of their patients
were described as 'relatively or severely mentally
retarded'.
Narabayashi's study is important, because it
represents the beginnings of a continuing use of
psychosurgery in the treatment of what is broadly
referred to as the episodic dyscontrol syndrome,
much of it on hyperactive children, and much of it
on people classified as mentally retarded.
In 1974, an Australian team headed by Professor
L.G. Kiloh published a study of the effects of
amygdalotomy on eighteen patients exhibiting severe
aggressive or self-mutilating behaviour. Several of
these patients were adolescents, the youngest aged
thirteen. According to the diagnostic chart, eight
were diagnosed as suffering from 'mental
subnormality', the remainder from what was
denominated either a 'personality disorder' or
'schizophrenia'. Presumably the disorder for which
they were treated was not mental subnormality
simpliciter, but erethistic subnormality. Seven of
the eight mentally subnormal patients were stated to
be severely retarded, the other moderately retarded.
Of the remainder, five were said to display mild or
borderline retardation.[3]
The reports above represent just two cases in
which studies indicate that mentally retarded
persons are subjected to psychosurgical operations,
sometimes for conditions which seem to link, albeit
indirectly, with their retardation. Other studies
could also be cited.[4] In one, twenty-two
epileptic mentally retarded children between the
ages of three and fourteen were operated on. The
main, though not exclusive, purpose of the surgery
appears to have been the control of their epileptic
seizures, and the lesions extended far beyond the

71

amygdaloid body.[5]   The largest long-term study of
amygdalotomy is Indian-based, and encompasses a
total of 235 patients.[6]   Although it is not stated
in the study, there is reason to believe that in a
country where adequate facilities for the special
care of the mentally retarded are lacking, some
retarded children with behavioural problems are
given psychosurgery in lieu, thus enabling them to
remain in the care of their families.   The
alternative would be their rejection or
abandonment.[7]

     I think I have said enough to indicate that
psychosurgery, even though primarily intended as a
treatment for certain psychiatrically defined
disorders, merges into a treatment for conditions
whose aetiology is more obviously neurological or
histological.   In the case of mentally retarded
persons, the psychosurgical treatment often appears
to be contemplated as a management option. At least
that is the way post-operative assessments read.
Understandably, this raises ethical questions about
the sort of interventions which are appropriate to
the situation of mentally retarded people, and the
conditions under which appropriate interventions may
be instituted.   Is it legitimate to contemplate the
use of psychosurgery in the treatment of 'behaviour
disturbances' of the kind outlined in these studies?
Ought psychosurgery to be imposed on people whose
consent either cannot be obtained or cannot be
assured?   Does the use of psychosurgery on mentally
retarded persons violate conventions against the use
of experimental procedures on non-competent
subjects?   These are some of the questions I hope to
address in this paper.

     I want to commence with a discussion of the
role of consent in therapeutic interactions, leading
from that to a consideration of the situation of
mentally retarded persons. This will give rise to
an examination of the character and limitations of
proxy consent in treatment decisions.   I then turn
to a more detailed investigation of the status of
psychosurgery as part of a treatment regime for
'behaviour disturbances', relating this finally to
the situation of mentally retarded persons.

THE SIGNIFICANCE OF CONSENT

     To consent to something is to accept
responsibility for it or be a party to it.[8]   In
therapeutic transactions, where the consent of

72

patients is sought prior to the initiation of treatment, consent is intended to signify their willing and open-eyed participation in the treatment regime. The securing of consent is important to and for both parties. For patients, it constitutes a recognition of their status as individuals with desires, reasons, values and life-plans of their own, whose choices carry considerable weight in the intersections and interactions of social life. For doctors, patient consent provides some protection against tortious or criminal action should the treatment be unsuccessful or attended by adverse side-effects. Other values, such as those relating to therapeutic success, are probably secondary to these.

Because consenting involves the acceptance of responsibility, those who consent must be able to understand what it is that they are consenting to, and must be sufficiently free from external and internal constraints and limitations for their agreement to express <u>their</u> will, and not merely reflect that of some other. 'Understanding' in this context has been articulated in the legal doctrine of 'informed consent', in which it is argued that for patient consent to be valid, patients need to have explained to them, in terms appropriate to their situation and background, the procedures to be followed, the benefits to be expected, the discomforts and risks which can reasonably be anticipated, and any alternatives they might reasonably contemplate. The disclosure process must also indicate whether any aspect of the treatment is experimental.

CONSENT AND MENTAL RETARDATION

Not surprisingly, it is difficult to generalize about the position of mentally retarded persons with regard to consent. Retardedness is not a simple phenomenon; nor is it without degrees. It is, moreover, still in the process of being understood.[9] Awareness of a reasonably determinate distinction between idiocy and insanity did not emerge until late in the seventeenth century. During the nineteenth and early twentieth century, aetiological differentiations of retardation became popular – attention was focused on the various genetic or environmental factors that were believed to have caused it. This worked well enough for cases in which the retardation was severe or profound, but did not help to isolate or understand cases where retardation was mild, and for which there was no clearly identifiable medical syndrome. The present emphasis tends to be on psychological and sociological factors.

The major theory in this connection is one which sees the mentally retarded as 'slow learners'. If we view human cognitive development in terms of a series of stages of maturity through which we progress, measureable by means of IQ-type tests, we can characterize mentally retarded persons as those whose passage through these stages is markedly slower than average and whose ultimate attainment, so far as the stage of cognitive development is concerned is markedly lower than that of others.

One of the chief merits of this theory is that it does not view mentally retarded persons as belonging to a race apart, but as continuous with nonretarded persons. It is not, however, without its problems. One concerns the methods used to discriminate retardation: the general problems associated with IQ-type tests are as relevant here as elsewhere. And social/emotional as well as cognitive factors are often considered to be important to any judgment of retardation. But here I don't propose to do more than flag the problem. The general practice has been to characterize as retarded those who score about 70 or below on standard IQ tests, with various subcategories of retardedness: mild (those with scores between 55 and 70), moderate (35 to 55), severe (20 to 35) and profound (under 20). That gives us enough to work with in the present context.

What does seem to me to be important is the fact that when we are considering the matter of consent to psychosurgery, there is a special burden on those whose task is to secure that consent, to determine whether the person is competent to provide it, and, if so, to ensure that the informational and environmental requirements for a voluntary and informed consent are satisfied. Except for the case of those who fall into the severe and profound categories, I don't think that a simple appeal to the category of retardedness will settle the question of competence. Those who are classified as mildly retarded show considerable variation in their capacity to consent to surgical procedures. The categorization should not be taken as settling the question of competence so much as placing a special burden of care on those charged with the responsibility of seeking consent to treatment.

One reason for this, not surprisingly, is to be found in the controversiality of criteria for retardation. If, as it is sometimes suggested, the various tests used to assess retardedness show as much about the cultural situation of the person concerned as they do about that person's own capacities, then we should beware of using the category of retardedness, at least in its milder varieties, as anything more than index of vulnerability. As it is, many who are classified as mildly retarded when young manage, through support, to develop into adults whose adjustment to and assimilation into adult society renders the continued use of the label inappropriate.

The problems of mentally retarded persons are to a certain extent compounded when their retardation is coupled with some psychiatrically defined disorder. On the one hand, the disorder is likely to raise additional questions about their competence to consent; on the other hand, psychiatric diagnoses are notoriously susceptible to cultural influences. Without wanting to pass judgment on the particular cases involved, it does not seem to me to be entirely accidental that psychosurgical operations for hyperactivity commenced in Japan, and are most commonly performed in India. The problems of psychiatric diagnosis tend to be exacerbated where the apparent or alleged disorder takes a form which is socially unacceptable. Where that is so, the temptation to cope with it in ways that will enable its suppression is often quite considerable.

My point in saying this is not to challenge the legitimacy of psychiatric classifications - that, it seems to me, involves a dogmatism as doctrinaire as that found in those for whom such classifications are entirely unproblematic - but to see such classifications as no more than cautionary so far as the issue of competence to consent is concerned. There is no direct path from 'psychiatrically disordered' to 'incompetent to consent'. This is so not only because the criteria for psychiatric disorder serve a wider and somewhat different purpose to those for competence, but also because even in the case of chronic disorders, their manifestations tend to be recurrent rather than continuous.

SOCIAL POLICY AND CONSENT

It is one thing to argue that mental retardation and psychiatric disorder do not *ipso facto* render a person incompetent to consent to therapeutic treatment. Is is another to incorporate this possibility into social policy. Where we propose to acknowledge such possibilities as part of social policy, we need to have publicly accessible and workable means of securing consent and monitoring its validity, and safeguards against the abuse of such provisions. The difficulties in the way of achieving this may be so formidable and the likelihood of mistake or manipulation so considerable, that wisdom will lie on the side of conservatism.

There is something to be said for the conservative approach. For one thing, the mentally retarded, and perhaps especially those who are also psychiatrically disturbed, are in a manifestly unfavourable bargaining position vis-a-vis their doctors, and should the latter decide that psychosurgical treatment would be appropriate, they would not find it difficult to structure the choice situation in favour of their judgment. This is even more likely where the person concerned is hospitalized. Not only does the hospital environment provide all sorts of subtle and not so subtle opportunities for coercion or manipulation, albeit in benevolent clothing, but it also tends to breed dependence. [10]

However, the conservative approach can sound more like a counsel of despair than a genuine attempt to acknowledge the real capacity for consent which at least some of the mildly retarded are able to exercise. They might well be sceptical of the importance which sacrifices them to the alleged welfare of others. I think the scepticism would be justified. Though there is little doubt that the mentally retarded are sensitive to environmental pressures and vulnerable to the manipulation of others, their interest in having the opportunity to give or withhold consent can probably be secured sufficiently by having their consent reviewed by a panel whose membership has no stake in the proposed treatment, and includes those who have as their interest a determination of the patient's unencumbered will.

PROXY/THIRD PARTY CONSENT

Although there are some whose retardation and
psychiatric disorder will be compatible with their
competence to consent to psychosurgery, it is likely
that many of those considered for psychosurgery
treatment will not be in this position. This at
least is strongly suggested by the published
clinical reports. The age of those involved, and
the severity of their retardation, makes it very
unlikely that they could proffer a valid consent.
In circumstances like these, it is common to
seek what is somewhat paradoxically called 'proxy
consent'. Unlike the granting of power of attorney,
where a person vests in another the authority to
make decisions on his or her behalf, in proxy
consent cases, the person's authorization is
lacking, and so it cannot really be claimed that
consent given or withheld is the consent of the
person on whose behalf it is given or withheld.
Nevertheless, there is some point to the
nomenclature, and in providing for what it attempts
to ensure. It is one way in which the interests of
the party concerned may be represented and secured.
There is, however, a problem about what 'proxy
consent' is intended to achieve, a problem which can
be articulated in terms of two senses of 'interest'.
A person's interests may comprise the ingredients of
his or her welfare, those conditions of life which
made the pursuit and achievement of his or her good
(whetever that may be) possible. Or they may be
constituted by those enterprises in which he or she
has a stake. What a person has an interest or stake
in may conflict with his or her interests or
welfare. This ambiguity has come to be reflected in
two doctrines of proxy consent, the so-called 'best
interests' doctrine and the doctrine of 'substituted
judgment'. The development of these two doctrines
provides additional complexity, but here I will take
what I understand to be their current
interpretation.
According to the 'best interests' doctrine, the
proxy consenter, the guardian, is expected to make
an assessment whether the treatment proposed will be
compatible with or will further the non-competent
patients's welfare interests, or as Rawls would put
it, primary goods. It is intended to ensure that
what is decided will be consistent with those
'things which it is supposed a rational man wants,
whatever else he wants'.[11] There is a certain
impartiality about the interests which the doctrine

of 'best interests' seeks to protect. This stands in potential contrast with the interests which it is the purpose of the doctrine of 'substituted judgment' to determine and secure. Here the intention is that the guardian should, so far as possible, both stand in the patient's shoes and imaginatively enter into the patient's point of view, so that what is reflected in the giving or withholding of consent preserves the patient's integrity as the particular individual he or she is.

Moral positions which place a high value on individuality-respecting autonomy will tend to give priority to the second of these doctrines, for it seeks to accommodate therapeutic interventions to what is known of the particular constellation of desires, values and life-plans of the individual patient. The doctrine of 'best intrests', on the other hand, may compromise that individuality in the name of some more general conception of welfare. However, what confronts us in the sort of cases with which this paper is concerned is not a simple either/or. In the case of patients who are very young, or whose retardation is fairly severe, or whose disorder is one of long standing, there may not be a pre-existing self with sufficient stability and coherence to give point and sense to an appeal to the doctrine of 'substituted judgment'. In such cases, an appeal to 'best interests' is most likely to safeguard what needs to be safeguarded in requiring proxy consent.[12]

One problem that constantly bedevils attempts to fulfil the proxy consent requirements is the determination of an appropriate agent. Traditionally, it has fallen to parents, spouses and/or close relatives to make such determinations, the presumption being that the bonds of consanguinity and care would most likely ensure protection of the patient's interests. But in certain cases, and particularly cases of the sort with which we are here concerned, that presumption is less compelling. Parents of retarded and/or disturbed children have often found that the pain of observing their plight and the burden of caring for them have interfered with their perception of and commitment to their interests, and decisions have been made which are more expedient than respectful. This is further complicated by their need to rely on medical expertise in assessing the appropriateness of treatment options. Doctors frequently have interests in particular treatment regimes, and these can interfere with the fair presentation of information to those charged with the responsibility for giving or withholding consent.

For this reason, various additional safeguards have been proposed and in some cases implemented. Independent hospital review committees and judicial review are most commonly considered. They do not eliminate all possibility of mistake, and in some cases may even introduce additional sources of distortion. But they do reflect the problems of a situation in which variously interested parties have widely disparate bargaining power.

The resort to proxies is not justified simply by virtue of the non-competence of the patient, particularly where some risk is involved. Unless there is some reasonably pressing need, we might be loath to entrust others with such powers. The probability of mistake and abuse is too high. In the case of medical treatment, it is usually presumed that the treatment recommended will be therapeutically beneficial. This raises two serious questions about treatments for 'behaviour disorders'.

First, is such treatment intended to be therapeutically beneficial, or is the object some social benefit - say, to make the person more manageable? These are not necessarily opposed or even unrelated goals, The aggressively antisocial person is likely to be his or her own worst enemy, as well as that of others. Nevertheless, there is a difference in focus which may be important in treatment decisions. In institutions, where scarcity of individualized resources is common, and there is consequently a strong emphasis on the management of patients, there will exist a continuing temptation to focus on the antisocial dimensions of aggressivity, rather than on its self-destructive character, and psychosurgery may be recommended for the benefit of staff rather than that of the patient. Obviously those who act in aggressively antisocial ways need to be restrained in some way, but it needs to be considered whether psychosurgery represents a proper option in such circumstances, unless there is some reason to believe that there will be a commensurate direct benefit to the patient.

The second question concerns treatments said to be 'experimental'. Should proxy consent be permitted where treatment has that status, or is it better to safeguard non-competent patients against abuse by forbidding all experimentation on them? Would the latter violate their 'right to treatment?'

or constitute an unfair discrimination against them? Some jurisdictions and codes prohibit experimentation on non-competent patients; others permit it, but hedge it round with conditions.

Before we puruse this further, we should first consider its relevance to the present question. Is psychosurgery of the kind practised on and envisaged for mentally retarded patients experimental?

IS PSYCHOSURGERY AN EXPERIMENTAL PROCEDURE?

Because of the somewhat more stringent requirements that are usually associated with the use of experimental procedures, there has, not surprisingly, been a continuing debate about the status of psychosurgery. The lines in this debate are not easy to draw. Quite a number of those who advocate the use of psychosurgery are prepared to call it 'experimental', and even some of those who don't regard it as experimental often want to differentiate some types of psychosurgery as experimental. We will be best served here if we focus on the status of amygdalotomy performed to alleviate uncontrollable rage behaviour.[13]

One of the complicating factors in this debate has been an unclarity about the character of experimentation.[14] I have been able to find at least three well-worked understandings in the literature:

(1) There are some writers who wish to argue that everything a doctor does, diagnostically and therapeutically, is experimental. Diagnostic and therapeutic options have to be matched up with particular patient symptoms and susceptibilities, and, it is claimed, this process of matching is essentially experimental.

I think we may use 'experimental' broadly enough to cover this exploratory activity on a doctor's part, but I think it is unhelpful and misleading if it is used as a way of conflating what is being done when a doctor tries a person out on a particular antibiotic and, say, the use of psychosurgery in the treatment of obesity. No doubt there are important duties of care involved when a doctor engages in this type of experimentation. But there are other and more important senses in which the psychosurgical operation would be experimental and which are obscured if we expand the term to cover everything a doctor does.

(2) The use of a particular therapeutic

procedure may involve a more radical ignorance. If its effects cannot be easily predicted, if the mechanisms whereby it achieves its effects are not reasonably well understood, if it involves significant, variable and unpredictable risks, and its benefits are debatable, then it can be regarded as experimental. In this sense, where 'experimental' tends to be contrasted with 'established', calling a procedure 'experimental' means that it cannot be said with any confidence that, say, the procedure is successful in 85% of cases, that its contra-indications are A, B, and C, that there is a 0.001% risk of adverse side-effects X and Y, and so on. Here we are not dealing with a residual ignorance arising out of the particularities of the doctor/patient transaction, but with an ignorance of a much more fundamental kind.

Is amygdalotomy experimental in this sense? We face some formidable difficulties in answering a question of this kind, though I think the data we have strongly favours an affirmative answer. Although several hundred amygdalotomies have been performed and followed up for upward of eighteen months, the reported results are not particularly encouraging. It would appear that in some 40% of cases there has been a 'marked improvement', often gauged by reference to the patients's manageability. At the same time, various adverse operative and post-operative sequelae have been reported: some operative deaths, seizures, short-term memory loss and hemiplegia being the most common. Risks (and improvement rates) tend to vary with the study, though it has to be said that in the case of amygdalotomy, post-operative judgments are heavily oriented to clinical assessments, and are fairly unsophisticated at the level of psychometric assessment.[15]

It is not surprising that the figures for amygdalotomy are not better. The procedure is based on animal studies reported by Kluver and Bucy in 1939.[16] They performed temporal lobectomies (which included the amygdala) on laboratory primates and found that the animals become tame and fearless, indiscriminate in their eating and sexual behaviour, and suffered from visual agnosia and hypermetamorphosis. Terzian and Ore reproduced the syndrome in a human being in 1955.[17] This was the background to Narabayashi's amygdalotomies, begun in 1958. What captured his attention was their taming effect, and this determined his use of the procedure, despite the evidence of other sequelae. In the event, he reported good results and an absence of other Kluver-Bucy features. This serendipitous result is rendered more intelligible and more worrying by later primate studies, particularly by Pribram and Kling, in which it was found that the appearance of the Kluver-Bucy syndrome depended to a large extent on environmental factors, and that visual agnosia was probably its most persistent element.[18] This helped to explain why, in certain circumstances, the destruction of amygdaloid tissue diminished aggressiveness: the animals failed to appreciate threatening elements in their situation which would normally have triggered off aggressive behaviour. What is disturbing about these later findings, even allowing for the problems of transferring data from animal studies, is that what appears to be a reasonably specific operative consequence may in fact be but one facet of a more generalized effect, whose deleterious character is not being picked up in post-operative assessments. These worries have been reinforced by more recent human studies which suggest that what is characterized as 'visual agnosia' may be simply an extrapolation from an even more general deficit produced by lesioning temporal lobe structures, a disruption in the ability to integrate perceptual experience. It is this 'seat-of-the-pants' approach to` psychosurgery which makes it very difficult to see it as being other than experimental.

One psychiatrist involved in amygdalotomy has claimed that the relatively low improvement rate can be partially explained as the consequence of mis-sited lesions, an inference made on the basis of some post mortem examinations.[19] That may be so, but it does little to improve the procedure's stocks. The amygdala is a fairly small almond-shaped structure, and, even with contemporary stereotactic and radioencephalographic techniques, can be easily missed. In the case of people who are moderately to profoundly retarded, where there is a strong likelihood of some brain deformation, the chance of mis-siting lesions is considerable. Add to this the functional importance of the amygdala itself, and the technical difficulties become crucial. It is now generally considered that the limbic system comprises two functional circuits, one largely concerned with modulating a person's behaviour with respect to the outer world, the other concerned with emotionality. That is not all the system is concerned with, but it indicates why

contemporary psychosurgery focuses there rather than
elsewhere in the brain structure. Within this
system, the amygdala constitutes one of the few
points of connection between the two circuits, and
so its lesioning is likely to have wide
ramifications for the person's total functioning.
Not only so, but different nuclei of the amygdala
seem to be more closely associated with different
emotional responses, so there is an additional risk
involved should lesioning be misplaced. Some
psychosurgeons have attempted to circumvent this
problem by implanting electrodes in the region and
stimulating them to determine the correct siting.
But there are various theoretical difficulties about
correlating the data from stimulation of this kind
with clinical data, and the practical outcome of
this operative procedure does not seem to have been
significantly better than achieved by less 'precise'
techniques.

(3) A further sense of 'experimental' can be
distinguished by considering the intentions of those
who treat. Interventions designed to increase or
confirm knowledge of a general kind, particularly
where some manipulation or control of variables is
required, are generally considered to be
experimental in nature. This does not mean that
they cannot also be therapeutic in intent. Indeed,
what is often sought is therapeutically significant
knowledge.

Nevertheless, the demands of therapy and the
demands of experimental design are not identical.
The requirements of scientific validity may
sometimes be in tension with the needs of a
particular therapeutic, or more broadly,
doctor/patient interaction, and a choice between
ends will need to be made. Doctors do not
automatically put the patient first, and that is one
reason why patients whose treatment is part of an
experimental project need to be made aware of this,
and be given the opportunity to determine the limits
of their participation. Obviously non-competent
patients are not in a position to make such
determinations, and in their case, if there is some
reason for including them in such a project, there
is a strong reason for ensuring that therapeutic
considerations take priority.

Whether or not amygdalotomy is experimental in
this third sense will obviously depend on the
particular team involved. Some will see themselves
as doing no more than using a procedure that others
have developed, perhaps recording their results for

posterity. Others will see themselves as pushing back the frontiers of their subject, and may well find themselves with choices generated by the dual purposes of their intervention. One of the more controversial contributions to the contemporary debate has been Mark and Ervins's study, Violence and the Brain, in which amygdalotomies were performed on patients in whom temporal lobe epilepsy and uncontrollable rage episodes appeared to be associated.[20] They reported favourably on their results, but performed only about twenty operations. When asked why, Ervin responded: 'Our concern is not to treat a lot of people but to figure out what is going on. I am persuaded that I now know the questions to take to the laboratory and do not need to do any more for a while'.[21] Mentally retarded people are particularly vulnerable to this kind of experimentation.

If, as I am suggesting, amygdalotomy is always experimental in the second sense, and is sometimes experimental in the third sense, what implications does this have where mentally retarded patients are concerned? I do not find this an easy question to answer. There is a lot to be said for prohibiting the use of amygdalotomy where a valid consent cannot be obtained. It is a highly intrusive procedure, associated with significant risks and relatively uncertain benefits, not in any obvious way in the patient's 'best interests', and it would be presumptuous for a proxy consenter to claim to do more than speculate what the patient would have chosen had he or she been competent to do so. Given the vulnerability of mentally retarded persons to exploitation and abuse, whether by doctors or relatives, it might seem fairer to exclude them from that treatment option. It might be replied to this that a 40% marked improvement rate is not so bad when you're considering a group of people for whom all other treatments have failed, and who in many cases would have to be closely supervised or even confined in protective harnesses lest they mutilate themselves or injure others. We can perhaps add to that our recognition that in these cases improvement could not amount to much in the way of personal autonomy, since the psychosurgery would not affect the retardation. Nor would any autonomy be violated, since there would have been none to start with. So one of the major grounds for concern about psychosurgery would not be relevant.

Closer inspection of the pro-psychosurgery argument, however, reveals some weaknesses that are

not immediately apparent. For one thing, the 40%
improvement rate contains no discounting for placebo
effects.[22] It is, moreover, a composite, heavily
influenced by the results of an Indian study. Here
we have some reason to ask whether the treatment was
really a 'last resort', or simply an easy and
effective way of dealing with a domestic/social
problem. Probably no more than 0.005% of India's
mentally retarded population has access to
institutional care, and the relatively high
improvement rate may partially reflect that (along
with a somewhat narrow conception of improvement).
In the Australian study, only 20% showed any marked
improvement, with an even worse showing for the more
severely retarded. The poorer prognosis in the case
of the more severely retarded seems to be reflected
in other studies.[23]

PSYCHOSURGERY AND HEALTHY BRAIN TISSUE

I do not think we yet have a decisive argument
against the therapeutic use of psychosurgrey on
non-competent, erethistic mentally retarded
patients. Nevertheless, it is very easy to feel
uneasy about employing a procedure of this kind.
One source of this unease is the belief that even in
the case of the mentally retarded, psychosurgical
lesioning is not normatively different from the
removal of a kleptomaniac's hand. Even if it stops
behaviour that needs to be stopped, it is an
inappropriate means to that end. A perfectly
healthy hand, useful for purposes other than
stealing, is removed just so that certain
unacceptable behaviour over which the person has no
proper control can be curtailed. Once removed, it
cannot be replaced. The argument may even be
broadened to accommodate cases in which consent is
obtainable. A parallel can be drawn with cases in
which self-mutilation and mayhem are consented to,
options consistently rejected by our legal
tradition.
Whatever the merits of the argument, it has
clearly bothered some advocates of the
psychosurgical treatment of the episodic dyscontrol
syndrome. Vernon Mark, who strongly advocates
surgical treatment, is no less insistent that it be
associated with temporal lobe epilepsy. He sees it
as the neurosurgical treatment of electro-chemical
malfunctioning in the brain. Others have thought it
sufficient that brain lesions would ameliorate the

condition, though they have often supposed that in
time some brain malfunction would be discovered.
Histological normality, they have insisted, should
not be taken to indicate functional normality.

If indeed the psychosurgical treatment of
aggression is premissed upon some brain malfunction,
as appears to be the case where the aggressive
behaviour is associated with temporal lobe epilipsy,
then much of the bad smell about psychosurgery is
dissipated. We have no qualms about brain surgery
to remove tumours that may be affecting behaviour;
lesioning the amygdala where temporal lobe epilipsy
is associated with episodes of uncontrollable rage
may seem to be no more than a modest extension of
this. Or if it does seem to be more than that,
since we do not usually have evidence that it is the
amygdala that is malfunctioning, but some other
region of the temporal lobe or its environs which is
overstimulating the amygdala, then we may liken it
to removal of normally functioning endocrine glands
in a bid to stop the spread of cancer.

But the bad smell cannot be dispersed quite so
readily, for the connection between temporal lobe
epilepsy and aggressivity is not as straightforward
as the advocates of psychosurgery sometimes claim.
There is, first of all, the problem of diagnosing
temporal lobe epilepsy. That is no great problem
where there is clinical evidence of seizures; but
sometimes doctors seem content to interpret abnormal
EEG activity as evidence of temporal lobe epilepsy,
and there have even been cases in which episodic
rage has been assumed to be the result of temporal
lobe disorder. This last assumption is particularly
pernicious, since few of those who have outbursts of
uncontrollable rage suffer from temporal lobe
epilepsy, and only a minority of those who suffer
from temporal lobe epilepsy display the episodic
dyscontrol syndrome. A further difficulty arises
when it is noticed that the rage episodes frequently
occur interictally, and not in conjunction with a
seizure. Compounding this, psychosurgical treatment
which diminishes episodic violence frequently leaves
the epilepsy (otherwise?) unaffected.

I mention these points because they need to be
accounted for by those who maintain that the
psychosurgical treatment of certain kinds of
aggression is not significantly different from the
neurosurgical treatment of parkinsonism. I think
they probably can be accounted for, at least in some
of the cases for which psychosurgical treatment is
thought appropriate. If the amygdala is not itself

disordered, but is simply one of the sites which is hyperactivated by abnormal discharges elsewhere in the temporal lobe, then it is possible to give a physiological explanation for both interictal violence and the persistence of epileptic seizures following amygdalotomy.

The claim that psychosurgery is directed at a physically based condition is also plausible in the case of erethistic mental retardation. Where retardation is severe or profound, there is usually some brain deformation or damage, and it is not unreasonable to see the disordered emotion and behaviour as a consequence of this. However as I noted earlier, amygdalotomy is not well indicated for people in this condition. That goes for other procedures which are sometimes attempted: posterior hypothalamotomy, dorsomedial thalamotomy, and leucotomy. There is a good reason for this. Except for certain tissue-type functions (e.g. heart beat, vomiting), brain functions cannot usually be localized in particular structures. This is especially so when we come to the so-called 'higher' functions, which appear to be systemically based. So, although the amygdala does appear to be more closely associated with aggression than some other parts of the brain, there is no reason to believe that it is necessarily or exclusively connected with it.

Let us leave these speculations and uncertainties, and consider those cases for which no evidence of deformation or damage can be provided. Many who are mildly retarded fall into this category. Ought they to be permitted to consent to or undergo psychosurgical treatment? Is there something sacrosanct about structurally and functionally normal non-replaceable tissue? I think not. I see nothing immoral about donating a kidney to someone who needs it, and if the removal of good tissue is intended to benefit not another but oneself, I don't see that that somehow makes it immoral. The problem of course is one of the risk-benefit ratio, and in psychosurgery, it has often been thought that the risks were more certain and substantial than the benefits. I doubt whether that holds generally. However, I think it may hold in the case of amygdalotomy, though I would be reluctant to prohibit it. What does seem to me necessary is that it be thoroughly reviewed and monitored, lest vulnerable persons are subjected to invasions of their persons which they could not or should not be expected to consent to.

87

NOTES

1   The development of psychosurgery is detailed in Valenstein, E.S. Brain Control: A Critical Examination of Brain Stimulation and Psychosurgery, New York: Wiley, 1973. An updated overview can be found in Part I of his edited collection, The Psychosurgery Debate: Scientific, Legal and Ethical Perspectives, San Francisco: W.H. Freeman, 1980, and in O'Callaghan, M.A.J. and Carroll, D. Psychosurgery: A Scientific Analysis, Lancaster: MTP Press, 1982.

2   Narabayashi, H., Nagao, T., Saito, Y., Yoshida, M. and Nagahata, M. "Stereotaxic Amygdalotomy for Behavior Disorders", Archives of Neurology, IX (July, 1963), II; cf. Narabayashi H. and Uno, M. "Long range results of sterotaxic amygdalotomy", Confinia Neurologica, XXVII (1966), 168-71.

3   Kiloh, L.G., Gye, R.S., Rushworth, R.G., Bell, D.S. and White R.T. "Stereotactic Amygdaloidotomy for Aggressive Behaviour", Journal of Neurology, Neurosurgery, and Psychiatry, XXXVII (1974), 437-44.

4   See, e.g. Hitchcock E. and Cairns, V. "Amygdalotomy'", Postgraduate Medical Journal, XLIX (1973), 894-904; Siegfried J. and Ben-Shmuel, A. "Long-Term Assessment of Stereotactic Amygdalatomy for Aggressive Behaviour" and Nadvornik, P., Pogady, J., and Sramka, M. "The Results of Stereotactic Treatment of the Aggressive Syndrome", in L. Laitinen and K.E. Livingston (Eds.), Surgical Approaches in Psychiatry, Lancaster: MTP Press, 1973, 000-006 and 125-8, respectively.

5   Ciganek, L., Benko, J., and Mr. Cackova, "Surgical Treatment of Epilepsy and Mental Disorders in Children" [trans.], Ceskoslovenska Psychiatrie, LXIX, 6 (December, 1973), 363-5, abstracted in Mental Retardation: An abstracted bibliography 1971-1980, Washington, D.C.: American Psychological Association, 1982, p. 249.

6   Balasubramaniam V. and Kanaka, T.S. "Amygdalotomy and Hypothalamotomy - a Comparative Study", Confinia Neurologica, XXXVII (1975), 195-201; cf. idem, 'Hypothalamotomy in the management of Aggressive Behavior', in T.P. Morley (Ed.), Current Controversies in Neurosurgery,

PSYCHOSURGERY

Philadelphia: W.B. Saunders, 1976, pp. 195-201.
7 Bridges, P.K. personal communication, 14 March, 1984.
8 My views on consent are developed and defended in "The Ethics of Consent", in Kai Nielsen and Steven C. Patten (Eds.), New Essays in Ethics and Public Policy, Canadian Journal of Philosophy, Supplementary Volume VIII, Guelph, Ontario: Canadian Association for Publishing in Philosophy, 1982, pp. 91-118.
9 For useful discussions of mental retardation, see Hayes, S.C. and Hayes, R. Mental Retardation: Law, policy and administration, Sydney: Law Book Co., 1982; R. Macklin and W. Gaylin (Eds.), Mental Retardation and Sterilization: A Problem of Competency and Paternalism, New York: Plenem Press, 1981.
10 A generalized claim to this effect was argued in the US case, Kaimowitz v. Department of Mental Health, Civ. No. 73-19434AW (Cir. Ct., Wayne City, Mich., 1973), reprinted with briefs in Shuman, S.I. Psychosurgery and the Medical Control of Violence: Autonomy and deviance, Detroit: Wayne State University Press, 1977. Although there were inadequacies in this argument, there is some evidence that in the case in question the court's concern was well-founded. See Burt, R.A. "Why We Should Keep Prisoners from Doctors", Hastings Centre Report, V, 1 (February, 1975), 25-34.
11 Rawls, J. A Theory of Justice, Cambridge, Mass.: Harvard University Press, 1971, p. 92.
12 Some have suggested that where a therapy is still experimental in character, the patient's assent, should be obtained. In circumstances where the patient's own will is unknown, and best interests moot, assent would provide an additional safeguard against exploitation.
13 Although the amygdala has been the major focus in this connection, several closely related structures have been targetted - particularly the posterior hypothalamus, and dorsomedial thalamus, or some combination of structures. Because of their functional interconnections, much of what is said about amygdalotomy can also be said about posterior hypothalamotomy and dorsomedial thalamotomy. If anything, the problem confronting amygdalotomy are more serious where hypothalamotomy is concerned.
14 I have developed this material at greater

89

length in Ethica Issues in Psychosurgery, London: Allen & Unwin, 1985, Ch. 4. See also Dickens, B.M. "What is a Medical Experiment?", Canadian Medical Association Journal, CXIII, 7 (4 October, 1975), 635-9.

15 For surveys of the clinical data, see Carroll D. and O'Callaghan, M.A.J. "Psychosurgery and the Control of Aggression", in Paul F. Brain and David Benton (Eds.), The Biology of Aggression, Alphen aan den rijn, The Netherlands: Sijthoff & Noordhoff, 1981, pp. 457-71; One factor that most of these studies tend to neglect is the extent of the placebo effect involved.

16 Kluver, H. and Bucy, P.C. "Preliminary Analysis of Functions of the Temporal Lobes in Monkeys", Archives of Neurology and Psychiatry, XLII (1939), 979-1000.

17 Terzian, H. and Ore, G.D. "Syndrome of Kluver-Bucy Reproduced in Man by Bilateral Removal of the Temporal Lobes", Neurology, V (1955), 373-80.

18 Rosvold, H.E., Mirsky, A.F. and Pribram, K.H. "Influence of Amygdalectomy on Social Behaviour in Monkeys", Journal of Comparative Physiological Psychology, XLVII (1954), 173-8; Kling, A. "Effects of Amygdalectomy on Social-Affective Behavior in Non-Human Primates", in B.E. Eleftheriou (Ed.), The Neurobiology of the Amygdala, New York: Plenum, 1972.

19. Kiloh, L.G. as quoted in McIlraith, S. "Psychosurgery is Still Going Ahead", Sydney Morning Herald, 3/10/1980, p. 2.

20 Mark, V. H. and Ervin, F.R. Violence and the Brain, New York: Harper & Row, 1970.

21 Ervin, F.R. "The Treatment of Rage - Implications for the Future", in J. Sydney Smith and L.G. Kiloh (Eds.), Psychosurgery and Society, Oxford: Pergamon Press, 1977, p. 80.

22 Cf. Beecher, H.K. "Surgery as Placebo: A quantitative study bias", Journal of the American Medical Association, CLXXVI, 13 (1 July, 1961), 1102-7, where it is argued that placebo effects in surgery may made a difference of up to 35%.

23 Cf. Heimberger, R.F., Whitlock, C.C. and Kalsbeck, J.E. "Stereotaxic Amygdalotomy for Epilepsy with Aggressive Behavior", Journal of the American Medical Association, CXCVIII (1966), 741-5; Narabayashi et al., 20.

Chapter Six

CAN WE AVOID ASSIGNING GREATER VALUE TO SOME
HUMAN LIVES THAN TO OTHERS?

Peter Singer

The question I have taken as my title arises
because it is frequently said that we must avoid
comparing the value of one human life and the value
of another. Each and every human life, it is said,
is equally sacred or is of infinite worth or of
infinite intrinsic value. To regard the life of a
severely and irreparably retarded human being as
less valuable than the life of a normal human, those
who take this position will suggest, is to violate
this fundamental notion of human equality. It is
also, some would go on to add, the first step down a
slippery slope, a slope that leads eventually to the
elimination of all those whom the rulers or elite in
a society regard as the unfit. Next will come the
anti-social, then the politically undesirable, and
perhaps in the end, all those who don't belong to
some self-decreed master race.
        In what follows, I shall focus on some cases
where this kind of attitude has practical
consequences. One such case was reported by Anthony
Shaw in an article entitled "Dilemmas of 'Informed
Consent' in Children" published in the New England
Journal of Medicine".

A baby was born with Down's syndrome
(mongolism), intestinal obstructions, and a
heart condition. The mother, believing that
the retarded infant would be impossible for her
to care for adequately, refused to consent to
surgery to remove the intestinal obstruction.
Without surgery, of course, the baby would soon
die. Thereupon a local child-welfare agency,
invoking a state child-abuse statute, obtained
a court order directing that surgery be
performed. After a complicated course of

surgery and thousands of dollars worth of
medical care, the infant was returned to her
mother. In addition to her mental retardation,
the baby's physical growth and development
remained markedly retarded because of her
severe cardiac disease. A follow-up enquiry
eighteen months after the baby's birth revealed
that the mother felt more than ever that she
had been done an injustice. [1]

That case is similar to a much more recent case
which was quite widely reported in the newspapers.
A baby identified only by the Christian name of
Alexandra, was born at the Queen Charlotte Hospital,
London in July of 1981. Alexandra also had Down's
Syndrome and an intestinal obstruction, but
apparently did not have the congenital heart disease
reported in the case by Shaw. Here too, it was
suggested in the discussion that one should not
distinguish between levels of life. That case went
to court because the municipal council sought to
order the operation performed.
The initial judge declined to make such an
order. The case then went to the appeal court where
Lord Justice Templeman ordered the operation
performed. Lord Justice Templeman did not say that
no matter what the particular circumstances, such an
operation must be performed. He held out the
possibility that there might be a case where the
life would be so "demonstrably awful" for the child
that it would not be right to order the operation;
but he said that in Alexandra's case, where Down's
Syndrome would be the only defect once the operation
was performed, the operation should go ahead. [2]
The Guardian then published a leader in which it
supported this decision and suggested that in
accordance with this judgement, it was necessary to
make this kind of distinction between forms of life.
[3] The result was a number of letters, some of
which complained that the Guardian was suggesting
that some lives are more valuable than others and
that this was contrary to the idea of human
equality. [4]
The final case, and perhaps the most tragic and
horrific of these cases, is the case of the Siamese
twins born in May, 1981 in Danville, Illinois.
These twins were joined in a particularly grotesque
manner, having two upper bodies but only one trunk,
with two legs and a vestigal third leg. Upon
delivery, the obstetrician stayed the hand of the
nurse who was about to rescusitate the twins. The

ASSIGNING VALUE TO HUMAN LIVES

father, who was present at the delivery, concurred in this; but as it turned out rescusitation was not necessary. The twins survived birth without medical intervention.

The doctor then, after consulting the parents, ordered that the twins not be fed, and should have nursing care only. This situation continued for a few days, but there were clearly some on the nursing staff who disagreed with it - apparently at one point the twins were fed by a nurse contrary to the doctor's orders. The case was finally reported to the Illinois Child Welfare Department which sought a court order to take over custody of the twins. It obtained such an order. Thereafter, the twins were fed. The State then went further and sought a prosecution for attempted murder against the doctor and parents. When the issue came to court, the Illinois State Attorney who was responsible for the prosecution, Edward Littak set it out like this:

> Quality of life has nothing to do with it. Under no circumstances do you take a life because you disagree with the quality of it. These kids would have lived and are living human beings. They are entitled to life as long as nature gives it to them. [5]

WHY QUALITY OF LIFE IS CRUCIAL

Let us consider this question then, whether indeed one can concur with the idea that where you have a living human being, the quality of life has nothing to do with it. Can this view be defended? It is my view that despite the fact that it is a view which fits with things that we would like to believe, ultimately it cannot be defended. When someone says to us: "These were living human beings," we have to ask: "What is so special about being human?" That question must be answered in a way that is morally relevant to these· decisions about keeping alive or not keeping alive; and the only morally relevant way of answering it is by reference to certain characteristics of the lives of human beings - in other words to certain points about the nature or quality of their lives. We have to ask: "Is there any quality, any characteristic, which is possessed by all human beings? And indeed only by human beings?" We must ask these questions. Because what people are saying here is that if a being is human, its life should be preserved whatever the quality is. They would also say, in general, that its life ought to be preserved above the value or the importance of preservation we place on the lives of any nonhuman animals.

Now, if we look at the cases that we are sometimes faced with - one could argue about exactly which cases should be discussed here, but if we take for example the most severe forms of retardation or of brain damage - then I believe that we cannot find any characteristic or quality of life which does single out these beings that are human (in the sense of members of the species homo sapiens) from those other beings who are not members of the species homo sapiens, who also have, obviously, a certain quality of life. Think about the notion that merely because a being is a living human being, its life must be regarded as having some infinite value or intrinsic worth, and this value is something about which you cannot even enquire as to its quality. This notion is one which singles out a biological species, and says of that species, that the lives of its members are somehow superior to the lives of members of other species. If that judgment is to carry moral conviction it must be a judgment that is based on some morally relevant characteristic of the species.

In the case of normal humans we can do this without any problem. We can say that normal humans have certain characteristics which no nonhuman animals have. Capacities to reason, to anticipate the distant future, to communicate in a sophisticated way, to plan their lives, to be as fully self-conscious as humans are: all these things one might say, mark off the normal mature human from most if not all other species. Those characteristics, however, are precisely the ones that will be lacking in some of the cases that here are being considered, the cases of extreme mental defect. Therefore, those characteristics cannot be used as a way of defending the claim that there is infinite worth, or a special unique intrinsic value, in the lives of all members of our species. I don't think we can find any such characteristic of all members of the species homo sapiens which does elevate them above others - at least, not if we confine ourselves to a broadly secular perspective.

No doubt, one could claim on the basis of religious revelation, say, that in fact all human beings, all members of the species homo sapiens, however defective, however retarded, have an immortal soul. If that could be established, then perhaps that would suggest a reason why there is

94

some difference between the intrinsic value of the lives of all humans, no matter how defective, and the intrinsic value of the lives of all nonhuman animals. However, I do not believe that such an argument can be made out. If it can be made, it can only be based on a religious faith which is not an argument that has any prospect of acceptance by those outside that faith.

Putting aside any such religious defence, it seems to me that there is no characteristic to which one can refer which suggests that the lives of all human beings have some intrinsic value which the lives of nonhuman animals do not. This suggests that the attitude I referred to at the beginning, the attitude that all human life is of intrinsic worth simply because it is human, cannot really be defended in terms of a soundly based ethical theory. This attitude, though widely held, is a legacy of a specific religious and cultural heritage which our society is now questioning in a variety of ways.

When people talk of the declining belief in the sanctity of life in our society, they are referring to the fact that our society no longer accepts uncritically a religious Judeo-Christian framework of thought. In rejecting this framework we are starting to think critically about this underlying religious idea that all human life is sacrosanct simply in virtue of being human, though we are perhaps not fully aware of what we are doing. It is important to realize that this is a doctrine specific to our Judeo-Christian culture, and not one widely shared among the hundreds, or indeed thousands, of human cultures known to us. In cultures that we would regard as highly civilized such as ancient Greece, Mandarin China or traditional Japan, the notion that life was sacred from conception or even from birth was not accepted in the way that it has been accepted during the last couple of thousand years in our society.

ERODING THE SANCTITY OF LIVE VIEW

The basic principle being discussed here, the principle of the sanctity of life, is being eroded by greater critical reflection outside the religious framework in which it most naturally fits. This critical reflection, however, has not been systematic. It has not dared to tackle the sanctity of life doctrine at its root. Therefore, it has led to patched solutions to particular issues. What I shall now do is to discuss some of the ways in which we are already accepting outcomes that are at odds with the sanctity of life principle. In other words, I shall examine some of the recent erosions of that doctrine.

Perhaps the most obvious of these erosions, if you look at the last 10 - 20 years, is the acceptance of abortion in a very large number of Western societies. There has been a dramatic change, if you consider statements to be found in medical journals no more than 20 years ago, which suggested that readily available abortion would have a very drastic role in undermining the nature of medical practice, and could lead to the collapse of the medical ethic that life is to be preserved, not taken. Since then, the majority of our society have accepted abortion and would not see it as in any way akin to the ordinary taking of life.

I do not wish to discuss all the arguments about abortion in this paper. One thing that can be said without discussing the entire issue, however, is that if there is a majority acceptance of abortion in general, there is a still greater acceptance of the idea that abortion is legitimate where a defect is detected during pregnancy. Defects like Down's Syndrome or spina bifida can now be detected during pregnancy and in these cases people would agree that the woman should be offered an abortion. This suggests that we do not regard all lives as of equal value. For if we did, then we would say: "Even though this fetus will become a Down's Syndrome child, or will suffer from spina bifida, nevertheless its life is of infinite value and for that reason abortion should be considered no more justifiable in that case than it should in any other case." Consider for a moment the fact that we do not think this way, and what it implies about our readiness to make decisions about the quality of life, and to hold that some lives are less worthy of carrying through to maturity because of the defects that they have.

A second case would come from the kind of practice that was illustrated by the two Down's Syndrome cases I described earlier, but is even more evident in the treatment of spina bifida babies. Here, I think it is quite clear that there is a growing practice of making decisions as to whether to treat vigorously or not to treat vigorously spina bifida babies on the basis of some assessment of the quality of their life. This has been described by John Lorber, one of England's leading physicians in this area. [6] Lorber examines the nature and location of the opening in the spine, and takes account of the presence of hydrocephalus or other complicating conditions.

Using these indicators, Lorber has developed a type of scale which guides him as to whether or not the baby should be treated vigorously. He was led to this result because for sometime previously, he simply treated all babies as vigorously as possible. The result was that there was a large increase in the survival of spina bifida babies, but the quality of life was so poor that he decided he was not doing the right thing. Hence he became more selective about the babies he would treat. The result of this selection, now widely practised in Britain and many other countries, is that fewer babies survive but those that do survive have a much better quality of life, on average, than used to be the case when all survived. Those that are not vigorously treated generally die within something like about nine months at the most.

Lorber himself does not endorse active euthanasia. He believes that there is a distinction between omitting to save life and actively taking life. I do not believe that there is an ultimate moral distinction here, but whether omitting to save life is, or is not morally equivalent to taking it, as long as we endorse the idea that we should not strive to save all these babies, we are also endorsing the idea that quality of life assessment is possible and that it is not the case that all lives have equal intrinsic worth.

The third example of cases which show an erosion of the sanctity of life principle is one which is widely used by those who are perhaps most likely to invoke the sanctity of life doctrine themselves: the distinction between ordinary and extraordinary means. Here, I think it can be shown that the distinction as it is commonly drawn is not a distinction between what are "ordinary means", recognized simply by their ordinariness, and "extraordinary means" recognized by the high technology that they use. Rather the distinction as it is used is related to the quality of life of the patient, so that in the case of a very severely defective child (let us say a spina bifida baby with very poor prospects) a doctor may well judge that the administration of antibiotics to ward off pneumonia would be the use of "extraordinary" means and therefore, the doctor would not do it. Whereas, if you had a normal baby suffering from a bout of pneumonia there would be no doubt whatsoever that one would consider the administration of antibiotics as perfectly ordinary. The point here is that the distinction between "ordinary" and "extraordinary" means is not a distinction in terms of the nature of the means themselves, but rather a distinction relating to what is appropriate for the circumstances, and what is appropriate for the circumstances will itself depend on an assessment of the quality of life that the patient would have. [7]

Fourth and finally, among these areas where we have already broken away from the idea of all life having equal and intrinsic value, there is the question of allocation of resources. It is sometimes said, for example in the American debate about whether or not the United States Government should pay for kidney dialysis for everyone, that it is impossible to place a dollar value on a person's life. The belief that a person's life is always of infinite value has the implication that as a society we ought to be prepared to commit <u>any</u> resources to the saving of life, that we must not quantify life and say that life is only worth a hundred thousand dollars, or half a million dollars, or whatever. And yet, I think we now realize that to avoid such estimates is simply not possible. As a society, we simply cannot save every life which it is technically possible to save. We have to apply our resources in such a way that we really are deciding that certain lives are too costly to save.

In making that decision I believe we are again guided by questions about quality of life rather than simply the number of lives saved. In some cases, a life could be saved but the resulting quality of life would be so poor that it is not worth the expenditure. It is better to put the resources available into saving lives that will have a better quality.

ASSESSING QUALITY OF LIFE

I have said that we are already making judgments about the different values of life in a covert and disguised way. I am proposing here that we bring these judgments in to the open a little, and begin to discuss the grounds on which such statements may be made. The final question is, how is one to do this? In what ways can one assess the values of lives and give weight to some rather than others? I am not going to make much in the way of concrete suggestions here. I think some steps have been made in that direction. For example, a recent paper by Dr. W. O. Spitzer and others describes a scale produced in an attempt to assess the quality of life in terminally ill patients (Spitzer, Dobson, Hall, Chesterman, Levi, Shepherd, Battistra & Catchlove, 1981). [8] Difficult as this task undoubtedly is, we could at least begin to develop a list of the kind of factors that we think of as making life particularly valuable and worthwhile.

One might begin with such simple things as the capacity to experience pleasure or joy, and conversely the absence of both physical pain and the absence of mental suffering. We would need to go on from there to take account of such things as the capacity to live a self-conscious life. By that I mean the capacity to understand that one is a being separate from the rest of the world, with a life of one's own to lead; that is, to look at one's life from a point of view that has some detachment from moment to moment existence and is able to see life as something that continues over time - to understand, for example, that one has had a past and that one will in the normal course of events have some kind of future. I think this is a significant characteristic, and we might well decide that it is something that contributes to the importance of preserving life. Similarly, ability to communicate with others, to recognize and respond to others, to relate to them in some way, could be an important characteristic that we would think makes a difference to the quality of life.

I do not intend to extend this list at this point. You can think of your own lists and then speculate about how you would try and weight or rank them. That is really a task for another paper, and certainly a very difficult task. I do not want to underestimate it. What I have been trying to suggest is simply that it is a task we need to attempt, a task we cannot avoid simply by making declamations to the effect that all life is of intrinsic and equal or infinite value, irrespective of the mental level of those under consideration. We are already in a situation in which we judge some lives as being of superior quality to, and having more value than, others. We will have to continue to go in that direction.

NOTES

1. Shaw, A. "Dilemmas of 'informed consent' in children", New England Journal of Medicine, 1973, <u>289</u>.

2. The decision of Lord Justice Templeman was reported in The Times Law Report, August 8, 1981.

3. For the Guardian leader, see Guardian Weekly, August 16, 1981.

4. The letters may be found in the Guardian Weekly, August 23, 1981.

5. Littak, E. Gannett News Service, Independent Journal, June 13, 1981.

6. Lorber, J. "Early Results of Selective Treatment of Spina Bifida Cystica," British Medical Journal, October 27, 1973, 202-204.

7. Kuhse, H. "Extraordinary means and the sanctity of life", Journal of Medical Ethics, 1981, <u>7</u>, 74-79.

8. Spitzer, W.O., Dobson, A.J., Hall, J.E., Chesterman, J., Levi, J., Shepherd, J.R., Battistra, R.N. & Catchlove, B.R. "Measuring the Quality of Life of Cancer Patients", Journal of Chronic Diseases, 1981, <u>12</u>, 585-597.

Chapter Seven

INFANTICIDE

Bonnie Steinbock

Current medical technology enables us to screen
pregnant women for many fetal abnormalities, such as
Down's syndrome and spina bifida. Some day such
diseases may be curable in utero; at present,
however, the main reason for performing these tests
is to give pregnant women the option of abortion.
Sometimes defects are not spotted, because the tests
are not carried out or because the results are
incorrect. What should be done with severely
defective babies who would have been aborted had the
defects been spotted before birth? Must their lives
now be protected? Do they have a right to life?

This issue was raised in the case of "Baby Jane
Doe" (we now know her name is Keri-Lynn), who was
born in New York in October, 1983 with serious
disorders: meningomyelocele, a form of spina bifida
in which part of the spinal cord protrudes, covered
by a thin membrane, forming a sac; hydrocephaly, or
fluid in the skull; and (possibly) microcephaly, an
abnormally small skull. Her physicians informed her
parents that unless she had surgery to correct the
spina bidifida and hydrocephaly, her life expectancy
ranged from a few weeks to two years. With surgery,
she might survive twenty years, but would be
severely retarded, epileptic, paralyzed and subject
to constant urinary tract and bladder infections.
After consulting with neurological experts, nurses,
religious counselors and a social worker, the
parents, Dan and Linda, declined to consent to the
proposed surgery, opting instead for antibiotics to
protect against infection of the spinal column.
Their intention was to keep their daughter
comfortable, but not to prolong her life.

At that point, a "right-to-life" lawyer,
Lawrence Washburn, Jr., received a confidential tip
that the infant was being denied life-preserving

surgery, and took her parents and Stony Brook
Hospital, where the surgery would have been
performed, to court. Justice Melvyn Tanenbaum of
the State Supreme Court, New York's lowest court,
authorized her court-appointed guardian to give
consent to surgery, but this ruling was reversed by
higher courts. The case went all the way to the
United States Supreme Court which declined to hear
it. Without comment, the justices let stand the
decision of New York's highest court, the Court of
Appeals, that the parents of the infant had the
right to withhold life-prolonging surgery.[1]

The case of Baby Jane Doe raises a host of
issues. Some are largely procedural, raising the
question of who has the right to decide to withhold
treatment, and when the state may intervene. The
New York Court of Appeals based its decision in
favor of the parents primarily on procedural
grounds. It held that the intrusion of a totally
unrelated person, with no knowledge of the infant's
condition or treatment, violated the parents' right
of privacy. Since procedures already exist to
protect children from neglect or abuse, procedures
which were not followed in this case, this intrusion
was unjustifiable.

The decision of the Court of Appeals should
protect the parents of future Baby Does from
illegitimate intrusion into their lives. However,
the central philosophical issue is not who should
decide when treatment should be withheld, or what
procedures must be followed to challenge the right
of parents to make such decisions, but what are the
criteria justifying the withholding of life-
prolonging treatment for defective newborns? Is
this always and intrinsically neglect? Or can it be
in an infant's own best interest to withold such
treatment?

It is important to distinguish here two
different questions, or sets of questions. One set
is factual and concerns the actual condition and
prognosis of the child in question. The other is
philosophical and concerns the relevance of various
factors to withholding treatment. Some argue that
such decisions should be made on medical grounds
alone, that "quality of life" considerations are
irrelevant. There is no such thing as "a life not
worth living"; any life is better than no life at
all. This position is called "vitalism". By
contrast, anti-vitalists think that life need not be
prolonged when prolonging it is not in the infant's
best interest, although they may differ widely on

what that is.

I wish to point out, parenthetically, that I have phrased the issue in terms of "withholding treatment" and "prolonging life" because that is how it is usually discussed. Parents may have the legal right to withhold life-prolonging treatment from their children; they never have the right to kill them, no matter how severely defective they are. Those who oppose withholding life-prolonging treatment from defective infants think that this is killing them, and they object to obscuring this by what they regard as mere euphemisms. While I think that it is simplistic to label every withholding of life-prolonging treatment as intentional killing,[2] I agree that the question raised in the case of Baby Jane Doe, and in many of the other Baby Does, is whether life itself is in the infant's best interest. In these cases, the point of discontinuing or withholding treatment is to end the child's life. Therefore, it is properly regarded as infanticide, and morally justified only if active killing would also be, whatever the legal situation. So I am quite willing to acknowledge that at least sometimes not treating is killing, but I take no position in this chapter on whether there is ever a difference between active and passive euthanasia, or killing and letting die. Nothing I say here depends on there being such a difference.

Vitalists maintain that treatment may not be withheld, regardless of prognosis. So even if the pessimistic prognosis offered by some of Baby Jane Doe's doctors was entirely correct, vitalists would maintain that treatment was morally necessary. By contrast, those who regard quality of life as relevant to treatment decisions would maintain that if withholding treatment is ever justifiable, it was justifiable in that case. Whatever the standards of a life not worth living, a life consisting of little more than pain surely qualifies. But was Keri-Lynn necessarily doomed to such a life? this brings us to the factual questions, concerning the accuracy of the prognosis. There was testimony that, with surgery, Keri-Lynn might escape retardation alogether, walk with braces, and enjoy, if not a "normal" life, a happy and meaningful one. This factual disagreement in turn refers back to the procedural questions: who should decide when the experts disagree about the child's condition? In addition, disagreement over condition and prognosis is not purely "factual", as doctors' views are conditioned by their ethical beliefs. Vitalists

tend to be optimists, while those who favor
infanticide - at least in some situations - tend to
paint more pessimistic pictures.

The parents of Keri-Lynn maintain that their
decision to withhold surgery was made out of love
for their daughter. They believe that condemning
her to twenty years of severe retardation,
paralysis, and pain would be cruel. They have not
abandoned her, but have taken her home to care for
her as long as she lives. Nor have they rejected
all surgical intervention; in the spring of 1984,
they consented to a shunt to make her more
comfortable. They regard all their decisions as
being in her best interest. Whether they are right
about this is a matter for debate.

At this point, however, I would like to raise a
different question, namely, whether decisions not to
treat must be limited to consideration of what is
best for the infant, or whether extraneous factors,
including the preferences of the parents, the impact
on the family, and financial considerations, are
morally relevant to such decisions. Such factors
are often mentioned in justifying the decision not
to treat, without any clear statement of why they
are thought to be relevant. Indeed, their relevance
is often confused with a separate issue, namely, the
right of the parents to decide whether treatment is
in the best interest of their child. However, the
question of who should decide is entirely separate
from the question of the basis for deciding; giving
parents the right to decide whether treatment is in
their child's best interests does not give them the
right to withhold treatment because the child's
death is in their best interest.

As we have seen, vitalists argue that
witholding life-prolonging treatment from newborns
is never justified, unless treatment would be
futile. I do not agree; I think infanticide in the
child's own best interest can be justified.
However, I wish to reject the view that extraneous
factors, such as the parents' desires, the impact on
the family, and so forth, are morally relevant to
killing the defective infant. In my view, the
belief that such extraneous factors are relevant
rests on an assumption, sometimes not explicitly
stated, that newborns do not have the same moral
status as older human beings. This claim must be
examined, and not confused with the separate issue
of who should make decisions about treatment: the
parents, or doctors, or courts.

The birth of a severely defective baby is a

terrible shock. Instead of pride and joy, the parents experience grief and fear. What will happen to this baby? Can they care for it? What will this do to their lives, to the rest of the family? Why has this happened to them? Parents of defective children sometimes point out the ways in which their lives have been enriched by what seemed at first to be a tragedy. However, whatever compensatory pleasures lie in store, great emotional burdens await them as well. Marriages are sometimes wrecked, other childen's needs are inevitably neglected. In view of all this, some people have wondered why the lives of such children must be prolonged. Wouldn't it be better if the defective newborn could be killed, and the parents given the chance to have another normal child? Furthermore, they may point out, if Baby Jane Doe's mother had had a simple bood test in her fourth month of pregnancy, the spina bifida probably would have been detected. She would have had the option of aborting and trying later for a normal child. Is there so much difference between a fetus of sixteen to twenty weeks gestation age (g.a.) and a newborn baby that the killing of the one is regarded as perfectly acceptable, while the killing of the other is regarded as unthinkable? Does birth, by itself, confer personhood and a right to life? These questions must be taken seiously by those who insist that life-prolonging treatment must be given to severely defective newborns.

Some of the most ardent supporters of the Baby Does do think that birth has no special significance for moral personhood. These are the right-to-lifers, who believe that the right to life begins at conception. Their championship of the Baby Does has made opponents of restrictive abortion laws understandably nervous. They are afraid that legislation proposed ostensibly to protect the lives of defective newborns is only a cover, the first step toward anti-abortion legislation. Nat Hentoff, who has written a series of articles defending the right to life of defective newborns,[3] dismisses this fear as craven. One ought not shy away from a position one knows to be right, simply because it is defended by people who hold other views one rejects, and with whom one does not wish to be associated. However, Hentoff, and others who support the right of the Baby Does to life-prolonging treatment, must consider whether the right-to-lifers are not correct in maintaining that opposition to infanticide is incompatible with tolerance of abortion. The

differing legal status of fetuses and newborns does
not settle the question; right-to-lifers would like
to see the legal status of fetuses changed because
they regard them morally as persons. Anyone who
regards abortion as morally permissible must be
prepared to say why infanticide is morally wrong.

In this chapter, I will defend the right to
life of newly born babies, even defective ones,
againt the view that newborns are not persons and so
do not have a right to life. In the first section,
I point out that this justifies the killing of
perfectly normal babies as well as defective ones, a
conclusion I find so intuitively implausible as to
require a closer look at the connection between
being a person and having a right to life.

In the second section, I distinguish between
the descriptive and normative senses of person, and
argue that neither Tooley nor Warren has given us
adequate arguments for thinking that only those
beings who meet their descriptive criteria can be
moral persons, or beings protected by a right to
life. There is no conceptual barrier to attributing
to infants a right to life, and there are good
reasons for ascribing the same privileged moral
status of full-fledged descriptive persons (that is,
ordinary people, like you and me) to newborns.
Admittedly, babies and small children are not
autonomous. They lack the intellectual ability to
make decisions for themselves, and so we must take
care of them and make decisions in their behalf.
Because of this, we cannot treat them with the
respect that is due full-fledged persons, who are
autonomous agents. However, this is no reason to
deny infants a right to life.

In the third section, I argue that the
recognition of an infant right to life does not
threaten the right to abortion. Recognizing the
moral personhood of infants does not commit us to
regarding first or second trimester fetuses as
persons. The "replaceability thesis"[4] does not
plausibly apply to infants.

In the fourth section, I argue that we are
morally justified in killing babies so severely
defective that their lives are not a good to them:
this does not violate their right to life. However,
in the fifth section, I acknowledge that our
inability to know with certainty at birth that a
given infant's life cannot be made worth living
makes infanticide rarely justifiable. In the last
section, I restate my view that infants have an
independent moral status, and that they may be

killed only when death is genuinely in their best interest.

ARE BABIES PERSONS?

    Mary Anne Warren and Michael Tooley defend abortion by arguing that since human fetuses are not persons, they do not have a right to life, and hence, there is no serious moral objection to killing them.[5]   Another way of stating their position is to say that the moral status of the fetus provides no reason - or perhaps no serious reason - to prohibit people from killing it. However, there could be serious moral objections to killing fetuses quite apart from the claim of a right to life; for example, if population were to fall drastically and more people were needed. We may call this an extrinsic reason not to kill fetuses. That a being has a right to life, provides an intrinsic reason not to kill it, whether or not other good ends are promoted by respecting it.
    I present my argument in terms of rights because Warren and Tooley do so, and I am willing to accept the existence of a right to life as the battlefield. Some theorists, notably utilitarians, are unhappy with talk of rights: they think that such talk adds nothing substantive to the discussion and may even cut it off prematurely.   I do not agree, though for present purposes, I will avoid this controversy by phrasing my claim hypothetically: if there is a right to life, human babies have it as much as do human adults, so the central issue is the moral status of babies. Anyone uncomfortable with the notion of moral rights can translate a discussion of rights into a discussion of reasons.   The issue then is whether the moral status of human babies provides us with the same reasons not to kill them as we have not to kill adult human beings.
    The lynchpin of Tooley and Warren's arguments is a distinction between genetic humanity (i.e., membership in the species homo sapiens) and moral humanity (i.e., personhood).   For both Warren and Tooley, a person is an entity with certain (mainly cognitive) capacities.   We may call this the descriptive aspect of personhood.   Personhood also has a normative aspect because to say that someone is a person is to imply that he or she or it is entitled to moral treatment of a certain kind, for example, a right not to be killed.   Tooley and

Warren believe that the claim that human fetuses have a right to life stems from a confusion between the genetic and moral senses of humanity.

Warren suggests that the traits most central to the concept of personhood are consciousness, self-consciousness, reasoning, self-motivated activity and the capacity for language. She thinks that if a space traveler landed on an unknown planet and met a race of alien beings, these are the criteria which he or she would use in deciding their moral status. Thus, these traits are supposed to capture the way we use the word "person". Hence, Joel Feinberg refers to criteria such as Tooley and Warren give as "commonsense personhood". These criteria serve to remind us of the distinction between genetic or biological humanity and personhood. The endearing alien, E.T., of the movie of that name, was clearly a person though not a human being. However, "common sense" also considers human babies just as clearly to be persons, although they are not rational, self-conscious, and so forth. I will follow Feinberg's usage, with the admonition that ordinary usage does not limit personhood to those who meet the criteria set out by Tooley and Warren. Warren thinks that this is the result of an error: confusing genetic humanity with personhood. I will argue that she has not shown this to be an error, but rather simply assumes that commonsense personhood is a necessary condition for moral personhood.

Tooley's requirements for personhood differ slightly from Warren's, and are chosen expressly to support a conceptual link between the descriptive and normative aspects of the concept. Tooley takes the sentence, "X is a person" to be synonymous with the sentence, "X has a (serious) moral right to life," and so the criteria of personhood are meant to explain and justify the claim that the being has a serious right to life. To that end, Tooley adds to Warren's criteria of personhood the requirement that a person has the capacity to envisage a future for itself and to have desires about its future states.

On neither account are newly born babies persons. (Warren would use the grammatically correct term "people", but I prefer "persons" to emphasize the stipulative or reformative nature of her definition, and its departure from ordinary usage.) This is a consequence which Warren accepts and Tooley positively welcomes, since it justifies killing babies with severe defects, something Tooley regards as a good thing. However, taken to its logical extension, their argument justifies not only infanticide of severely deformed babies, but also of perfectly normal babies who are, for any reason, unwanted. Tooley glosses over this point, but Warren bravely faces up to it: "... it follows from my argument that when an unwanted or defective infant is born into a society which cannot afford and/or is not willing to care for it, then its destruction is permissible."[6]

Furthermore, on this account older babies, as well as newborns, cannot be said to be persons. Even if language acquisition is not a prerequisite to meeting Warren and Tooley's requirements, such attributes as self-awareness, self-consciousness and the capacity to envisage a future for oneself about which one has desires are clearly not present in young babies, and may not be present even in relatively older children.[7] Tooley admits that it may be difficult to draw a line, but denies that this is troubling:

> It is not troubling because there is no serious need to know the exact point at which a human infant acquires a right to life. For in the vast majority of cases in which infanticide is desirable, its desirability will be apparent within a short time after birth.[8]

This is scarcely comforting. It makes infanticide permissible not only for good reasons, but also for terrible reasons - a small deformity (such as a hare-lip or club foot), or because the baby is female. It also prevents us from saying that a kidnapper who kills an eight month old baby has committed murder.

Obviously Tooley and Warren would not wish to appear to support indiscriminate baby killing. They would say that while killing babies is, in general, wrong, it is wrong for extrinsic reasons, and not because babies have a right to life. We may be unable to call the killing of an infant murder, but when we think of the terrible effects on its parents if it is wanted, or of the sad deprivation of those who would love to have a baby to care for, we can condemn the killing very strongly. Nevertheless, Tooley and Warren would have to agree that if there is nobody who has these feelings, then killing the baby is neither murder nor wrong.

If that conclusion seems wrong - crazy, even - then we must reconsider the notion of personhood, particularly in its moral aspect. I suggest that we do so by examining the alleged conceptual link between having a right to life and Tooley's requirements for being a person. If Tooley cannot sustain the claim that only those who meet his criteria of personhood have a right to life, then the issues of moral status and whose lives are protected, are open.

PERSONHOOD AND THE RIGHT TO LIFE

Why does Tooley think that there is a conceptual link between being a person, meeting his requirements, and having a right to life? He says:

> My basic argument in support of these ... requirements rests upon the claim that there is a conceptual connection between, on the one hand, the rights an individual can have and the circumstances under which they can be violated, and, on the other, the existence in him of the corresponding desires. The basic intuition is that a right is something that can be violated and that, in general, violation of an individual's right to something involves frustrating the corresponding desires.[9]

Tooley provides a skimpy defense of this intuition, merely giving the example of taking someone's car to illustrate his position. He says that the obligation not to take it is not unconditional: it depends, in part, upon the existence of a corresponding desire in the owner. "If you do not care whether I take your car, then I generally do not violate your right by doing so."[10]

This claim is false. It is superficially plausible because if I do not care whether you take my car, I may well give you permission to take it, and in this case you do not violate any right of mine by taking it. However, the crucial element is not the presence or absence of my desire, but the permission. I may give you permission even though I mind very much (perhaps I feel under a moral obligation to lend you my car); and unless I give you permission, it is quite irrelevant to the question of rights violation whether or not I cared. Suppose I am unaware that I have a right to something: for example, a legacy left to me in a will, or a constitutional right, such as the right to remain silent. If I don't know that I am entitled to it, I am unlikely to mind not having it. But it certainly doesn't follow that my rights regarding the thing in question cannot be violated. Why should only beings who have the high-level intellectual ability to envisage a future existence for themselves have a right to life? Such a view results from a misunderstanding of what an entity needs in order to have a right.

According to Joel Feinberg,[11] the function of rights is to protect interests. (Not all interests are protected by rights, of course; only those deemed sufficiently important, and this is a matter of moral debate.) Feinberg suggested that the capacity to have interests is both necessary and sufficient to be a rights holder; that is, the kind of being which can have rights. Adult human beings clearly can have interests and rights. Mere things, on the other hand, cannot have rights because they have no interests. This is not to say that particular kinds of treatment are not good or bad for things; we can take care of things, or fail to do so; preserve them or allow them to be ruined. But however we treat a thing, we cannot do what is in its interest, for a mere thing does not have interests of its own. We cannot preserve it for its sake, for it has no sake of its own. Thus, it does not make sense to ascribe rights to things. So even if changing the oil can be said to be good for a car, we should not think that we do it for the sake of the car. If we do it for anyone's sake, it is for the sake of the owner who has an interest in the car's running well.

If cars clearly cannot have rights and persons clearly can, what about borderline cases, such as trees? Living things like trees might be thought to have a welfare, a good of their own, for it is not solely the interests of people that determine what is good for them. They can be healthy or sick, and what constitutes health or sickness is independent of our purposes. Nevertheless, if we water a plant and keep it healthy, it does not seem that we can be said to do this for the plant's sake. It does not matter to a plant whether it is healthy or sick, alive or dead, because plants have no conscious life, no experiences. Life, therefore, can neither be a good to trees, nor can they be said to have a welfare of their own.

The case is quite different for babies, who are conscious and sentient. Babies can be not only healthy or unhealthy, but happy or miserable.

Babies have a welfare of their own: things can be done for their sakes. So babies, unlike trees, can have rights. But what rights can they have? Are their rights limited to things which they can envisage and want? Tooley thinks that for a being to have a right to something, it must have an interest in it. By contrast, I hold that to have a right to something, all that is necessary is that it be in one's interest. A baby cannot want to be inoculated against disease, yet it is in his or her interest to be inoculated. Therefore, we can talk about the right to be inoculated. Similarly, a baby cannot want not to be killed tomorrow, but it can be in his or her interest not to be killed. Life can surely be - indeed, ordinarily is - in the interest of an infant. Therefore there is no conceptual bar to ascribing to infants the right to life.

If Tooley's argument for restricting the right to life to commonsense persons is flawed, Warren gives no argument at all. She simply assumes that the "moral community" - those who have full moral rights, as opposed to those to whom we owe some, but not equal, moral consideration - consists of all and only commonsense persons. Indeed, Warren thinks it is part of the <u>concept</u> of personhood that all and only people have full moral rights.

However, the concept of personhood is ambiguous between its descriptive and its normative sense. Warren's criteria belong to the descriptive sense. In its normative use, the term 'person' ascribes moral properties, such as rights and duties. In claiming that it is part of the concept of personhood that all and only people have full moral rights, Warren fails to distinguish between the descriptive and normative senses of 'person'. All and only moral persons may have full moral rights, but it is not self-evident, nor a mere matter of linguistic usage, that all and only commonsense persons (those who meet Warren's criteria) are moral persons. This has to be supported by an independent argument.[12] We need to know what it is about capacities such as reasoning, language, and the presence of self-awareness that endows all and only beings which have them a privileged moral status and full moral rights, including the right to life. Without an argument connecting the descriptive aspect of personhood with the normative, restricting the moral community to those who have such capacities is as arbitrary as restricting it to members of our species. Warren gives no such argument.

Nevertheless, it seems to me that there are good reasons for regarding both the lives and the interests of person as morally more valuable and important than the lives and interests of non-persons. Of course, this does not mean that we owe no moral consideration to sentient beings who are not persons (such as most animals). Rather, I am basing the privileged moral status of human beings over animals on our ability to participate fully in the moral life; to have duties as well as rights; to be autonomous and act on altruistic reasons. These capacities make us special and justify taking both the lives and interests of people more seriously than those of animals; indeed, they justify killing animals and inflicting pain on them where this is necessary to preserve the lives and essential interests of people.[13]

However, if we are to argue for inequality and a differentiated moral status, based on rationality and capacities dependent on it, then what makes human babies moral persons? Obviously, they are not rational or self-aware or possessed of a desire for continued existence. What, then, makes them special,and entitled to privileged moral status? What makes most of us so certain that even the tiniest baby. counts as a moral person, whose needs and interests must be considered, and who has numerous rights including a right to be cared for and a right to live?

One answer is that, despite `the present absence of commonsense personhood, the newborn is still a human being. Warren thinks that this answer betrays a confusion of genetic humanity with moral humanity. However, there need be no <u>confusion</u>; rather, genetic humanity can be a ground for moral humanity. We regard the newly born baby as a person because, from the moment of its birth, it is a member of the family, a blood relative, and as such, entitled to the same consideration as any other family member. Indeed, because of their helplessness and vulnerability, we think they are entitled to extra care and attention, which other family members may have to forego to accommodate the newest member.

Some people will regard this as mere "speciesism" and a moral mistake. It is arbitrary, they say, to give privileged moral status to some non-persons, and not others, simply because they are members of our species. Even if the privileged moral status of persons can be defended, there is no non-speciesist way to include all humans in this

113

privileged group.[14]

Of course, most babies, unlike most (perhaps all) other animals are potential persons. While it would be a logical error to ascribe to them an actual right to life based on their potential personhood,[15] their ability to become persons provides us with reasons to protect their lives. This point aside, we have obligations to care for our children. It is not speciesist to acknowledge this special obligation, even though it is of course true that we cannot have this relationship to a member of any other species. In the same way, people may have special obligations to members of their own group: Jews to help Jews, blacks to help blacks. So long as this does not lead them to deny to others what they are entitled to, it is not arbitrary or morally unjustifiable. Our according to human babies a special place in the moral community is in no way inconsistent with denying such a place to other non-persons, such as animals, who will never become persons, and who are not blood relatives.

So far I have been arguing that babies do have, and are entitled to have a privileged position in the moral community, and therefore should be accorded the same right to life as all other moral persons. At the same time, it must be acknowledged that we cannot regard them as full-fledged moral persons, that is, as autonomous moral agents whose preferences - even irrational ones - must be respected. Their inability to be full-fledged moral persons does have significant implications for our treatment of infants, but it does not prevent them from having a right to life.

Babies are moral persons in that their interests and their lives must be protected, but they are not full-fledged moral persons; in that it is logically impossible to accord them the respect due to full-fledged persons. Respect for persons includes respecting the preferences they have concerning their own lives, preferences which may be irrational and contrary to their own best interests. This respect is manifested in the recognition of a right of bodily self-determination, which includes the right to refuse treatment, even treatment necessary to prolong life or treatment clearly beneficial to the patient. It makes no sense to ascribe such a right to infants. The right of parents, in some cases, to refuse treatment for their minor children should not be understood as a right of the child to self-determination. It is rather the right of the parent to act as he or she deems best for the child.

My point is that there can be, in the case of adults, a divergence between what the person wants and what is best for him. Furthermore, respect for persons often requires allowing the person to do what he wants, even when it is not in his own interest to do so. Such respect is not appropriate in the case of infants because in a wide range of cases they cannot be said to have preferences. They cannot be said to prefer death to living with x amount of suffering even where they would be better off dead. We <u>have</u> to act paternalistically where babies and young children are concerned, if we consider their interests at all.

I conclude that, while babies are not full-fledged moral persons, there is no conceptual bar to according them rights, including the right to life. So long as continued existence can intelligibly be said to be <u>in their interest</u>, a good <u>to them</u>, then it is meaningful to ascribe to them the right to life. I maintain, against Tooley, that one need not have a desire for some good for it to be in one's interest and capable of being protected by a right. So the mere fact that babies have no concept of continued existence in the future, and hence cannot be said to have the desire to go on living, does not rule out an infantile right to life.

However, demonstrating that babies <u>can</u> have a right to life, that it is meaningful or intelligible to ascribe such a right to them, is only half the battle. The substantive moral question of whether the lives of newborn infants ought to be protected as a matter of right must be addressed. For I have conceded that infants are not commonsense persons. There is no inconsistency in maintaining that all and only commonsense persons have the right of life. Furthermore, I fully acknowledge the considerations in favor of permitting the infanticide of defective newborns.

As Tooley reminds us:

> Most people would prefer to raise children who do not suffer from gross deformities or from severe physical, emotional, or intellectual handicaps. If it could be shown that there is no moral objection to infanticide, the happiness of society could be significantly and justifiably increased.[16]

This point can be made even more strongly. It is not just that most people <u>prefer</u> not to raise children with severe handicaps; the emotional and financial toll is enormous. Furthermore, we must admit that the newborn who is killed need feel no pain, nor can it fear death or experience sadness or loss at the thought of being killed. Why, then, it may be asked, must parents be forced to go through a lifetime of anguish? Why shouldn't infanticide be a permissible option?

It may be that in fact few parents of handicapped babies would want to have them killed. Many instead want the help that will enable their child to live the fullest life of which he or she is capable (and it is a tragic irony that the administration that has sponsored the Baby Doe hotlines has also cut back on the very social services necessary to enable handicapped people reach their full potential.) Such parents would not regard the offer of infanticide as a compassionate gesture. No doubt they wish fervently that their child was not defective, but to wish that a child had been born without a defect is not to wish the child had not been born, still less to wish that he or she could now be killed. Nevertheless, the issue before us is not whether most people would choose infanticide, if they had children with serious defects, but whether such a choice would be wrong.

THE REPLACEABILITY THESIS

Like Tooley and Warren, Jonathan Glover and Peter Singer have argued that parents should be able to choose the death of their seriously handicapped infants, and not just in those cases where death is probably in the infant's best interest. They think that even if the baby could have, with help, a life which was a good to it, it could still be permissible to kill. Glover says:

> But even where the worth-while life argument does hold, it is no stronger against infanticide than against not conceiving a child. In either case, there is one less person with a worth-while life. And, considering this reason in isolation, babies are replaceable. Just as it may be right to defer conception if later you stand a better chance of having a normal child, so, in terms of this consideration, it can be right to kill

a defective baby and then have a normal one you would not otherwise have.[17]

Surely everyone would agree that it would be permissible, perhaps even obligatory, to defer conception if by doing so one could avoid having a seriously defective child. However, there are many other good reasons to defer conception, e.g., if one's financial situation is likely to improve. It would be appalling to kill a baby, with the intention of having another later on, yet the number of worthwhile lives is the same. This should make us skeptical of the replaceability thesis.

Perhaps the strongest argument for replaceability comes from the similarity of newborns to fetuses. Singer says:

> When death occurs before birth, replaceability does not conflict with generally accepted moral convictions. That a fetus is known to be defective is widely accepted as a ground for abortion. Only those who believe in the sanctity of human life from conception would think it wrong for a woman to abort a fetus she knew to be seriously defective. Yet in discussing abortion, we saw that birth does not mark a morally significant dividing line. I cannot see how one could defend the view that fetuses may be 'replaced' before birth, but newborn infants may not be.[18]

However, from the fact that birth does not mark a morally significant dividing line, it does not follow that the acceptance of abortion in the second trimester commits us to accepting infanticide. There are significant differences between the fetus in utero and the born baby which affect moral status.

The most likely tactic for the defender of the right of women to choose abortion is to argue, as Judith Thomson has, that regardless of the status of the unborn, the pregnant woman is not morally required to act as its life-support system.[19] Its having a right to life does not automatically give it a right to use the woman's body. However, as Thomson realizes, the fact that the unborn has no right to the use of the woman's body does not necessarily mean that it is morally permissible for her to eject it at the cost of its life. Indeed, as several of Thomson's critics, including Warren, have suggested, this argument probably justifies abortion only in a fairly narrow range of cases. It justifies abortion in the case of rape, when the woman has no responsibility for the presence of the fetus, but is less persuasive in ordinary cases of pregnancy where the woman bears partial responsibility for the existence of the unborn. Warren dubs the limitations of Thomson's defense of abortion "an extremely unsatisfactory outcome, from the viewpoint of the opponents of restrictive abortion laws, most of whom are convinced that a woman has a right to obtain an abortion regardless of how and why she got pregnant."[20]

In Thomson's defense, it should be pointed out that her main concern was to attack the assumption of right-to-lifers that the wrongness of abortion follows from the presumption of a fetal right to life. At the least, Thomson has shown that this does not follow. Nevertheless, the critics seem to be right; any pro-abortion argument based solely on the woman's right of bodily autonomy is too weak and too narrow. A general defense of abortion requires an argument against the personhood of the unborn: hence, Warren's argument.

However, a monolithic view of the status of the unborn throughout pregnancy seems both unnecessary to defend the right to abortion and counter-intuitive. After all, most people think that the reasons necessary to justify a late abortion must be much stronger than those needed to justify an early abortion, if reasons are needed then at all. "I don't want to have a child," is regarded by many as a good reason to have an abortion in the first trimester of pregnancy, but no reason at all in the third trimester. This suggests a very different attitude to the mature fetus than to the early one, and helps explain why the United States Supreme Court, in Roe v. Wade, retained the right of the states to prohibit abortions in the third trimester, except where necessary to preserve the life or health of the pregnant woman. This is consistent with regarding the nearly born fetus as having the same moral status as the newly born baby: the pregnant woman is not required to allow even a moral person the continued use of her body at the cost of her life. It is difficult to think of other reasons that could justify abortion in the last months

It must be admitted that any cut-off point designed to establish moral personhood, before which the being may be killed, but after which its life must be preserved, is inevitably somewhat arbitrary.

There are no sudden and dramatic changes, enabling us to say with conviction, "Now we have a person!" The development of a person is a slow and gradual process. However, the about-to-be-born fetus is sufficiently like the newly born baby that recognition of the latter's moral personhood plausibly commits us to recognition of the former's as well. This does not commit us to further extensions of personhood to the fetus at earlier stages. Significantly, extension of moral personhood into the womb need not make us fear that the unborn has this status from the moment of conception. For the reasons for regarding the newly born and nearly born as moral persons are absent in the early stages of fetal development.

A human embryo cannot think or feel or have any experiences at all; life is no more a good to it than to a plant. Admittedly, unlike plants, human embryos develop into beings for whom life can be a good. This may provide us with reasons to allow them to develop into experiencing beings, whose lives will be a good to them, but those reasons do not seem to be any stronger than similar reasons we have for creating experiencing beings. That is, it is one thing to claim that we ought to value and protect the lives of beings whose lives are a good to them. It is quite another to claim that we have an obligation to value and protect the lives of beings whose lives will be a good to them if we do protect their lives. The former obligation is based on the good to the being in question. It is because babies, unlike embryos, have a welfare, a good of their own, that we can intelligibly ascribe to them a right to life. Without a welfare of their own, it is hard to see how embryos can have a right to life, any more than merely potential people can have a right to be brought into being. Of course, this does not rule out other rights for embryos, contingent on their being born (and hence having a welfare). A woman who intends to have a child may well have an obligation to that child not to smoke or drink excessively during pregnancy. A child has the right, if born, to be free of preventable defects; this in no way commits us to ascribing to the unborn a non-contingent right to be born.[21]

If an embryo is not a moral person, and a nearly born fetus is, what about those in between? Most elective abortions take place between eight and twelve weeks gestation age (g.a.) when the unborn has none of the characteristics of a person. However, abortions to prevent the birth of a defective child may not be possible until considerably later. Amniocentesis is usually performed at around sixteen weeks, it may take a couple of weeks to get back the laboratory results, and schedule an abortion, by which time the fetus may be twenty weeks g.a. Is it, by that time, a moral person, with a right to life? If so, arguments from the woman's autonomy alone would not justify abortion. However, I do not think that we are committed to regarding the twenty-week old fetus as a moral person. As I have claimed, in order for the fetus to qualify as a moral person, with a right to life, it must have a welfare of its own. And, as Feinberg plausibly argues, to have a welfare of one's own, one must have experiences of some kind: desires, preferences, feelings, however inchoate these may be. It is far from clear that the second trimester fetus even experiences pain. According to one science writer, "most experts" maintain that the capacity to suffer is not present until 28 weeks g.a.:

> The nerve endings in the skin have not yet extended outward with any of the degree of the affluence to be seen later on; the surface of the brain is relatively smooth, showing little in the way of the convolutions seen in the mature brain cortex. The nerve endings have not yet developed their fatty myelin sheaths - and without these sheaths, which play some crucial role in the transmissions of nervous "messages" from one nerve cell to the next, it is hard to imagine sensations of pain "getting through".[22]

If the capacity to suffer is not present until 28 weeks g.a., it is difficult to imagine that any other experiencing is going on. Without experiences, the fetus has no welfare; without a welfare, there seems to be little reason to ascribe to it a right to life. When we add to this consideration of the woman's right of bodily autonomy, there is no reason why a woman should be morally required to give birth to a defective child. The recognition of an infantile - or even a late fetal - right to life in no way endangers the right to abort defective fetuses in the second trimester.

DOES INFANTICIDE NECESSARILY VIOLATE THE NEWBORN'S RIGHT TO LIFE?

It does not follow from the fact that an individual has a right to life that killing him violates that right. Philippa Foot argues, rightly I think, that voluntary euthanasia does not violate a right to life, because in that case the right to life has been waived.[23] She also maintains that withholding treatment needed to sustain life (passive euthanasia) need not violate a right to life; it depends on whether or not the treatment is owed to the patient. This in turn depends on what the patient is entitled to expect, which is largely (though not entirely) a matter of standard medical practice. Foot maintains that active euthanasia is different. The right to life creates a general duty of noninterference: if someone does not want to die, no one has the right to practice active euthanasia on him. This rules out nonvoluntary euthanasia (where the patient's preference is unknown) as well as involuntary euthanasia (where he is killed against his will).

Now euthanasia in the case of infants is always nonvoluntary. So does active euthanasia necessarily violate their right to life? Foot writes:

> ... if it is ever right to allow deformed children to die because life will be a misery to them, or not to take measures to prolong for a little the life of a newborn baby whose life cannot extend beyond a few months of intense medical intervention, there is a genuine problem about active as opposed to passive euthanasia. There are well-known cases in which the medical staff has looked on wretchedly while an infant died slowly from starvation and dehydration because they did not feel able to give a lethal injection. According to the principles discussed in the earlier part of this paper they would indeed have had no right to give it, since an infant cannot ask that it should be done. The only possible solution - supposing that voluntary active euthanasia were to be legalised - would be to appoint guardians to act on the infant's behalf.[24]

In other words, Foot recognizes that sometimes active euthanasia may be desirable in the case of newborns. However, she argues that active euthanasia violates the right to life unless that right is waived, so she introduces the idea of guardians "acting on the infant's behalf". It should be noted that such guardians could not waive the infant's right to life in the sense of expressing his wishes for him: they could only act in the child's best interest, a distinction which is glossed over by the ambiguous phrase "act on the infant's behalf". So even with the introduction of guardians we do not have a genuine case of voluntary euthanasia. Instead, I think we should realize that some instances of active nonvoluntary euthanasia do not violate the right to life, namely, where active euthanasia is in the best interest of the individual and that individual has no desire for continued existence. Foot's reluctance to say this stems, I think, from the failure to distinguish being incapable of expressing a preference from being incapable of having a preference. If someone prefers not to die, but cannot communicate that preference, then we do violate his right to life in killing him, even if he really is better off dead. Furthermore, in most cases, we cannot confidently say what someone's preference is, if he or she is incapable of expressing it. Therefore, in the case of autonomous individuals, active nonvoluntary euthanasia violates, or runs the risk of violating, the right to life. However, in the case of infants, who do not even have a preference regarding life or death, because they lack the relevant concepts, their right to life is not violated when they are killed if death is genuinely in their own best interest.

Of course, it is no easy matter to give criteria specifying when death is in someone's best interest, nor would it be easy to apply such criteria if we had them. Physical suffering does not necessarily make a life not worth living, nor does (even serious) mental handicap. The crucial idea seems to be, as Foot suggests a minimum of basic human goods such as freedom from pain, pleasurable experiences, loving relationships, the ability to work and play. If an infant's life were likely to be totally lacking all these goods, it could hardly be a life worth living, and euthanasia, passive or active, would be justified.

EPISTEMOLOGICAL VITALISM

At the same time, it must be acknowledged that it is extraordinarily difficult to predict at birth the capabilities of a defective child, so we rarely are in a position to know whether conditions justifying infanticide are met. At times, parents have been told that their child's chances for a meaningful life were low and that it would be better to let the child die. When the parents have refused to accept the prognosis, and insisted on treatment, the infants have sometimes not only survived, but exceeded the expectations of the doctors. Nat Hentoff tells the stories of some of these children in a series of articles on the Baby Does.[25] One boy, Patrick, was born with a severe case of spina bifida. His natural parents decided to withdraw medical treatment. It took some months before the parental rights were terminated, and during that time, the opening in the spine was not closed. Eventually he was adopted by a couple, Carl and Rachel Rossow, who have a dozen handicapped children living with them. Now eight, he is in a wheelchair, he's had some brain damage, parts of his brain are missing. But he reads at a third grade level, he's good at singing, and hopes to be a professional drummer in a rock band one day. His mother describes him as "bubbly" and "full of life". He's attracted to people and people are attracted to him. There can be no doubt that this is a child whose life is worth living, a good to him.

The position that children like Patrick must not be deprived of life-prolonging medical treatment is one I call "epistemological vitalism".[26] It claims, not that every life is work saving, regardless of quality, but rather than, most of the time, we just don't know which lives will be worth saving.

However, Hentoff juxtaposes the story of Patrick with a very different story, that of Benjamin, who suffers from anencephaly. He just has a brain stem; he has no brain at all. If such a life must be preserved, it is not because we might be wrong about his capacities and potential. Yet the Rossows think that his life is precious: "... this little boy ... is kind of what we are about ... The hope of the human spirit".[27]

Rachel Rossow elaborates on this belief in the following anecdote:

(Benjamin) doesn't have any memory, he doesn't

have any balance ... He does have the ability
to chuckle and to laugh, and when he does, he
makes people feel good ... A young girl down
the street from us lost a very dear friend in a
traffic accident. She was a senior in high
school at the time. And she stopped by and she
asked if she could hold Benjamin. And she held
him for several hours, just rocking in a
rocking chair. And as she went to leave, she
cam over and she just said, 'Thank you, I feel
better'.

What Benjamin did for her at that moment I
really don't think a psychiatrist or perhaps
even a priest or a minister could have done at
that time. He allowed her to touch the core of
her own humanness, and helped her set her own
priorities straight. She was alive and she was
breathing and what was she going to do from
then on with her life.[28]

Though the story is moving, it is not clear
what its ethical implications are. In the first
place, what is the significance of its being
Benjamin that the girl held? She might have derived
comfort from holding any living thing, such as a
puppy. More importantly, why should the value of
Benjamin's life depend on his effect on other
people? Surely Benjamin's ability to make people
feel good is irrelevant to his moral status. The
important question is not how he makes others feel,
but what he feels; what his life is like, and
whether it can plausibly be said to be a good to
him. It may be that we simply cannot know what the
life of an anencephalic child is like, and that
therefore we should not risk depriving him of a life
that may be a good to him. However, we must
remember that Benjamin is not merely severely
retarded. He is not like the Down's syndrome child
whose life may seem to be a tragedy from our point
of view, but well be a good to that child. Benjamin
has no brain at all. It is difficult to believe
that without a brain, he can be said to have a
welfare of his own, or that his life can be a good
to him. For whose sake, then, must we keep him
alive? It is important to distinguish the cases of
Patrick and Benjamin, because while the former
provides an example of the force of epistemological
vitalism, the latter has nothing to do with our
fallibility in predicting future capacities. The
view that infanticide is never justified, not even

in the case of anencephalic infants, is vitalism pure and simple; but stripped of its implicit appeal to epistemological vitalism, it does not seem to have any justificatory force.

WHAT'S WRONG WITH KILLING BABIES?

Maintaining that babies are not persons, and yet wishing to reject wholesale infanticide, Warren, Tooley, Glover and Singer must appeal to "side effects", primarily in terms of the effects on the feelings of the rest of us, to explain why killing babies is wrong. It seems to me that this explanation is deeply unsatisfactory. It would mean that there would be nothing wrong with a society which thought it unnecessary to provide life-saving medical treatment to normal infants if their parents did not want to spend the money, or preferred just to "try again" for a healthy child. I think we would regard such parents and such a society not merely as different from ours, but as morally defective, and the tendency in our own society to move in this direction is I fear, evidence of moral decay. As Mary Warnock has said regarding other bioethical issues, "The question must ultimately be what kind of society can we praise and admire? In what sort of society can we live with our conscience clear?"[29] I do not think we can live with our conscience clear in a society which is callous toward infants, or which regards their moral status as dependent on the feelings others happen to have for them.

What is lacking in the approach of Tooley, Warren, Glover and Singer is any recognition of infants as beings who have a welfare of their own which must be taken into consideration. New-born babies are admittedly not full-fledged moral persons. At the same time, they are members of the moral community and entitled to care and concern. They are members of the family, and we have moral obligations to family members, even when - especially when - they are very young and vulnerable. Even the children of other people have a claim on us. They are still part of the human family and members of the moral community.

There is another reason for regarding babies as having the privileged moral status of persons, while acknowledging that they are not persons. Becoming a person is a complicated procedure, involving relationships with other people, which being at

125

birth. It is unlikely that a baby will become a person unless it is treated right from the start with the concern we accord persons. This does not mean that we can or should treat them just as we treat persons. As we have seen, we cannot give them the respect due to persons. We cannot respect their choices where they are incapable of making choices. Appreciation of this point makes it clear that if death is truly in an infant's best interest, we do not violate its right to life by killing it. At the same time, babies are entitled to be treated as unique, valuable individuals. Killing them can be justified only when it is in their best interest. Anything else does violate their right to life.

NOTES

1. Steinbock, B. "Baby Jane Doe in the Courts". The Hastings Center Report. February 1984, 13-19.
2. Steinbock, B. "The Intentional Termination of Life". Ethics in Science and Medicine, Vol.6, No.1, 1979, 58-64. Reprinted in B. Steinbock (Ed.), Killing and Letting Die. Englewood Cliffs, New Jersey: Prentice-Hall, Inc., 1980.
3. Hentoff, N. Weekly columns in The Village Voice, December 20, 1983 - May 15, 1984.
4. Glover, J. Causing Death and Saving Lives. Hardmonsworth, Middlesex, England: Penguin, 1977; and see also Singer, P. Practical ethics. Cambridge, England: Cambridge University Press, 1979.
5. Warren, M.A. "On the Moral and Legal Status of Abortion". In R. Wasserstrom (Ed.), Today's Moral Problems (2nd ed.), New York: Macmillan, 1979; and see also Tooley, M. "A Defense of Abortion and Infanticide". In J. Feinberg (Ed.), The Problem of Abortion. Belmont, California: Wadsworth, 1973. (The second edition of this collection (1984) contains a new essay by M. Tooley: In defense of abortion and infanticide.)
6. Warren, p. 51
7. Blumenfeld, J. "Abortion and the Human Brain". Philosophical Studies, 32 (1977), 251-268.
8. Tooley, p. 91
9. Ibid, p. 60
10. Ibid
11. Feinberg, J. "The Rights of Animals and Unborn Generations". In W.T. Blackstone (Ed.),

Philosophy and Environmental Crisis. Athens, Georgia: University of Georgia Press, 1974, Reprinted in R. Wasserstrom (Ed.), *Today's Moral Problems* (2nd ed.). New York: Macmillan, 1979.
12. Feinberg, J. "Abortion". In Tom Regan (Ed.), *Matters of Life and Death*. New York: Random House, 1980.
13. Steinbock, B. "Speciesism and the idea of equality". *Philosophy* 53, April, 1978, 247-256.
14. Singer, *Political Ethics*.
15. Benn, S.I. "Abortion, Infanticide and Respect for Persons. In J. Feinberg (Ed.), *The Problem of Abortion*. Belmont, California: Wadsworth, 1973, 2nd Edition, 1984.
16. Tooley, p. 54
17. Glover, pp. 162-163
18. Singer, *Political Ethics*, p. 136
19. Thomson, J. "A defense of abortion". *Philosophy & Public Affairs*, Vol.1, No.1, 1971. Reprinted in J. Feinberg (Ed.), *The Problem of Abortion*. Belmont, California: Wadsworth, 1973.
20. Warren, p. 126
21. Feinberg, "The Rights of Animal and Newborn Generations", *Op. Cit.*
22. Scarf, M. "The Fetus as Guinea Pig". *The New York Times Magazine*, October 19, 1975, p.13 passim.
23. Foot, P. R. "Euthanasia". In P. Foot, *Virtues and Vices*. New York: Random House, 1980.
24. *Ibid*, p. 57
25. Hentoff, N. Weekly column in *The Village Voice*, December 20, 1983, May 15, 1984.
26. Steinbock, "Baby Jane Doe in the Courts", *Op. Cit.*
27. Hentoff, N. Weekly column in *The Village Voice*, April 24, 1984, p. 11
28. *Ibid*
29. Warnock, M., quoted in the *Manchester Guardian Weekly*, July 29, 1984.

ADDITIONAL REFERENCES

Annas, G. "Disconnecting the Baby Doe Hotline". *Hastings Center Report*, Vol. 13, No.14, June 1983, 14-16.
Duff, R. S. and Campbell, A.G.M. "Moral and Ethical Dilemmas in the Special Care Nursery". *New*

England Journal of Medicine, 289 (October 25, 1973).

Koop, C. E. "Ethical and Surgical Considerations in the Care of the Newborn with Congenital Abnormalities". In D. Horan and M. Delahoyd (Eds.), Infanticide and the Handicapped Newborn. Provo, Utah: Brigham Young University Press, 1982.

Maciejczyk J. "Withholding Treatment from Defective Infants: 'Infant Doe' Postmortem". Notre Dame Law Review, Vol.59, 1983. 224-252. (This article contains an excellent bibliography in its footnotes.)

Murray, T., Arras, J., Kett, J. and Fiedler, L. "On the Care of Imperiled Newborns". Hastings Center Report, April 1984, 24-42.

President's Commission for the Study of Ethical Problems in Medicine and Biomedical and Behavioral Research. Deciding to Forego Life-Sustaining Treatment. United States Government Printing Office, March, 1983, chap.6.

Singer, P. and Kuhse, H. "The Future of Baby Doe". The New York Review, March, 1, 1984, 17-22.

Steinbock, B. "The Removal of Mr. Herbert's Feeding Tube". The Hastings Center Report, October 1983.

Weir, R. Selective Nontreatment of Handicapped Newborns. New York: Oxford University Press, 1984.

Chapter Eight

LONG DAYS JOURNEYS INTO NIGHT: THE TRAGEDY
OF THE HANDICAPPED AT RISK INFANT

George P. Smith, III

Each year, approximately thirty thousand
genetically handicapped at risk infants are born in
the United States.[1]   In Australia alone, it has
been estimated by the New South Wales Health
Commission that approximately $500,000.00 will be
spent during an average lifetime for one
institutionalized person with a genetic
abnormality.[2]
Initial decisions regarding the administration
of care - heroic and extraordinary or nursing and
ordinary - to the defective newborn present a number
of vexatious issues.   The purpose of this article is
to explore a number of those very issues.   Toward
the achievement of this end, it has been developed
into six parts dealing with: the establishment of a
working definition - philosophically, legislatively
and administratively - of handicapped individuals;
the British and the American judicial postures
regarding the matter;   the medical profession's
response;   triage as a viable principle for the
allocation of scarce neonatal support systems;   the
expanded role of ethics review committees; and the
development of a construct for effecting humane
decision-making.
Both the thesis and the major conclusion of
this article are identical and state - very simply -
that no matter what the physicians, lawyers, judges,
social welfare workers, philosophers or ethicists
posit re the structuring and validation of treatment
or non-treatment of handicapped newborns, the final
reality of decision-making is tied to a complex
balancing test of weighing economic costs of
nonmaintenance against the social benefits of
maintenance.   Stated another way decisions of this
scope and dimension are reached by balancing the
gravity of the economic harm that will accrue in a

particular case of maintenance against the utility of the social good that will occur for non maintenance.

DEFINING THE HANDICAPPED

Since the mid-1960's, neonatalogy has developed as a sub-speciality in pediatrics and "neonatal intensive care units" have emerged.[3] These new units make it possible to save the lives of newborns who would have died previously. While this technological progress must be recognized with excitement, its continued development has intensified the critical moral dilemmas now faced by health care providers. Sophisticated neonatal care is not only costly, but scarce, with demand often exceeding the supply of beds, equipment and personnel. What is seen, then, is that physicians and hospitals are being forced not infrequently to choose which newborns receive intensive care and which ones do not.[4] Decisions of this nature - in turn - involve a plethora of medical, moral, legal and economic problems - with the central most issue being how best to distribute scarce neonatal intensive care resources.

As observed, costs are of considerable importance in this sphere of decision making. The United States Department of Health and Human Services reported the Nation's health bill shot up 15.1% in 1981, outpacing the 8.9% inflation rate for the year. Overall medical costs, both public and private, rose to $287 billion dollars. This sum represented a record of 9.8% of the gross national product averaging out of a cost of $1,225.00 for each American.[5] Over the past ten years in the United States, hospital care expenditures quadrupled to $118 billion dollars; with the costs of physicians' services more than tripling to $54.8 billion dollars.[6]

A PHILOSOPHICAL APPROACH

The term, "handicapped human being," is not a technical description. In fact, attempts to define it as a precise concept meet with difficulty. Hence, what must be realised is that what constitutes a handicap is stipulative.[7] A "handicapped human being" is designated to be one because of a negative consequence of genetic

inheritance, a flaw in constitutional make-up, or even because of social attitudes which place him at an actual or potential disadvantage in respect to the living of life vis-a-vis the access to goods and services and the enjoyment thereof when compared with other human beings.[8] Accordingly, to carry an imperfection as a human means strictly to suffer a handicap. It is obvious, however, that most human beings   suffer   -   to   one   degree   or   other, imperfections, either as to sight, hearing, taste, speech, skin, limbs, etc. Unless the imperfection presents   a   serious   disadvantage   to   living, therefore, it is not to be considered a handicap.[9]
      The range of human handicaps is - indeed - vast, some springing from defects of reason (low or limited   intelligence   memory   defects)   and   others relating to sensory capacities (blindness, deafness, etc.) while still others relate to malformed limbs, exaggerated heights and genetic predispositions to certain diseases (e.g., diabetes, hemophilia). To be remembered is the fact that some imperfections termed "handicaps" in one social structure are not considered to be as such in others. Thus, one born left-handed, short but not a dwarf, or excessively tall but not a giant, is rendered a handicapped person only as a consequence of human attitudes and social   arrangements   in   different   societies.   If social attitudes were to be altered in some way, these   imperfections   would   cease   to   be   considered handicaps.[10] In sum, then, one may be said to be handicapped in modern society only if he is lacking an   excellence   or   perfection   of   a   kind   possessed naturally by homo sapiens.[11]
      It has been argued that the handicapped possess special or derivative rights which have evolved from such basic rights as those to life and liberty and, which in turn, are to be recognized as moral rights or   entitlements   which   are   directed   at   doing, demanding,   enjoying   or   receiving.[12]   Going further, it is submitted that a right to liberty - for   example   -   is   co-ordinate   with   a   right   to self-development [13], a right to moral autonomy [14] and, for that matter, a right to life.[15] Thus, the right to life carries not only a negative right not to be killed, but is to be recognized as really more of a positive right - more specifically, a   right   of   recipience,   a   right   to   protection, vis-a-vis those aids and facilities necessary for basic enjoyments of life, itself.[16]   If one embraces this philosophy, then not only must heroic or   extraordinary   measures   be   undertaken   for   all

handicapped at risk newborns, but one must accord the greatest respect for a new, one-minute-old embryonic life as well - this even though at present, the law refuses to recognize such organisms as protectable.[17]

A LEGISLATIVE APPROACH

The Rehabilitation Act of 1973 enacted by the United States Congress [18] and modeled in large part from the Civil Rights Act of 1964 [19] and the Education Amendments of 1972 [20] sought, through Section 504, to enunciate a federal policy which would mandate non discrimination against handicapped individuals who participated in programs which received federal financial assistance.[21]   The Congress chose to define "handicapped individual" in vocation terms such as:

... any individual who (A) has a physical or mental disability which for such individual constitutes or results in a substantial handicap to employment and (B) can reasonably be expected to benefit in terms of employability from vocational rehabilitation services provided ... [22]

In 1974, the Act was amended, the concept of "handicapped individual" redefined and Section 504 impliedly extended to all government programs receiving federal financial assistance. The new, expanded definition of "handicapped individual" was held to apply to:

... any person who (A) has a physical or mental impairment which substantially limits one or more of such person's major life activities, (B) has a record of an impairment, or (C) is regarded as having such an impairment. [23]

The Rehabilitation Act has involved the full spectrum of legal interest - from employment discrimination [24] and discrimination in education [25] to discrimination as a result of inaccessibility.[26]

It remained for President Ronald Reagan in 1982 to interpret and apply Section 504 to treatment decisions regarding defective newborns.[27] Accordingly, an Interim Final Administrative Rule was promulgated by the United States Department of

Health and Human Services which modified presently
existing regulations in the Department by including
provisions for the medical care of defective
newborns.[28] Specifically, the Department advised
all federally assisted hospitals (which number over
seven thousand) that their failure to comply with
the expanded definition of section 504 as applied
specifically to newborns could well subject those
hospitals to termination of their federal financial
support.[29]
     The novelty of expanding Section 504 as a basis
for preventing discrimination has been fraught with
difficulty and misunderstanding since its early
operation. In fact not until February 23, 1984, was
it finally determined by a federal court that
Section 504 of The 1973 Rehabilitation Act was not
applicable to treatment decisions involving
defective newborn infants.[30] Prior to this
decision, the role and application of Section 504
actions were ill-defined. President Reagan's 1982
actions regarding this Section were thwarted by a
federal district court decision in 1983 in the case
of American Academy of Pediatrics v. Heckler [31]
which held the Rule promulgated by the United States
Department of Health and Human Services, consistent
with the Reagan Directive, was arbitrary and
capricious.[32]
     The impact of the February, 1984, judicial
opinion in United States v. University Hospital,
State University of New York at Stony Brook et al
has yet to be fully understood. For, on January 12,
1984, new, revised rules and regulations were issued
concerning nondiscrimination on the basis of
handicap relating to health care for handicapped
infants based upon what was understood as the
enabling authority of Section 504.[33]
     On March 12, 1984, several medical groups
including the American Medical Association, and the
American Hospital Association, filed an action in
the United States District Court for the Southern
District of New York which seeks to prohibit the
Department of Health and Human Services from
implementing the new, revised rules issued in
January. Elsewhere, the United States House of
Representatives is studying proposed legislation
designed to amend The Child Abuse Prevention and
Treatment Reform Act and establish procedures
designed to facilitate appropriate modalities of
treatment for infants at risk with life threatening
congenital impairmants implemented through each
state child abuse agency.[34] The Senate, also, is

considering action [35] designed to establish a
Depratment of Health and Human Services advisory
committee on seriously ill newborns which would
conduct a comprehensive study of local
decision-making procedures involving the medical
management of seriously ill newborns with health
care facilities and to make recommendations
concerning appropriate procedural mechanisms to be
utilized by health care facilities which treat
seriously ill newborns.[36]

A REGULATORY APPROACH

        The federal regulations on non discrimination
in the care of defective newborns as promulgated on
January 12, 1984, even though under current
challenge in the courts, declare in essence that
where medical care is clearly beneficial, it should
always be provided to a handicapped newborn.[37]
Although recognizing a presumption should always be
in favour of treatment. Reasonable medical
judgments will be respected regarding treatment and
nourishment so long as those decisions to forego or
withhold are not made on the basis of present or
anticipated physical or mental impairments.[38]
Thus, decisions not to commence futile treatment
which would not be of medical benefit to the infant
and would in fact present a risk of potential harm
will be respected.[39]
        Infant Care Review Committees are encouraged,
although not mandated, to be structured in the seven
thousand health care providers receiving federal
financial assistance.[40] These Committees will not
only be charged with developing and recommending
institutional policies concerning the withholding or
withdrawal of medical treatment for infants with
life-threatening conditions, but with providing also
counsel in specific cases presently under
review.[41] Adhering to various principles approved
by such groups as The American Academy of Pediatrics
and The National Association of Children's
Hospitals, the ICRC's will conduct their operations
under the premise that where medical care is clearly
beneficial, it should always be provided.[42]
Although recognizing a presumption should always be
indulged in favour of treatment according to the
principles, reasonable medical judgment will be
respected regarding treatment and nourishment so
long as such decisions to forego or withhold are not
made on the basis of present or anticipated physical

or mental impairments.[43] Presumably the validity of the test of reasonableness will depend upon the facts of each case-situation that arises.

Informational notices of the application of the Federal Law, posted where nurses and other medical professionals may view them are required to include a statement of non-discrimination of health services (consistent with the specific provisions of Section 504 of the Rehabilitation Act 1973) on the basis of handicap. The poster must be of a size no smaller than five by seven inches and list a twenty-four hour toll free "hot line" telephone number at the United States Department of Health and Human Services and/or state child protective services agency where violations of the Act may be reported.[44]

Perhaps as important as the new Rules is an Appendix, "Guidelines Relating to Health Care for Handicapped Infants," which - while not independently establishing rules of conduct - are to be recognized as "interpretive guidelines" designed to assist in interpreting the application of Section 504.[45] Considering Appendix C(a)(1)-(3) ad C(a)(5)(ii), (iii), (iv), one finds a recognition that where any of the following situational standards are in operating focus or application, no discrimination will be acknowledged and, thus, no federal intervention undertaken:

1. Where treatment based upon reasonable medical judgment would be futile;
2. Where treatment is too unlikely of success given the complication of a particular case; or otherwise not of medical benefit to the infant; or,
3. Where there is a recognition of improbable success of a modality of treatment or risk of potential harm.[46]

It is interesting to observe that as of December 1, 1983, of the forty-nine cases of alleged discrimination of treatment of seriously handicapped newborns in federally assisted maternity wards, "no case resulted in a finding of discriminatory withholding of medical care."[47]

JUDICIAL POSTURING

<u>The British</u>
        The Sunday Times of December 4, 1983, carried
an absorbing article concerning the plight of
handicapped newborns in the United States and raised
the question of whether such a similar condition
could ever obtain in Britain.[48]   Only time, of
course, can provide a definitive answer; but two
important cases perhaps point to the recognition of
a judicial attitude or temperament regarding the
matter.
        A case determined by the Court of Appeal on
August 7, 1981, gives the closest indication of a
judicial perspective in this area.[49]   The facts
showed that B, a female child, was born suffering
not only from Down's syndrome but an intestinal
blockage - as well - and would require a surgical
intervention in order to relieve the obstruction if
she were to have the life of more than a few days.
Although the surgery provided no guarantee of long
life - in fact, there was a possibility that B might
die within a few months - the evidence pointed to
the fact that she could have an expectancy of normal
mongol life anywhere from twenty to thirty years if
the operation were successful.   Her parents decided
that in "the kindest...interests of the child" [50],
no operation should be performed.   Accordingly, they
advised the doctors of this decision and it was
respected.   The local authority thereupon made the
infant a ward of the court and sought an order
authorizing the operation be performed by other
surgeons.   The lower court respected the parental
decision and refused to order the surgery.   On
appeal by the local authority, the Court of Appeal
reversed and held that parental wishes were
secondary to what was in the best interests of the
child.   The parents made a strong argument that,
owing to the fact that the child would be severely
handicapped both mentally and physically, no measure
of the qualitative life of a mongoloid could be
evaluated properly during its predicted limited life
span.   The Court determined that insofar as a "happy
life" could be provided a mongoloid, baby B was
entitled to that life.[51]
        Noting that a judicial decision in a case of
this nature requires the court to consider the
evidentiary proofs as well as the views of the
parents and their doctors, the court acknowledged
that "at the end of the day it devolves on this
court in this particular instance to decide whether

the life of this child is so awful that in effect the child must be condemned to die, or whether the life of this child is so imponderable that it would be wrong for her to be condemned to die."[52] The court continued, stating, that "There may be cases, I know not, of severe proved damages where the future is so certain and where the life of the child is so bound to be full of pain and suffering that the court might be driven to a different conclusion."[53]

Of interest also is Regina v. Arthur, an unreported case decided at the Leicester Crown Court on November 5, 1981, but three months after the In re B decision. Here, a mongoloid was born on June 28, 1980, and thereupon rejected by his parents. The consultant pediatrician, Dr. Leonard Arthur, prescribed "nursing care only" (i.e. a regime which included no food) for the child and prescribed regular doses of the drug DF118 for purposes of sedation. Originally Dr. Leonard was charged with murder, but during the course of the trial the charge was reduced to attempted murder and a subsequent degree of acquittal rendered by a jury. In his summation, the judge indicated - without apparent reference to the In re B decision - that it was lawful to treat a baby with a sedating drug and offer no further care by way of food or drugs or surgery provided two criteria are met: the child is "irreversibly disabled" and rejected by its parents. Thus, the Arthur case seems to suggest the issue of treatment of a severely handicapped newborn child is a private matter between physician and parent and - in light of In re B - places the law in an uncharted sphere of disequilibrium.[54] While it is clear the Arthur verdict does not legitimize the use of drugs in order to accelerate death, it is unclear whether it establishes a uniform policy of nontreatment as legal and whether "holding procedures" are valid in all cases.[55]

The American

Baby Jane Doe was born on Long Island, New York, on October 11, 1983, with spina bifida and an abnormally small head which was swelling with excess fluid. After consultation with physicians and members of the clergy, her parents refused to allow corrective surgery. If successful, the operation might have allowed the infant to live some twenty years - but in a state of retardation, constant pain, epilepsy, and paralyzed below the waist.[56]

The highest court in the State, the Court of Appeals, decided that the parents' decision must be respected. It refused to enumerate the circumstances which would trigger judicial protection of an infant of this type's interest - merely observing that there may be occasions where it would be appropriate to intervene. Rather, it noted that the Legislature had designed a statutory scheme designed specifically for protecting children from abuse - and, at the same time safeguarding familial privacy and relationships - and that this procedure would be adhered to unless the Legislature, again, decided to amend the process.[57]

Although refusing to deal directly with the need to establish criteria for validating decision-making in cases of this nature, a key lower court decision in New York has indicated that only if there is a "reasonable chance" to lead a fulfilling and useful life, parental inaction regarding needed surgical intervention will not be permitted.[58]

The very first Baby Doe case to be found and popularized by the press, involved a six pound baby boy born with Down's syndrome in Bloomington, Indiana, in 1982 who lived but six days. His death precipitated a national re-thinking of issues of infanticide, parent decision-making and power under the Common Law to exercise jurisdiction over the care of children and perhaps the central most issue of all: whether quality of life standards are more significant and fundamental than principles of sanctity of life. In addition to being born a mongoloid, with consequent mental retardation, "Baby Doe" (as he was dubbed by the press) had a malformed esophagus, together with multiple physical problems. The esophagal condition prevented food from reaching the stomach. Rather than authorize corrective surgery, the parents chose to direct a withholding of food and medical treatment, save pain killers, from their son. Before an emergency appeal to the United States Supreme Court could be taken of an unwritten decision of the Indiana Supreme Court not to overturn two Monroe County Circuit Court orders preventing interference with the parental decision, "Baby Doe" succumbed.[59]

In an officially unreported 1981 case, In re Jeff and Scott Mueller, [60] Siamese twins were born connected at the waist. The parents and their attending physicians decided against corrective surgery and discontinued efforts to feed the infants. The Illinois Department of Children and Family Services thereupon filed a petition of neglect against the parents in the Illinois Family Court and sought to gain custody of the twins. The court in due course awarded custody of the infants to the Department for the express purpose of authorizing the necessary surgery and additional medical treatment. While the court found neglect on the part of the parents in that they failed to provide treatment for the infants, it refused to impose civil or criminal liability for the neglect - which it implied - occurred in an unintentional manner.[61] Subsequent efforts by the State Attorney-General to secure an indictment from a grand jury against the parents and the attending physician on various charges of attempted murder, conspiracy and solicitation to murder, met with failure.[62]

The English Court of Appeal precedent and the officially reported United States cases draw persuasive if not conclusive authority for their decisions by utilization (whether understood as such, or not), directly or indirectly, of a principle of a "substituted judgment." Thus, the Court will seek to place itself in the position of the infant in extremis and determine whether, given its medical condition, it would wish to live under present or altered conditions - whether a meaningful or qualitative life could be achieved. Inherent in the effectivensss of application of such a principle is the employment of a cost-benefit analysis or balancing test. Or, stated simply, the costs (social, economic) of maintaining life are weighed against the benefits (religious, ethical, spiritual, etc.) of preserving it.

THE MEDICAL ATTITUDE

A startling study of special care nursing treatment of neonates undertaken at the Yale-New Haven Hospital was released in 1973 and showed that fourteen percent of the two hundred ninety-nine deaths recorded during the period of the study - eighteen months - were related to actions which withheld treatment.[63] The publication of this study initiated a public dialogue and raised issues regarding the treatment of defective newborns or neonates which heretofore had been raised only privately by attending physicians, with or without familial consultation.[64]

In 1975, questionnaires were sent to all members of the Surgical Section of the American Association of Pediatricians and to all the chairmen of teaching departments of pediatrics in the United States, as well as to chiefs of divisions of neonatology and to chiefs of divisions of genetics in the departments of pediatrics. Two hundred and sixty-seven physicians from the first two groups and one hundred ninety-seven from the latter groups returned completed questionnaires. The results showed "broad support" for the propositions that: physicians need not attempt to maintain the life of every severely impaired newborn simply because the technology and skills to do so existed; parents and physicians (in that order) bear the ultimate responsibility for making decisions regarding the withholding or administration of treatment for handicapped at risk newborns; such decisions should be made on the basis of the best medical predictions regarding longevity and quality of life; under certain "egregious" circumstances physicians could seek judicial intervention in order to effect treatment and, finally , decisions to treat or not to treat defective newborns were best made on a "case-by-case" or situational basis.[65]

It would appear that the majority of the members of the medical profession are of the opinion that the autonomy of the parent-physician relationship should be maintained in this critical area of concern.[66] It is submitted that the affected or involved physicians and the families to which they attend are the most informed parties in a case involving treatment or non treatment decisions of handicapped at risk newborns and that they should be accorded both respect and latitude in making these necessary decisions.[67] Contrariwise, there are a minority of physicians who maintain that parents - traumatized emotionally by the birth of a defective child - are in no position to make life or death treatment decisions regarding it.[68] No less than the Surgeon General of the United States, C. Everett Koop, has asserted that decisions which withhold treatment for handicapped newborns are acts of "infanticide."[69] He opposed the exclusive reliance that is placed upon the precincts of the physician-parent autonomy in this area of concern.[70]

In its 1983 Report, <u>Deciding to Forego Life-Sustaining Treatment</u>, The President's Commission for the Study of Ethical Problems in Medicine and Biomedical and Behavioral Research examined critically governmental intrusions into the parent-physician decision-making process and concluded that an approach should be followed which allows for and recognizes that the non treatment of genetically defective newborns is not necessarily unethical and should be made by the concerned parents with the advice of an attending or consulting physician, without government intervention.[71] The Commission urged that the entire process of decision-making be opened to include the formation of ethic review committees and that their deliberations be considered - in order to assure an objective assessment - in those cases where the greatest degree of complexity and difficulty exists.[72] Thus, by the establishment of an internal review process, judicial intervention would be obviated and be permissible only when a "rapidly deteriorating medical status" of a handicapped newborn required parents and physicians alike to act without this internal review.[73]

The American Medical Association Judicial Council reached a similar conclusion to that of The President's Commission. More specifically, however, the Council put forth the proposition that as to quality of life decisions affecting the treatment of seriously deformed infants,

...the primary consideration should be what is best for the individual patient and not the avoidance of a burden to the family or to society. Quality of life is a factor to be considered in determining what is best for the individual. Life should be cherished despite disabilities and handicaps, except when prolongation would be inhuman and unconscionable. Under these circumstances, withholding or removing life supporting means is ethical provided that the normal care given an individual who is ill is not discontinued. In desperate situations involving newborns, the advice and judgment of the physicians should be available, but the decision whether to exert maximal efforts to maintain life should be the choice of the parents. The parents should be told the options, expected benefits, risks and limits of any proposed care: how the potential for human relationships is affected by the infant's condition; and relevant information and answers to their questions.
The presumption is that the love which parents usually have for their children will be

dominant in the decisions which they make in
determining what is in the best interest of
their children. It is to be expected that
parents will act unselfishly, particularly
where life itself is at stake. Unless there is
convincing evidence to the contrary, parental
authority should be respected.[74] (Emphasis
added.)

TRIAGE

Ironically, the alleged miracles of modern
medicine may, when performed, be little more than
curses to those who are the recipients. A vivid
description of such a "victim" of modern medicine
brings poignantly to the fore the major point and
illustrates it graphically:

The child lies motionless inside the plexiglass
incubator ... She weights 24 ounces and is two
months old. Tubes, five in all, carry
nutrients into her body and carry wastes away.
She is covered with scabs. Her skin is yellow
and slowly dying. Two weeks ago, infection
ravaged her small intestine. Her body is
stiff: poor circulation and blood teeming with
bacteria have caused a condition similar to
rigor mortis. When this little girl begins to
die, she will not be resuscitated, her parents
and her doctor have decided. She is taking up
a bed that could be used for a potential
survivor.[75]

The classical definition of <u>triage</u> may be
acknowledged as being:

The medical screening of patients to determine
their priority for treatment; the separation of
a large number of casualties, in military or
civilian disasters medical care, into three
groups: those who cannot be expected to
survive even with treatment, those who will
recover without treatment, and the priority
groups of those who need treatment in order to
survive.[76]

Even before "<u>triage</u>" found significant
application to military or civilian catastrophes,
its root meaning in French - "sorting, picking,
grading or selecting according to quality" - was

142

subsequently first applied in the English language to the process of separating wool according to quality and even later, to the separation of coffee beans into three categories: "best quality", "middling" and "triage coffee", with the last consisting of beans which had been broken and were thus the lowest in grade.[77] Over the course of time, the use of triage has been expanded to other situations where it has become, in practice, a metaphor for social, economic and even political decisions.[78]

Both the idea and the process of sorting casualties of war were developed by Napoleon's chief medical officer, Baron Dominique Larrey.[79] One of the Baron's early goals in his efforts to organize an efficient system of medical services to the injured was to perform surgeries as soon as possible after soldiers sustained their injuries. To this end, he developed "ambulances" whose purpose was not only to transport the wounded from the battle area but whose purpose was also to serve as mobile units for providing instantaneous medical assistance.[80] Additionally, he put into operation a scheme for sorting casualties on the basis of their medical need. Thus,

> Those who are dangerously wounded must be tended first, <u>entirely without regard to rank or distinction.</u> Those less severely injured <u>must wait until</u> the gravely wounded have been operated on and dressed.[81]

Medical personnel, then, were concerned centrally with finding ways to conserve scarce resources - the first and foremost being their time and their energy.[82]

During the Civil War the United States did not classify wounded soldiers essentially for purposes of medical treatment, providing such care instead without regard to physical condition. During World War I, however, it did in fact adopt from the French and the British, the principle of <u>triage</u>.[83] To this day, in fact,the current military policy of the armed forces of the United States is recognized as a policy of <u>triage</u> which involves both the evaluation and the classification of casualties for purposes not only of treatment but of evacuation. The motivation for this policy is tied to the principle "accomplishing the greatest good for the greatest number of wounded and injured men."[84] This being so it is clear that an explicit utilitarian rationale is embraced and extolled.

PRINCIPLES OF ALLOCATION; UTILITARIAN VERSUS EGALITARIAN

Since the law at present provides no uniformly agreed upon principles which may be applied in order to regulate the allocation of scarce medical resources, current medical practice draws upon a structure for decision-making evolved as such from a number of philosophical and ethical constructs.[85] There are five utilitarian principles of application which are operative in the hierarchy of triage: the principles of medical success; immediate usefulness; conservation; parental role and general social value.[86] Translated as such into decisional operatives, what emerges is a recognition that priority of selection for use of a scarce medical resource should be accorded to those for whom treatment has the highest probability of medical success, for whom treatment would be most useful under the immediate circumstances, to those candidates for use who require proportionally smaller amounts of the particular resource, to those having the largest responsibilities to dependants or to those believed to have the greatest actual or potential general social worth.[87] The utilitarian goal is - simply stated - to achieve the highest possible amount of some good or resource.[88] Thus, utilitarian principles are also commonly referred to as "good maximizing strategies."[89]

On the contrary egalitarian alternatives seek either a basic maintenance or a restoration of equality for persons in need of a particular scarce resource.[90] There are five basic principles utilized here: (1) the principle of saving no one - thus priority is given to no one simply because none should be saved if not all can be saved; (2) the principle of medical neediness under which priority is accorded to those determined to be the medically neediest; (3) the principle of general neediness which allows priority to be given to the most helpless or generally neediest; (4) the principle of queuing where priority is given to those individuals who arrive first and - lastly - (5) the principles of random selection where priority of selection is given to those selected by pure chance.[91]

To the utilitarian, maximizing utility, and hence what is diffusely referred to as the "general welfare", are both the primary Ground and Subject of

all judgments.[92] That which is required in order
to maximize utility overall may, thus, infringe upon
an individual's own entitlements or rights to
particular goods.[93] Accordingly, moral rights are
either rejected generally or recognized as certainly
not absolute.[94]

Philosophy and religion may well provide us all
with the necessary balance and direction for life
and allow us to develop an ethic for daily living
and a faith as to the future, but in cases of
neonatology where law, science medicine and religion
interact, great care must be exercised in order to
prevent inexplicable fears and emotions - oftentimes
fanned by journalistic prophets of the "what if"
shock culture - taking hold of and thereby blocking
powers of rationality and humanness.[95] The basic
challenge of modern medicine should be, simply, to
seek, promote and maintain a level of real (and when
the case may dictate, potential) achievement for its
user-patients, thus allowing for full and purposeful
living.[96] Indeed, man should himself, seek to
pursue decision-making responsibilities and in doing
so, to exercise autonomy in a rational manner and
guided by a spirit of humanism. He should seek -
further - to minimize human suffering and to
maximize the social good, though defining the extent
and application of the social good will vary
obviously with the situation of each case.[97]

BALANCING COSTS AND BENEFITS

The conundrum of seeking to maintain purposeful
living while at the same time protecting the
recognition of the very sanctification of life,
finds reality and force when dealing with the plight
of genetically defective newborns. This connundrum
is also to be recognized as presenting a duality of
goals. One goal is and must be balanced against
another in attempting to reach a level of
distributive justice in the hard decision required
here. The situation ethic must be predominant over
a harsh, unyielding a priori standard. Viewed from
another perspective, this balancing test underscores
recognition of the fact that human life is, in all
actuality, but a resource - as are natural, physical
and environmental resources. Thus, the primary goal
for the conservation of every resource is the
maximization of its full use or potential - be it
viewed as economic, social, cultural or political.
Waste must be avoided. Considered as such, then, in

seeking to maximize the good of this precious resource of life, the right of personal autonomy and spiritual awareness are but vectors of forces which must be additionally factored into any balancing equation. State interest is yet another positive force and also a constraint on autonomous or, in this area, parental-familial medical decision-making.[98]

When considering the severely defective newborn, vis-a-vis its quality and extent of life, the costs to the individual must be weighed against not only the side effects on the parents from a social, emotional and economic level, but on the hospital staff in the nursery watching the infant die and listening to its strangled cries.[99] Similarly, the effects on society as to the loss of a young citizen must be considered along with the potentially dangerous recognition that such deaths may legislate precedents for future citizens. Indeed, the goal of achieving a manageable level of sustenance may well involve incalculable levels of suffering for both the active and passive participants.[100]

Lord Justice Ormrod, a qualified medical practitioner and a Fellow of The Royal College of Physicians, observed in 1978, that the "cost-benefit" equation was no longer ignored in making modern medical treatment decisions.

> The medical profession has ... recognized that it is concerned with something more than the maintenance of life in the sense of cellular chemistry, and so implicitly accepted the concept of 'quality of life' from which it has in the past always fought shy, for obvious reasons. It has implicitly accepted that considerations of cost-benefit cannot be completely ignored...Ten or fifteen years ago, mere mention of either was enough to precipitate an emotional response from non doctors. Now they are explicit and can be discussed and debated rationally - an important advance from many points of view.[101]

THE ROLE OF THE ETHICS COMMITTEES

Ethics committees have been utilized since the 1970's - with greater or lesser degrees of success as either advisory or enforcing bodies.[102] In fact, a 1976 decision by the New Jersey Supreme

Court was the progenitor of these committees.[103] There, it was determined that ethics committees, composed variously of physicians, social workers, attorneys and theologians, endeavour to review the circumstances of specific ethical dilemmas in hospital settings. Such dilemmas normally involved the issue of whether to maintain or remove life-sustaining treatment modalities and thus to assist both patients, their families, and the attending physicians in finalizing decisions, at the same time conditioning civil or criminal liability that might otherwise arise from such undertakings.[104]

Sparked by the recent Infant Doe case in Indiana [105] and the Baby Jane Doe case in New York [106] involving the birth of genetically handicapped newborns, together with recently promulgated federal administrative regulations by the United States Department of Health and Human Services,[107] a new and sustained level of interest has emerged in both refining and utilizing a variant of ethics committees.

While the federal regulations apply only to handicapped to risk newborns, there are strong indications that ethics committees are being formed to assist in aiding situations other than the critical ones found in neonatal units.[108] California, New York, New Jersey, Connecticut and Massachusetts are examples of states whose hospital systems have responded in advancing the development of ethics committees which participate in, one level or another, the clinical decision-making process.[109]

Although the popularity of ethics committees admittedly has increased, it is clear that even the proponents of these committees recognize that they should not become an ultimate decision-making body.[110] Rather, they would "strive to emphasize the role of attending physicians and surrogates as the primary decision-makers for incapacitated patients."[111] Yet, depending upon the nature of the particular case under review, the degree of patient incompetency, level of informed or proxy consent given, and rationality of argument given for refusing medical treatment, there should be an understanding that the ethics review committee might in fact require a level of authority to order a (temporary) postponement of decisions which it has counseled against or even to initiate judicial proceedings in order to seek a review of decisions which it opposes.[112]

147

The positive values which ethics committees provide can be found not only in their structuring of a sound system for careful, humane decision-making, but in their service as a valuable bridge "between societal values and the actual developments occurring in the institutions that care for and treat the particular patients who manifest these dilemmas."[113] Not only do they assist in efforts to distinguish between ethical dilemmas where consensus may exist and in those cases where none is achievable, but also in developing policies and guidelines designed to facilitate decision-making, advancing an educative component targeted at the medical and nursing staffs which would better enable them both to comprehend and to resolve ethical dilemmas arising from the administration of modern health care.[114] Finally, the institutional ethics committees would serve as a consultative and case review mechanism whereby its individual members would be available to discuss the ethical and social concerns of interested parties, and by having the committee provide advice to parties that seek it.[115] The scope of individual case review would - as noted previously - vary necessarily with the facts of each case under consideration. Some cases would require more aggressive posturing by the committee than others.

The value of such committees will increase if courtroom adversarial situations can be prevented. Toward the achievement of this end, government regulation in this field should be avoided. In its place, concerted efforts should be taken toward following the example of hospice care in the United States (a system which developed as local and independent - but connected - entities in the health care system) rather than follow the path of institutional review boards, which were created by federal regulation to protect the subjects of human biomedical experimentation.[116] If concerned individuals in present health care institutions - be they pediatric, acute care or geriatric - work toward establishing a viable structure designed both to protect patients' rights and to ensure that reasonable and fair decisions are guaranteed for those unable to decide for themselves, the advances of governmental regulation will be halted and the goal of improving patient care will be enhanced.[117]

SEEKING A CONSTRUCT FOR DECISION-MAKING

The underlying principle of application should always be to minimize suffering and maximize the qualitative potential for fulfilling human relationships, thereby promoting a purposeful life for the at risk infant.[118] The extent to which this principle, inquiry or test should be applied depends solely upon the facts of each situation as it arises to present a problem. To have an unyielding a priori standing of mandated care for all seriously handicapped newborns would be unjust and promotive of undue suffering not only for the infant, itself, but equally unjust and harsh for its parents, presenting an unreasonably heavy economic burden to society for its maintenance and allocation of scarce and expensive medical support resources and mechanisms. Efforts must always be made to ensure, however, that if a class is structured and labeled, "disabled", it is drawn as narrowly as possible and as strictly defined as possible.[119] Thus, the overriding issue, is whether a construct can in fact be designed in such a manner as to assist the supervising physicians, the family and their religious counselors and the state (when involved) in defining the parameters of a class of nonsalvageable defective newborns?

At various times it has been suggested that the capacity for consciousness,[120] social interaction, human relationships (and especially love)[121] and rational thought were the four most important considerations in determining who was to be placed in the "non-salvageable" classification.[122] The importance of each capacity in the hierarchy of the classification depends, very obviously, upon one's particular social, ethical, religious and philosophical perspective. One leading ethicist has stated that, "..the warmth of human interaction, the love of one person for another, the emotional bonding that links people in moral communities does not require a capacity for consciousness."[123]

What is crucial in assessing these various capacities, no matter which are regarded as more central or primary by the philosopher-ethicists, is the actual physical condition of the handicapped newborn. If some agreement or at least a consensus could be reached that certain genetic afflictions were not correctable by surgery or medical treatment in any significant manner so as to promote a humane, qualitative life, free of intense pain and suffering, then better, more informed

149

decision-making could be considered by the family and its expanded circle. Such decision making would be aided by the medical recognition or determination that the at risk infant was one member of a classification for whom sustained living would be inhumane.

THE SHEFFIELD CRITERIA

Perhaps the most impressive effort toward developing a classification of at risk infants may be found in the results of a study undertaken at Children's Hospital in Sheffield, England. In the early 1970's at this hospital a list of six defects were found and agreed upon as being of such a nature as to preclude the possibility of an independent, dignified life - or, for that matter - a life which might be said to be meaningful in the sense that interpersonal relations could be enjoyed. The classification is as follows:

1. Thoracolumbar or thoracolumbosacral lesion.
2. Gross paralysis with neurologic segmental level at L 3.
3. Kyphosis or scoliosis.
4. Gross hydrocephalus with a head circumference at least 2 cm about the 90th percentile related to birth weight.
5. Other gross congenital defects, such as cyanotic heart disease.
6. Intracranial birth injury.[124]

AN EXPANDED CRITERIA

Recently it has been suggested that termination of a pregnancy during the third trimester (in the twenty-fifth week) can be morally justifiable - that is to say permissible in accordance with the mother's wishes - when two conditions are fulfilled. The conditions are:

1. that the fetus be afflicted with a condition that is (a) incompatible with postnatal survival for more than a few weeks or (b) characterized by the total or virtual absence of a cognitive function; and,
2. That highly reliable diagnostic procedures be available for determining prenatally that the fetus in fact fulfills either conditions

1(a) or 1(b).[125]

One condition, anencephaly, or the marked effective development or the brain, together with the absence of the bones of the cranial vault, clearly fulfils both conditions.[126]
Several other disorders fulful condition 1(a) in the sense that a fetus afflicted with them cannot survive for more than a few weeks after birth. Examples are renal agenesis, or failure or imperfect development of the renal system, infantile polycystic kidneys with resultant hypoplastic or under developed lungs and Mackel's syndrome.[127] The difficulty here is that these disorders do not fulfil the second condition, in that there are no highly reliable diagnostic procedures available to determine prenatally the presence of the disorder.[128]
Contrariwise, Tay-Sachs, a genetic anomaly, can be reliably diagnosed in utero but when the afflicted infant is born, it may well and usually does in fact have a number of months of normal life before rapid deterioration occurs and - as such - does not fulfil the first condition, namely that postnatal survival be for no more than a few weeks or be characterized by the total or virtual absence of cognitive functions.[129]

LOW BIRTH WEIGHTS

A recent report of infant births in the United States disclosed the fact that infants in the 501-750 gm range (1 lb. 11\2 ox. - 1 lb. 101\4 oz.) are oftentimes treated aggressively; those in the 751-1,000 gm range (1 lb. 101\4 oz - 2 lb. 3 oz.) are commonly treated in an aggressive manner while those infants weighing more than 1,001 gms (2 lb. 3 oz.) at birth are routinely · treated aggressively.[130]
Unless substantive reasons exist for the withholding of treatment, intensive care in Britain and Sweden is generally reserved for infants over 750 gm. Similarly, when an infant weighs less than 750 gm., it is seldom subjected to aggressive care (e.g., machine assisted respiration). As a consequence of this practice or unstated policy, fewer disabilities result in British and Swedish infants of low birth-weight from aggressive treatment than in the United States. Interestingly, the report concluded that the major difference

between infants provided with intensive care in Britain and Sweden and the United States was not based on genetic grounds - for which there is considerable consensus - but, rather, on the weight below which aggressive therapies should be withheld.[131]

Since the infant with a very low birth-weight is susceptible not only to brain injuries which in turn may result in associated handicaps such as mental retardation and cerebral palsy, (the sustained outcome being obtained only at considerable financial expense) it has been suggested that a cut-off weight of 1,000 grams be set (or, in other words, about two pounds, three ounces) below which aggressive treatment could be withheld justifiably. Another suggestion would be to withhold aggressive infant care when a birth weight of 1,000 grams or less is recorded for those born in a state of severe asphyxiation.[132]

It should be noted with clarity that non-aggressive care does not mean "no care". Rather, it has been termed conservative care and is recognized as a less intensive modality of therapy designed to promote comfort and well-being by, for example, keeping a distressed infant warm, providing fluids for him when indicated and - where necessary - placing him under oxygen hood in order to prevent cyanosis.[133]

Underlying these suggestions is the ultimate realization that selective non treatment would be administered on the basis of a determination made by the family and its physicians regarding the potential for quality of life. Such a decision would be sustained and developed and derived in part from economic considerations of cost-effectiveness in saving and promoting a particular life. Thus, an infant who, from a neurophysiological consideration has no conceivable potential to engage in rational deliberations and from a sociodemographic index would be unable to enjoy a qualitative life, would not be assisted in an aggressive manner with its struggle for life.[134]

Perhaps the most commonly agreed upon genetic factors which would justify the withholding or the withdrawing of aggressive therapies are tied to severe abnormalities, diseases or damages to an infant's central nervous system - especially the brain. More specifically, such agreement would include cases of hydroanencephaly, severe neural tube defects, gross hydrocephalus (if complicated by infection) and specific chromosomal disorders such as trisomy 13 and 18. Additional cases might include infants with extensive and fully documentated brain damage (asphyxia and) hemorrhage.[135]

CONCLUSIONS

Life - viewed as a human resource - should be developed and preserved along those lines which allow for the achievement of its fullest potential for total economic realization, maximization or productivity. Indeed, human life - at whatever state of development - is both a precious and a sacred <u>resource</u>. Its initial advancement or abrupt curtailment should be guided always by a spirit of humanism. Viewed accordingly, attainment of the quality of purposeful, humane living becomes a co-ordinate to total economic utility.[136]

Child protection laws are, of course, necessary. Their design and promulgation by the government are crucial if standards of equal protection for all its citizens - regardless of age or physical stature - are to be assured. It is a dangerously thin line to tread between familial privacy in decision-making matters and government intervention.[137] The judiciary, when called upon to evaluate cases of alleged abuse for handicapped newborns, can be aided by a close working partnerships with the medical profession in seeking to determine those situations where the withholding of needed medical or surgical modalities of treatment would be in the infant's best interests - as well as all others immediately concerned.[138] This is a proper judicial inquiry and a proper role for it to pursue. The construct for decision-making proposed herein is of value to not only the courts - but also to the parents of a handicapped infant who, themselves, must confront the initial decision regarding sanctified or qualitative living either alone, or with their physician or with the use of an ethics review committee. In fact, the refinement and wider utilization of Ethics Review Committees denominated Infant Care Committees or whatever, will go far toward forestalling not only the legislature, but the judiciary as well from intruding into the privacy of the doctor-patient relationship and parental autonomy.

In the absence of the pursuit of this suggested course of action, or for that matter in addition to it, and given the medically agreed upon components

of the modest construct that has been posited in
this article, together with the laws already in
place protecting children from abuse,[139] there is
no need for further direct government involvement or
intrusion into the sensitive area of familial
autonomy by way of federal regulatory schemes of the
nature being structured currently in the United
States.

NOTES

1.   Ellis, T. "Letting Defective Babies Die: Who
     Decides?" Am. J. Law & Med. 7, 1981, p.393, n.
     1.
2.   Hayes S. & Hayes, R. Mental Retardation: Law,
     Policy and Administration pp.48-49, Sydney: Law
     Book Co. Ltd., 1981.
3.   Childress, J. "Triage in Neonatal Intesive
     Care: The Limitations of a Metaphor", Va. L.
     Rev. 69, 1983, p.547.
4.   Ibid.
5.   Time Mag., Aug 9, 1982, p.42.
6.   Ibid.
7.   McCloskey, H. "Handicapped Persons and The
     Rights They Possess: The Right to Life,
     Liberty, Self-Development, Development of
     Self", in R. S. Laura (Ed), Problems of
     Handicap, Melbourne: Macmillan Press, So. 1980,
     p.86.
8.   Ibid.
9.   Ibid.
10. Ibid, p.88.
11. Ibid, pp.88-89.
12. Supra footnote 7.
13. Ibid, p.101.
14. Ibid, p.93.
15. Ibid, p.98.
16. Ibid.
17. Chief Justice Gibbs of The High Court of
     Australia held on March 30, 1983, in Attorney
     General for the State of Queensland (Ex Rel.
     Kerr) and Another v. T. that a foetus has no
     rights of its own until it is born and has a
     separate existence from its mother.   57 ALJR
     285.
18. Pub. Law No. 93-112, tit. v S.504, 87 Stat. 394
     (1973).
19. 42 United States Code S.2000d (1976).
20. 20 United States Code S.1681 (1976).
21. Supra, footnote 18.

22. Ibid.
23. 29 United States Code S.706(6) (1976).
Since originally Section 504 did not grant
either civil or criminal sanctions for
violations lodged under it, in 1978 the Act was
amended to make all those remedies which were
available under The Civil Rights Act of 1964
applicable to Section 504 claims. Pub. Law No.
95-602, 92 Stat. 2955, Rehabilitation
Comprehensive Services and Developmental
Disabilities Amendments of 1978.
24. Gurmankin v. Costanzo, 411 F. Supp. 982 (E. D.
Pa. 1976).
25. Camenisch v University of Texas, 616 F. 2d 127
(5th Cir. 1980).
26. Ferris v. University of Texas 558 F. Supp. 536
(W.D. Tex. 1983) (plaintiff sued to require the
University to make its shuttle busses
accessible to wheelchairs).
27. "Discrimination Against the Handicapped by
Witholding Treatment or Nourishment: Nature of
(sic) Health Care Providers", 47 Fe. Register
26, 027 (1982).
28. Nondiscrimination on the Basis of Handicap, 48
Fed. Register 9630 (1983).
29. Ibid.
30. U.S. v. Univ. Hospital, State Univ. of N.Y. at
Stony Brook, et al. Memorandum Opinion at
pp.43, 47.
31. 561 F. Supp. 395 (D.D.C. 1983).
32. Ibid.
33. 49 Fed. Register 1622 (Jan. 12, 1984).
34. H.R. 1904.
35. S.1003.
36. See, Legal Update Memorandum: Recent
Governmental Action Regarding The Treatment of
Seriously Ill Newborns, March 16, 1984,
Pierson, Ball & Dowd Law Offices, Washington,
D.C.
37. Supra footnote 33 at p.1652.
38. Ibid.
39. Ibid pp.1653-1654.
40. Ibid p.1652.
41. Ibid.
42. Ibid p.1652.
43. Ibid.
44. Ibid p.1651.
45. Ibid pp.1653-1654.
46. Ibid.
47. Ibid pp.1646-1649.
48. Marton, J. "Fight for Baby Jane", Dec., 4 1983,

155

col.1, at p.45.

49. In re B (A Minor), C.A. 1981, 1 W.L.R. 1421.
50. Ibid p.1422.
51. Ibid p.1423.
52. Ibid p.1424.
53. Ibid. See B. Dickens, "The Modern Function and Limits of Parental Rights", Law Quarterly Rev., 97, 1981, p.462.
54. Kennedy, I. "Reflections on The Arthur Trial", New Society 59, Jan. 7, 1982, p.13.
55. Glover, R. "Letting People Die", Lond Rev. of Books, Mar. 4-17, 1982, p.3.
56. Newsweek, Int'l Edition, Dec. 12, 1983, p.27.
57. In the Matter of William E. Webster, Guardian Ad Litem for Baby Jane Doe v. Stony Brook Hospital, et al, Oct. 28, 1983. Slip Opinion No.676 at pp.4, 5; 456 N.E. 2d 1186 C N.Y. 1983).
58. Application of Frank T. Curio, M.D., 421 N.Y.S. 2d 965, 968 (1979).
59. See, Van der Dussen, J. "High Court May be Asked to Save Baby", Bloomington Herald-Telephone, April 15, 1982, at p.1, col.1; Van der Dussen, J. "Infant's Death Ends Feverish Appeal for Life", Bloomington Herald-Telephone, April 16, 1982, at p.1, col. 1; Van der Dussen, J. "Givan: Court's 'Doe' Action Set No Legal Precedent", Bloomington Herald-Telephone, April 23, 1982, at p.1, col. 1. In re Infant Doe, No. GU 8204-00 (Cir. Ct. Monroe County, Ind., April 12, 1982) writ of mandamus dismissed sub nom. Infant Doe v. Baker, No.482 - S 140 (Ind. Sup.Ct., May 27, 1982) (case mooted by child's death).
60. Robertson, J. "Dilemma in Danville", Hastings Center Report, Oct. 1981, p.5.
61. See, "The Moral Dilemma of Siamese Twins", Newsweek, June 22, 1981, at p.40.
62. "State Drops Siamese Twins Case", N.Y. Times, April, 17, 1983, col.2, at p.6.
63. Campbell, W. & Duff, J. "Moral and Ethical Dilemmas in the Special Case Nursery", New Eng. J. Med., 289, 1973, p.890.
64. Ellis, T. "Letting Defective Babies Die: Who Decides?" Am. J. Law & Med. 7, 1981, pp.393, 399; Robertson, J. "Involuntary Euthanasia of Defective Newborns: A Legal Analysis", Stanford L. Rev., 21, 1974, p.213.
65. Shapiro, M. & Spece, Jr., R. Cases, Materials and Problems on Bioethics and Law, pp.702, 703, West Pub. Co., St. Paul, Minn., 1981.

66. Supra, footnote 63. Harvard, J. "Legislation is Likely to Create More Difficulties than It Resolves", J. Med. Ethics 9, 1983, p.18.
67. Supra, footnote 63 at pp.893-894.
68. Fost, J. "Counselling Families Who Have a Child with A Severe Congenital Anomaly", Pediatrics, 1981, pp.321-323; "Editorial, Severely Handicapped Infants", J. Med. Ethics 7, 1981, p.115; Diamond, J. "Treatment Versus Non-Treatment". In D. Horan & N. Delaboyd (Eds.) Infanticide and The Handicapped Newborn, pp.55, 62, Brigham Young Univ. Press, Provo, Utah, 1982.
69. Koop, D. "Ethical and Surgical Considerations in the Care of Newborns with Congenital Abnormalities" in D. Horan & N. Delaboyd supra, p.89.
70. Ibid.
71. The President's Commission for The Study of Ethical Problems in Medicine and Biomedical and Behavioural Research, Deciding to Forego Life-Sustaining Treatment: A Report on Ethical, Medical and Legal Issues on Treatment Decisions, (Committee Print, Mar. 21, 1983) pp.226, 228. This Commission ceased operating in 1983.
72. Ibid.
73. Ibid.
74. Current Opinions of The Judicial Council of The American Medical Association, A.M.A., 1982, p.9.
75. Sternberg, S. "Lying Hopelessly Ill, Infant Tests Law of Hospital Survival", Wash. Post, Apr. 3, 1983, at p.A4, col.1.
76. Stedman's Medical Dictionary, 4th unabridged lawyer's ed., W. Cornette (Ed.), Anderson-Jefferson Co., Cincinnati, 1976, p.1476.
77. Childress, J. "Triage in Neonatal Intensive Care: The Limitations of a Metaphor", Va. L. Rev. 69, 1983, pp.547, 549.
78. See Rund, D., Rausch, T. Triage pp.3-10, C.V. Mosby Co., St. Louis, Mo., 1981.
79. Winslow, G. Triage and Justice p.1, Univ. Cal. Berkeley, 1982.
80. Ibid p.2.
81. Ibid.
82. Ibid p.5.
83. Supra footnote 77 at p.550.
84. Ibid.
85. Note, "Scarce Medical Resources", Colum. L.

Rev. 69, 1969, p.620.
86. Supra footnote 79 at p.106.
87. Ibid pp.63-86.
88. Ibid p.87.
89. Ibid.
90. Ibid.
91. Ibid pp.88-106.
92. Gewrith, A. "Can Utilitarianism Justify Any Moral Rights?" in J. Pennock. & J. Chapman (Eds.), Ethics, Economics and The Law, New York: N.Y. Univ. Press, 1982, p.167.
93. Ibid pp.167-168.
94. Ibid p.168. Bentham in effect rejected moral rights generally. Hart, H.L.A. "Bentham on Legal Rights" in A. Simpson (Ed.), Oxford Essays in Jurisprudence (2nd Series), Oxford: Clarendon Press, 1973, pp.171-201.
95. See generally, Smith, G. "Intrusions of a Parvenu: Science, Religion and The New Biology", Pace Univ. L. Rev. 3, 1982, p.63; Smith, G. "Uncertainties on the Spiral Staircase: Metaethics and The New Biology", The Pharos 41, 1978, p.10.
96. Smith, G. "Genetics, Ethics and The Law", pp.2, 8, Associated Faculty Press, Port Washington, N.Y., 1981.
97. Ibid.
98. Ibid.
99. Young, R. "Infanticide and The Severely Defective Infant" in R. S. Laura (Ed.), Problems of Handicap, Melbourne: Macmillan Press, 1980, p.131.
100. Ibid.
101. "Editorial, Bioethics and The Law, Reform", The Law Reform Commission, p.10 Jan. 1979.
102. Cranford, R. & Doudera, A. "The Emergence of Institutional Ethics Committees", Law, Med. & Health Care, Feb. 1984, p.13.
103. In re Quinlan, 355 A 2d 647 (N.J. 1976).
104. Ibid.
105. Supra footnote 59.
106. Weber v. Stony Brook, et al 52 U.S.L.W. 2267 (N.Y. Oct. 28, 1983). 456 N.E. 2d 1186 (N.Y. 1983).
107. Supra footnote 33.
108. Supra footnote 102 at p.14.
109. Ibid pp.14, 15.
110. Ibid p.17.
111. Ibid.
112. Ibid.
113. Ibid p.15.

114. Ibid p.16.
115. Ibid.
116. Ibid p.19.
117. Ibid.
118. Supra footnote 96.
119. Supra footnote 54.
120. Fletcher, J. "Indicators of Humanhood: A Tentative Profile of Man", Hastings Center Report, Nov. 1972, p.1.
121. McCormick, R. "To Save or Let Die: The Dilemma of Modern Medicine" in R. McCormick (Ed.), How Brave A New World?, Doubleday, New York, 1981, p.339.
122. Veatch, R. A Theory of Medical Ethics 244, New Haven : Yale Univ. Press, 1981.
123. Ibid p.245.
124. Lorber, J. "Early Results of Selective Treatment of Spina Bifida Cystica", Br. J. Med, 4, 1973, pp.201, 203.
125. Chervenak, F., Farley, M., Walters, L., Hobbins, J., Mahoney, M. "When Is Termination of Pregnancy during the Third Trimester Morally Justifiable?", New Engl. J. Med. 318, Feb. 23, 1984, p.591.
126. Ibid.
127. Ibid p.502.
128. Ibid.
129. Ibid p.503.
130. Young, R. "Caring for Disabled Infants", Hastings Center Report, Aug. 1983, p.15.
131. Ibid p.16.
132. Ibid.
133. Strong, R. "The Tiniest Newborns", Hastings Center Report, Feb. 1983, p.14.
134. Kuge, E. The Practice of Death p.191, New Haven: Yale Univ. Press, 1975.
135. Supra footnote 130.
136. Supra footnote 96.
137. Dickens, supra footnote 53.
138. Burger, W. "Reflections on Law and Experimental Medicine" in G. Smith (Ed.), 1 Ethical, Legal and Social Challenges to a Brave New World, Associated Faculty Press, Port Washington, N.Y., 1982, p.211.
139. See eg. in England, The Child Care Act, 1980; Children Act, 1975, Children and Young Persons Act, 1963; Children and Young Persons Act, 1933; and the Infant Life (Preservation) Act, 1929. In the United States, each of the fifty states have laws designed specifically to protect the health and welfare of its

children-citizens from abuse.

Chapter Nine

GENETICS AND MENTAL RETARDATION

Jacquelyn Ann K. Kegley

        The German philosopher, Hegel, has counseled us
that the important questions, the crucial issues in
life are rarely clearly black or white, but rather
almost always varying shades of brown. In what
follows I will essentially argue that this is
precisely the case with the issues and questions
arising out of the use of various genetic
technologies to treat and prevent mental
retardation. The complexities arise out of a number
of factors including some contradictory operating
assumptions, rapid changes in the state of knowledge
in genetics and medicine, and the essential private
nature of reproductive decisions. I shall treat
each of these in turn, in addition to a number of
ethical and legal issues. First, however, I shall
discuss basic genetics, genetic diseases, and
available genetic technologies for treatment and
prevention of mental retardation if necessary.

BASIC GENETICS AND CATEGORIES OF GENETIC DISEASES

        Each living cell contains in its nucleus
hereditary particles called chromosomes. These are
made up in part of strands of deoxyribonucleic acid
(DNA).   Every inherited characteristic has its
origin somewhere in the code of each individual's
complement of DNA. DNA itself basically consists of
three types of ingredients: simple sugars known as
deoxyribose, phosphate units and the chemical bases:
adenine, thymine, cytosine and guanine. Genes can
be thought of as code words made up of triplet
arrangements of these bases. The triplet code are
biochemical instructions used in the ordering of
amino acids and synthesizing of different proteins.
        Proteins are either structural (the building

blocks of living things) or they can inhibit or act as enzymes or biological catalysts in directing chemical or metabolic reactions in cells. The absence or malformation of any enzyme can destroy the normal sequence of metabolism and thus potentially give rise to a biological deficit. In other words, genetic activity can be looked upon as a biochemical process with the DNA determining the formation of proteins, whether they be constructions of living structures or enzymes to regulate the living processes. However, all genetic diseases are, in one sense, primarily metabolic defects.[1] As we shall see, many genetic diseases involve an inability to produce a needed enzyme.

Turning to the genetics of the human species, we find the genetic material linearly arranged on 46 chromosomes. Chromosomes come in pairs. Twenty-two of these pairs are autosomes (non-sex-determining) and the remaining parts are the X,Y sex chromosomes. The X chromosome carries a full complement of genetic material. The Y chromosome appears to be primarily important in sex determination. Most traits that are readily recognized are classified as dominant or recessive. For example, when an organism carries both a recessive and dominant characteristic, say eye color, the dominant character (say, brown eyes) will, when crossed, be expressed or dominate the other character (say, blue eyes), called recessive.

In human reproduction both parents contribute half of the genetic makeup to the offspring, that is, the sperm and the egg each contribute 23 chromosomes. In order for this to happen meiosis or reduction division occurs which separates pairs of chromosomes, reducing the chromosome number in each gamete. During this process chromosome reshuffling takes place. It is crucial that one chromosome from each pair be included in each offspring gamete. This is necessary because each pair has a specific set of functions based on its unique DNA sequence. [2] If things do not go right in the meiosis process, chromosomal alterations can occur, resulting in chromosomally based genetic diseases. There may be a change in the amount of chromosomal material or changes in their basic arrangement. Trisomy is an excess of genetic material; monosomy refers to cases in which one chromosome from any pair is missing. This meiotic disjunction occurs in females with a much higher frequency than males and its possibility increases with the age of the mother.[3] However, some data suggest that it could equally be the male's age.

Some of the better known genetic diseases caused by meiotic disjunction are Down's Syndrome, which involves an extra chromosome 21, and which occurs in one out of every 600 live births; and XO Turner's Syndrome (1 out of 400 male live births). Both of the latter involve abnormal sexual development. The controversial XYY "aggressive male" syndrome (one in 250 males) is also a chromosomal disorder. In fact, over 15,000 infants are born each year in the United States with a debilitating chromosomal disorder and 3,000 of them have Down's Syndrome.[4]

However, the largest number of genetic disorders are single-genetic factor defects and these are not necessarily a function of malfunction during meiosis. There are mutations and many of them involve inadequate or non-enzyme or protein production. A National Institute of Health (NIH) report predicted that 1 to 2 percent of all live-born infants will suffer from one of these conditions.[5] All these diseases involve a malfunctioning of a single gene, but there are three ways hereditary transmission occurs. The first is the passing of a dominant gene from parent to child with a 50% risk of the child receiving the dominant gene and thus having the disorder. A well known dominant gene disorder is Huntington's disease, a disease which does not manifest itself until later in life, but which involves neurological deterioration, including memory and mental loss.

A second category of single gene disorders are those caused by autosomal (not involving the sex chromosomes) recessive genes. Conditions such as phenylketonuria, galactosemia, sickle cell anemia, Tay-Sachs, and cystic fibrosis are common examples. In this type of genetic transmission, two carriers of the particular gene must reproduce, the offspring having a 25 percent chance of being affected and a 50 percent chance of being a carrier. X-linked recessive disorders comprise the third category of genetic diseases. These are very rare and only males are affected. The most common of this type of genetic disorder is hemophilia (1 in 10,000 live births) and Duchenne muscular dystrophy (1 in 5,200 live births).[6]

A final category of genetic disorders are polygenic (multigenic) and/or involve interaction between genetic and environmental causes. Among these disorders are the neural tube defects such as anencephaly (1 in 700 Caucasian live births; 1 in

2450 Negro live births) and spina bifida (1 in 1800 Caucasian live births and 1 in 1900 Negro live births).[7]

GENETIC TECHNOLOGIES

Having identified the basic genetic causes of disease, it is now time to look at the genetic technologies available for prevention and treatment of disorders. The major instrument for prevention and treatment of genetic disease is genetic screening which involves also some new medical procedures. One of the major types of screening is prenatal screening which is aimed at detecting Down's syndrome and other chromosomal abnormalities as well as neural tube defects (those associated with increased alpha beta protein in the amniotic fluid.[8] This type of screening can also be used to detect inborn metabolic or biochemical disorders (about 80 in number) such as Tay Sachs. RH incompatibility between the fetus and the mother, and the recessive X-linked Lesch-Nyhan disease are also detectable.[9]

This type of screening, of course, involves amniocentesis, a procedure in which amniotic fluid is withdrawn from the amniotic sac at about 14-18 weeks from the last menstrual period. The fluid and cultured cells from the fluid are subjected to biochemical and cytogenetic analysis.[10] It is generally concluded that there is little potential medical risk involved in this procedure and that it is highly accurate.[11] Amniocentesis is now supplemented by ultrasound monitoring and detection, which directs high-frequency sound waves into the abdomen of the pregnant woman to gain an "echo-visual" representation of the fetus, placenta, uterus, and so on.[12] It too seems to be a safe technique. A less safe technique, fetoscopy, which carries a miscarriage risk of 3-10% and an increased rate of prematurity, can offer visualization of the fetus and access to fetal blood samples.[13]

A second type of genetic screening is carrier screening, the primary objective of which is to diagnose the carrier status of individuals for specific genetic traits, to inform them of the risks of affected offspring, and presumably, to thereby reduce the number of children with genetic disorders. This kind of screening is most effective: (1) when the disease occurs predominantly in a well defined population, and (2) when there is a simple, accurate, and inexpensive method to identify heterozygotes is available. That both these are met perhaps explains the success of the most extensive types of carrier screening in the United States, namely, screening for Tay Sachs.[14] Affecting primarily Jews of eastern European background, this fatal neurodegenerative disease strikes the child after six months and results in paralysis, blindness, and severe mental retardation. Care for an afflicted child, until its death at about age 4-5, is about $40,000 per year. It has been estimated that, since 1969, more than 200,000 childbearing individuals in North America have voluntarily submitted to the Tay-Sachs carrier screening; 600 pregnancies at risk for Tay-Sachs have been monitored through amniocentesis, and the births of approximately 150 afflicted infants have been prevented.[15]

A much less successful carrier screening program has focused on sickle cell anemia, an autosomal recessive disease affecting primarily American blacks, which can lead often to a painful and early death. Though there are some new techniques being explored (Kan & Dozy, 1978), the usual and often only option for detection and prevention of sickle cell anemia is carrier screening. Unlike Tay-Sachs, however, the disease is not as well understood by the population most susceptible (Blacks) and education of the population has not been thorough. As a result, there has been opposition to this type of screening, even though many of the first laws including The National Sickle Cell Control Act of 1972 were written and/or sponsored by blacks.[16] About 1/3 of the states in the U.S. offer screening for sickle cell anemia. [17]

A third kind of genetic screening is neonatal and the prototype is screening for phenylketonuria (PKU), an autosomal recessive disease caused by the inactivity of the enzyme phenylalanine and which results in severe mental retardation. This screening has been cited as one of the most extensive and successful of recent preventive public health programs[18], and well it might. In the past about 1% of residents in mental institutions were PKU afflicted. Since screening was instituted, not one admission for PKU has occurred.[19] With early detection and administration of a diet low in phenylalanine content, mental retardation can be averted. At present all 50 states offer PKU tests, though 7 have no enabling legislation.[20]

Screening is the primary genetic technology for
prevention and treatment of genetically caused
mental retardation, though perhaps gene-splicing
will provide some promise in the future. Artificial
insemination, in vitro fertilization and embryo
transfer are reproductive options that also might
provide couples facing risk of genetic disorders in
offspring with other avenues of prevention.
Whatever technologies that are available, it is
clear that genetic disease is a serious problem.
For example, the National Center for Health
Statistics (in 1978) has reported that
gene-determined disorders are responsible for 20% of
all infant deaths; are the second cause of death in
the 1-14 year old category; and are among the
important causes of mental retardation and physical
disability. In a pamphlet entitled What Are The
Facts About Genetic Disease? published by the
Department of Health, Education and Welfare, there
are some estimates of the financial burden of
genetic disorders. The estimated lifetime cost of
maintaining a seriously genetically defective
individual is given as $250,000. The estimated
burden for the yearly care of new Down's syndrome
cases is cited as about $1 billion.[21]
It is clear that genetic disease is a serious
health economic problem and must be dealt with, but
in dealing with genetic diseases and associated
technologies a number of complexities arise for
various reasons and of varying types. It is to
these I shall now turn.

SOME COMPLEXITIES OF GENETICS AND RETARDATION

One of the factors contributing to the
complexity of issues and questions arising out of
attempts to prevent and/or treat mental retardation
by means of genetic technologies is that there seem
to be contradictory operating assumptions. First of
all, to prevent and treat mental retardation by
means of genetic screening and its related
technologies is to assume: (a) that genetic factors
play a primary causal role in mental retardation;
and that (b) mental retardation is a biochemically
based "disease" and therefore medically treatable.
Most of literature discussing Down's syndrome,
Tay-Sachs, and PKU, as well as the other "genetic
diseases" make these assumptions.
In spite of these causal and medical
assumptions, however, it must also be recognized

that the nature-nurture, hereditary-environment issue is a very real one and that caution is necessary. Thus, Mare Lappe and Richard O. Roblin, writing on genetic screening, tell us that although there is a tendency to assume that each genetic disease has a purely endogeneous cause, nevertheless,

> ... this is only partially true, for all genetic defects only, become manifest after interactions with some environmental or metabolic component. [22]

Lappe and Roblin believe that in viewing genetic screening as a preventive measure against mental retardation, some questions must be raised about any single cause assumptions. They write:

> ... the crux of the medical argument for neonatal genetic screening is whether or not one can accurately predict future sequelae of environmental exposure by a momentary look at the metabolic state of the newborn. [23]

Dr. Aubrey Milunsky, Medical Geneticist, Massachusetts General Hospital and Center for Human Genetics, Harvard Medical School, would also issue a word of caution about causal assumptions. Arguing that recognition of the cause is the first step in the prevention of mental retardation, Dr. Milunsky, however, also agreed that this will not be a simple task. The matter is complicated by the fact that in the past, the etiology was unknown in 60% to 70% of the cases.[24] Dr. Milunsky offered us the following picture of diagnosing causes of mental retardation:

> Elucidating the exact etiology of mental retardation in many cases may be extremely difficult and further compounded by such major effects as genetic/environmental interaction, low birth weight, prematurity, and perinatal complications. In addition, the causes of mental retardation, congenital malformations, and other developmental disabilities not only overlap but also are inextricably related ... [25]

Irving M. Gottesman, a behavioral geneticist claimed that there are three important questions to be answered by molecular geneticists, developmental

167

biologists, and developmental psychologists.[26]
They are:

1. How much of the variability observed within
   a group of individuals in a specified
   environment on a particular trait measure is
   attributable to hereditary differences among
   them?
2. How modifiable by systematic environmental
   manipulation is the phenotypic expression of
   a trait?
3. How does heredity interact with the
   environment to produce trait variation?

If a purely genetic model is adopted, giving
top priority to the genotype and to genetic
manipulation to improve our human condition, then
certain very important factors may be ignored at
least by the layman, though perhaps not by the
geneticist. First is the concept of genetic
diversity and a related fact, namely, that our
society is one which has traditionally been
committed to regarding the individual as a primary
social unit, as of ultimate social and political
value.[27] Biologist Dobzhansky argued that an
interactive model of genetic factors and environment
must be our operating model in all discussions of
genetic intervention and indeed, that genetic
diversity is the joint product of genetic and
environmental differences even at the micro level.
He wrote:

> ... an individual's physical and mental
> consitutions are emergent products, not a mere
> sum of independent effects of his genes. Genes
> interact with each other, as well as with the
> environment ... gene B may enhance some
> desirable quality in combination with another
> gene A, but may have no effect or unfavorable
> effects with gene A2 ... For this reason ... it
> is not at all rare that talented parents
> produce some mediocre offspring, and vice
> versa.[28]

To say that environment and genetic factors
interact is not necessarily to say that they have
equal influence, but rather that (1) we must
function with a complex rather than simplistic
model; (2) that genotype is not all paramount; and
(3) that genetic inheritance interacts with
multienvironmental influences to produce a

phenotype. In the words of E. White, "...
individuals with similar genotypes will vary
significantly in their phenotypes as a result of
environmental differences, and there is the
possibility that within similar environments
individuals with varying genotypes will differ
accordingly in observed behavior".[29]   Genetic
diversity is, says Dobzhansky, "a treasure," and we
must not ignore or cover up individual differences,
individual uniqueness. It has been estimated that
humans hold 95% of their genetic endowment in common
and 5% of each individual's genetic endowment is
unique.[30]   Both our commonality and our uniqueness
need to be stressed.

Genetic diversity and uniqueness must not be
ignored, but neither must we be beguiled into
ignoring environmental factors. To do so would be
dangerous both for prevention and treatment of
genetic diseases. Consider the fact that radiation,
including X-ray, and the use of chemicals and drugs,
would all seem in varying degrees to cause genetic
changes. We are a society heavily dependent on
chemicals and drugs, some of which we often take for
granted, such as those used for agricultural and
food enhancement. Widely prescribed drugs such as
Valium are used to cope with life, and others such
as marijuana, LSD, caffeine, alcohol and nicotine
are used for pleasure. Attention must be paid to
these environmental factors in a comprehensive and
intelligent approach to preventing genetic disease
and mental retardation. Thus, G.J. Stine and others
admonish:

On the basis of over 75 years of scientific
investigation, it appears that an increase in
the human mutation rate (by any means,
radiation or chemical) would prove detrimental
to humankind - both present and future
generations. On the basis of such knowledge,
the greatest caution must be exercised in
avoiding human exposure to mutagens.
Furthermore, the investigations of mechanisms,
causal factors, and effects of mutations, in
order that we avoid the suffering of inherited
diseases, must be continued.[31]

In other words, we cannot ignore environment
nor can we put the burden of prevention just on the
individual parents. Society must ask itself about
the conditions it is creating which may cause
genetic mutation, e.g., nuclear power plants which

give off radiation.

Marre Lappe has demonstrated dramatically how following rigidly a simplistic model of genetic causation can affect treatment. He tells of his search for "the ultimate paradigm for a genetically-determined condition." The condition he was directed to was the Lesch-Nyhan syndrome, an X-linked recessive condition, an enzymatic defect, which results in mental retardation (IQs of 20 to 40), self violence, and self-destructive behavior. In a visit to Dr. Nyhan in San Diego, he was introduced to an afflicted child named Jimmy. Not only did he discover a higher level of mental functioning than presumed, but also that the only assumed treatment of the disease was heavy restraints and excess amounts of 5-hydroxytryptophane. Believing that these children were not "simply programmed to be self-destructive, as would be predicted by a strictly genetically determined model of self-destructive behavior",[32] Lappe continued his research and discovered that Doctor Dancis at Columbia University was successfully treating Lesch-Nyhan children with behavioral modification techniques, "dampening the same reflexive biting behavior with purely behavioral means that Nyhan believed only chemical controls could suppress".[33] Lappe's conclusion, after this research is sobering and worth highlighting.

> The message of this case appears to be that a realm of indeterminancy exists in the best biologically classified systems, an indeterminancy that allows room for human invention and intervention. And that perspective provides opportunities for an overlay of hope against what would be an otherwise fatalistic diagnosis. Even the most simplistic formulas appear to actually work. If you take children with Down's Syndrome and their mothers and teach both of them to interact in a two week or three week course, you can raise the IQ of Down's Syndrome children 20 to 25 points.[34]

In light of these facts and questions it must be understood that causal diagnosis and behavioral and developmental prognosis is a complex and difficult affair. This is true because of the complexity of the genetic facts themselves, but also because of the continual change in the state of knowledge in the field. There remain many unknowns in genetic and brain research as well as in medical technology. New 'genetic-determined' traits, as well as new neurotransmittors are being discovered almost every day. Likewise there are continually new developments in fetal surgery. Two important cases were recently reported. The first concerns a "selective abortion" performed in 1981 at New York's Sanai Hospital. The mother learned through testing that she was carrying twins, one of whom had Down's syndrome. Rather than keep both or abort both, the genetically-diseased fetus was destroyed by drawing its blood through a needle and the mother later delivered the healthy twin.[35]

The second case is even more dramatic for the prevention of mental retardation. Terry Bennett, five months pregnant, discovered through ultra-sound that she was carrying a fetus with hydrocephalus, and that the prognosis for her child was a lifetime of institutionalization. Being Catholic, abortion was not an acceptable option. However, at the University of Colorado Health Sciences Center, a plastic shunt was snaked through a hollow needle into the fetus's skull. The one-way valve in the shunt permitted the fluid that was crushing the brain to drain into the amniotic sac. The baby survived his prenatal trauma and now, at 16 months, appears to be normal. Because of these dramatic developments in fetal surgery, decisions made on prevention and treatment in the near future may be quite different from those made now.

Furthermore, even in the treatment of fairly understandable genetic diseases, there are changing assumptions and facts. Take the case of PKU. PKU screening has had a mixed history. Criticisms of this screening, especially in its early stages, are worth noting. There was criticism of the fact that tests were made compulsory before there was sufficient knowledge to make informed decisions. In fact some have claimed that the tests were inaccurate.[36] Bessman and Swazey for example, put the point as follows:

> The tests are not accurate; they miss a number of cases of PKU and yield false positive reactions in an even greater number. Given a positive test, physicians will very probably put the child on a low phenylalanine diet ... But a child who does not have PKU is actively endangered by the diet and can suffer physical deterioration at the least; a number of

171

children died from being treated for PKU, and it is likely that they did not have the disease.[37]

Phillip Reilly also raised questions about PKU screening and cites the study of the Committee on the Study of Inborn Errors of Metabolism of the National Academy of Sciences (National Academy of Sciences, 1975).[38] There is a concern with false negative results and with a wide discrepancy in performance by laboratories charged with testing. Reilly recommended (1) that all newborn screening be made the responsibility of one lab, and (2) that the parents of newborn children be provided with a urine specimen mailing kit.[39]

There has even been change in the treatment of PKU and more change may be in the offing. Through diet therapy is now discontinued at about age six or seven, there is new evidence to suggest that it might be better if the diet was continued until the teen years.[40] Furthermore, data suggested great concern for PKU women who do not follow a diet before or early in pregnancy. There is evidence that as a result the fetuses will be poisoned.[41] Once again, this demonstrates the complexity of genetic disease as well as the complexity of treatment and prognosis and the need for continual monitoring, follow up, and education.

Indeed, even to use the word "disease" when dealing with mental retardation is perhaps not correct. There are those who shun looking at mental retardation in this manner and rather speak in terms of levels of development or levels of function. They argue that biological and psychosocial deprivation must be clearly distinguished and, once again, point to the necessity of noting the role of both kinds of factors in causing mental retardation.[42] Moreover, as indicated in Lappe's example of the Lesch-Nyhan child, it must be recognized that our predications about functioning are not always very clear or even good. Surveys have shown that in favorable circumstances mental defectives may achieve much higher degrees of social competence than could have been predicted on the basis of IQ score.[43] The key to achieving higher levels of social competencies seem to be in having a carefully worked out and individualized plan. H.C. Gunzberg, Consultant Psychologist, Monyhill Hospital, Birmingham, made the following point:

There is a general recognition that cultural

deprivation accounts for a large proportion of the social malfunctioning of the mentally handicapped and thus the main task appears to be to compensate for deficits and missed learning situations.[44]

Before we leave the issue of the role social and environmental factors, play in treatment and prevention of mental retardation, it must be seen that genetic screening does or could affect individual and parental feelings of personal worth, as well as the individual's ability to establish and/or maintain social relationships. Health is seen as functional adequacy, incorporating physical, psychological, and social aspects. This being so, illness "... can be conceptualized as one form of social deviance".[45] Different diseases have different degrees of social adaptability depending on visibility, physicalness, social disruption, and the fear it stirs in the nondisabled. Mental retardation seems to stir fear and have a low degree of social acceptability. A strong philosophical foundation of Western thought has been the belief that a pivotal test of full personhood and humanhood involves the ability of an individual to engage in rational thought. Even in the medical world brain function plays a crucial role in determining adequate functioning including the test of life and death. Much thought has to be given to the question of intellectual and brain functioning and here again, issues of great complexity arise, especially given the ignorance we still have of brain functions and the factors involved in "intelligence". A recent article on meningomyelocele and the spinal bifida research carried out by J. Lorber of Sheffield, England and J.M. Freeman of Baltimore, Maryland was concerned to show, that priorities must be established and that "we must establish criteria for considering a particular condition hopeless". [46]

All of this affects both offspring and parent carrier. As for carrier status, there is generally no bodily illness or disability, but there are serious implications for one's desire to get married, the choice of an acceptable mate, and the desire for children. A study of sickle cell anemia screening in a small Greek village demonstrated that being identified as a carrier has serious social consequences, serving to discourage engagements and to encourage downright lying to potential mates. [47]

Parenthood has high popular status in our society, and thus it is in the role of parent that the repercussions of carrier status are most likely to alter life expectations and self-esteem. It is important to be a parent and have the child be as perfect as possible. In fact, there seems to be a social attitude developing that "if congenital abnormality can be avoided, then it should be and those individuals who do not partake of these advances will be socially ostracized".[48] Moreover, there is some evidence that parents take genetic deformity in an offspring as a form of punishment, and thus as their personal responsibility. Along with this personal responsibility comes severe guilt feelings. This is all the more reason why there must be careful counseling and education of the public about genetic disease and about each specific disease. Indeed, there is general agreement that the following conditions should be met by any genetic screening program.
1. That the disease is clearly and precisely understood.
2. That a reliable and accurate technique is available for detection of the disease.
3. That there is evidence of substantial public benefit and acceptance and that benefits outweigh costs.
4. That means are available to evaluate the effectiveness and success of each step in the process.
5. That appropriate and effective public education can be carried out.

A major concern should be to promote public education both about genetic disease and about mental retardation. Such an approach is much needed and should be given top priority by public agencies. There is, however, another point and a crucial one with which we must deal, namely, that traditionally for the West, reproductive decisions have generally been a private matter, a decision made by the individuals involved. The decision to become a parent has long been considered a right within the democratic context of individual freedom. This decision is no longer thought to be an inalienable right. The new genetic technologies, because of their complexity and the public's lack of preparedness, have brought others automatically into the circle of this decision-making process, and this has raised new and unprecedented legal and ethical questions. It is to these issues I now turn.

174

ETHICAL AND LEGAL ISSUES

Since our particular concern is with mental retardation, it should be clear from the start that the mentally retarded person has not been traditionally granted the right to make those reproductive decisions that are considered so essential to individual freedom. The practice has more often been sterilization of the mentally defective person. Phillip Reilly has documented this history very well and I shall provide only a brief summary of it. The first state to enact a sterilization law was Indiana in the United States in 1907. From this time to 1925 the legislation was challenged in court, but sterilization continued to be performed. In 1925 there was a famous challenge of Virginia legislation, the Buck vs. Bell case. The Supreme Court, likening compulsory sterilization to compulsory vaccination, upheld sterilization legislation as an appropriate exercise of the state's police power. This led to a flood of sterilization laws in 20 states. In the 30's there were legal challenges, but sterilization continued. The issue again went to the Supreme Court. They did not overrule Buck vs. Bell, but the justices did show a greater sensitivity to the gravity of a compulsory sterilization program. Justice William O. Douglas, on behalf of the court asserted:

> We are dealing here with legislation which involves one of the basic civil rights of man. Marriage and procreation are fundamental to the very existence and survival of the race. The power to sterilize, if exercised, may have subtle, far reaching and devastating effects ... There is no redemption for the individual whom the law touches ... He is forever deprived of a basic liberty.[49]

A shift of attitude occurred in the 50's and 60's due to three factors: (a) new information about genetics and mental retardation; (b) the concern of the Supreme Courts to defend civil rights legislation; and (c) the defence of the rights of institutionalized patients by the legal community. Today the trend is towards the creation of medical review boards, and it is far more difficult to obtain sterilization for retarded persons. Reilly summarized the pros and cons of sterilization. The cons are as follows:

... Critics of sterilization usually offer three major arguments: that there is no substantial evidence that retardation is highly inheritable, that sterilization confers no benefits, and that the reduction in welfare costs accomplished by sterilization should not be used to justify state violation of a "fundamental interest".[50]

Reilly agreed that the fact that 83% of retarded children are born to nonretarded parents seems to support the arguments against sterilization, but he also asks us to consider that ...

17 percent of retarded children are born to retarded parents. Retarded persons comprise only 2 percent of the population. Two well-known behavioral geneticists recently concluded that the relative risks of retardation are much higher among the offspring of retarded persons than among the normal. In addition, sterilization may confer freedom on the retarded person. Many people feel that retarded persons that are educable can lead relatively independent lives so long as they are not burdened with the care of children.[51]

Once again, it becomes apparent that the issues are complex, that individual cases must be assessed carefully and that all factors must be weighed.

Turning to decisions made by parents and others on behalf of offspring, potential or real, the issues are many. First, there are the basic questions of individual freedom and the right to procreate. How do we weigh individual rights versus social benefit? There is a definite conflict between the view that child bearing is an inalienable and absolute right and the position that with knowledge and expertise to do so, society has the right and obligation to require couples to refrain from producing genetically defective children. The social costs are enormous, as we have seen, both the financial burden of care and the psychological and sociological effects on the family. It can be argued that the state does have an interest in the family, in the quantity and quality of the progeny of its citizens. Furthermore, although the concept of "socially useful" is problematic, there is an obligation to maximize the number of socially useful people and minimize the number of socially burdensome people.[52] The psychological, social, legal, ethical and economic costs and benefits of producing and maintaining an "unhealthy" individual must be carefully weighed and balanced. Included in this analysis must be a clear cut answer to the question "What counts as a serious genetic defect?" and in specific cases, what is the best prognosis we can give, viewing all the factors? Furthermore, individual freedom must be respected and maximized.

A second issue is that of the principle of the sanctity of life. The issue is this:

> The new emphasis on prevention of disease of genetic origin is the prevention of the existence of persons who might have the potential for disease. To prevent disease in this context means preventing people.[53]

There is a difficult question yet to be asked, namely, "Is abortion for genetic indications justified?" Second, if abortion is not chosen for whatever reason, does this imply that a parental decision to have a genetically affected child is morally irresponsible and blameworthy? The abortion issue, of course, is difficult in and of itself in every way, and becomes even more so in this context because of the uncertainty of some of the prognoses. There are, however, some outcomes which are quite clear. Consider, for example, Tay-Sachs disease. Here one cannot ignore questions about quality of life, and emphasis must be placed on the obvious value of preventing suffering. To have meaningful and rewarding life requires assurance of enough longevity to develop physical and mental capacities. Few, I believe, would argue that the first six months of a Tay-Sachs child's life is enough to compensate for the tremendous deterioration, physical pain and suffering for the child until its death, not to mention the mental anguish for the parents or the economic suffering. Further, one must also count the suffering of the siblings and other members of the family. In the studies that were made in England of spina bifida children and their families, it is clear that much social and psychological disruption occurs for all members of the family, including divorce. Each individual's life, health and development must be valued. Moreover, primary emphasis must be on freedom and fairness. In a democratic society can we afford to do otherwise? It seems to me that this means we must provide both genetic services to those who freely choose to control their reproduction, and to withhold support for those who freely choose to take the risk of reproduction even when they know the risk and suffering that may well befall them.

At the same time we must work for the broadest education of our citizenry on matters of genetic disease and its complexity, along with mental retardation and its varying degrees. For individual parents, of course, it is the job of the genetic counselor or physician to establish the risks and to interpret these risks in as meaningful terms as possible. The right to informed consent as well as to confidentiality are rights which must be upheld morally and legally and in fact. Furthermore, there must be respect for the dignity of each individual; the parents should be carefully counseled, not advised by the expert. It is they that must make the decision. Further, to avoid unnecessary guilt, and anxiety, it must be recognized by all concerned that all humans are carriers of mutant genes. Stigmatization must be fought when possible. In counseling, we also have the problem of truth-telling. When, if ever, should information be withheld from the parents, for example, in the case of questionable paternity. I find myself in agreement with Hastings Center Guidelines which include the stipulation that "... findings should not be withheld from parents, even when they are of disputed importance, e.g. XXY condition."[54]

Of course, there will be controversial requests for genetic services. Should amniocentesis be provided for cases where there is no history of genetic disease or any indication of risk? How much do we want to encourage the expectation of physical perfection in our children? I would again agree with the Hastings Center Guidelines which argue for "... opposition to amniocentisis for sex choice alone, but also opposition to any legal restriction of this option in the interest of protection of parental choice."

Finally, the difficult question of distributive justice will have to be sorted out for gentic services. What justification will we allow for the expansion of genetic services and what public priority will be given to genetic services? Further, how will we weigh and balance support for preventive measures vis-a-vis treatment measures and who will decide? We will need to work simultaneously to improve the societal treatment and respect accorded to those born with defects and to extend our genetic knowledge and apply it to genetic counseling. It will not be an easy task, but nevertheless it is one we must resolve to pursue.

New technology always brings in its wake a diversity of positives and negatives, and this is no less true in the case of genetic technologies, particularly as they are applied to the treatment and prevention of mental retardation. What is needed is the wisdom and compassion of a King Solomon or a Socrates. We need the wisdom to deal with the complexities of both genetics and mental retardation as well as those human complexities involved. We need compassion and resolve to treat all with dignity and respect. Somehow we must conquer genetic diseases which produce mental retardation without eroding personal freedom or losing our humanity.

NOTES

1.   Cortazzo, A.D. "Basic Genetics." pp. 25-26. In A.D. Cortazzo, R.M. Allen, & R.P. Toister (Eds.), The Role of Genetics in Mental Retardation. Coral Gables, Florida: University of Miami, 1971.
     Crome, L., & Stern, J. The Pathology of Mental Retardation. Baltimore, Md.: Williams & Wilkins, 1972.
2.   See Blank, R.H. The Political Implications of Human Genetic Technology. Bolder, Colorado: Westview Press, 1981; and
     Cavalli-Sforza, L.L. "The Genetics of Human Populations," Scientific American, 1974, 231, 80-89.
3.   Carr, D.H. "Heredity and the Embryo". Science Journal, 1970, 6, 75-79.
4.   Blank, Op. Cit.
5.   National Institute of Health. Antenatal Diagnosis; Predictors of Hereditary Disease or Congenital Defects. Washing, D.C.: Department of Health, Education and Welfare, 1979.
     Neel, J.V., & Bloom, A.D. "The detection of environmental mutagens". In A.S. Baer (Ed.), Heredity and Society. New York: Macmillan, 1977.
     Nitowsky, H.M. "Prescriptive screening for metabolic disorders". New England Journal of Medicine, 1978, 280, 1299-1300.
     Powledge, T.M. "Genetic Screening as a

Political and Social Development". In J. Wortis (Ed.), <u>Mental Retardation: Annual Review II</u>. New York: Grune & Stratton, 1970.

6. Blank, <u>Op. Cit.</u>

7. <u>Ibid.</u>

8. Chedd, G. "Who Shall Be Born?" <u>Science 81</u>, Jan/Feb. 1981, 33-41.

9. Blank, <u>Op. Cit.</u>

10. Golbus, M.S. Loughman, W.D., Epstein, C.J., Halbasch, G., Stephens, J.D., & Hall, B.D. "Prenatal Genetic Diagnois in 3000 Amniocenteses," <u>New England Journal of Medicine</u>, 1979, <u>300</u>, 157-163.

11. Culliton, B.J. "Amniocentesis: HEW Backs Test for Prenatal Diagnosis of Disease," <u>Science</u>, 1975, <u>190</u>, 537-540.

12. Frankel, M.S. <u>Genetic technology: Promise and problems</u>. Washington, D.C.: Program of Policy Studies in Science and Technology, George Washington University, 1973.

13. <u>National Institute of Health</u>, Op. Cit.

14. Kaback, M.M., & O'Brien, J.S. "Tay-Sachs: Prototype for Prevention of Genetic Disease," In V.A. McKusick (Ed.), <u>Medical Genetics</u>. New York: H.P. Publishing Co., 1973.

15. Powledge, T.M. "Genetic Screening as a Political and Social Development," In D. Bergsma (Ed.), <u>Ethical, Social and Legal Dimensions of Screening for Human Genetic Diseases</u>, New York: Stratton Internal Medical Book Corporation, 1974.

16. Blank, <u>Op. Cit.</u>

17. Reilly, P. <u>Genetics, Law and Social Policy</u>, Cambridge, Mass.: Harvard Univerisity Press, 1977.

18. Hansen, H., Shahidi, A., & Stein, Z.A. "Screening for Phenylketonuria in New York City: Threshold Values Reconsidered," <u>Public Health Reports</u>, 1978, <u>93</u>, 246-251.

19. McCready, R.A. "Admissions of Phenylketonuria Patients to Residential Institutions Before and after Screening Programs of the Newborn Infant," <u>Journal of Pediatrics</u>, 1974, <u>25</u>, 383-385.

20. Steiner, K.C., & Smith, H.A. "Survey of Departments of Health about PKU Screening Programs," <u>Public Health Reports</u>, 1975, <u>90</u>, 52-54.

21. Reilly, <u>Op. Cit.</u> pp. 28-29.

22. Lappe, M., & Roblin, R.O. "Newborn Genetic Screening as a Concept in Health Care

Delivery," In D. Bergsma (Ed.), Ethical, Social and Legal Dimensions of Screening for Human Genetic Diseases, New York: Stratton Internal Medical Book Corporation, 1974, p.4.

23. Ibid, p.5.

24. See Berg, J.M. Proceedings of the 2nd International Congress of Mental Retardation. Part I. Basel, Switzerland: S. Krager, 1963; and
Moser, H.W., & Wolf, P.A. "The Nosology of Mental Retardation: Including the Report of a Survey of 1378 Mentally Retarded Individuals at Walter E. Fernald State School," Birth Defects, 1971, 7, 117.

25. Milunsky, A. "The Causes and Prevalence of Mental Retardation," In A. Milunsky (Ed.), The Prevention of Genetic Disease and Mental Retardation, Philadelphia: W.B. Saunders, 1975, p.22.

26. Gottesman, I.I. "Behavioral Genetics," In A.D. Cortazzo, R.M. Allen, & R.P. Toister (Eds.), The Role of Genetics in Mental Retardation, Coral Gables, Florida: University of Miami, 1971.

27. See Lappe, M. "Reflections on the Cost of Doing Science". Annals of the New York Academy of Science, 1976, 265, 102-109; and
Lappe, M. Genetic Politics: The Limits of Biological Control. New York: Simon and Schuster, 1979.

28. Dobzhansky, T. Genetic Diversity and Human Equality. New York: Basic Books, 1973.

29. White, E. "Genetic Diversity and Political Life: Toward a Populational Interaction Paradigm," Journal of Politics, No. 4, November, 1972, 34, 1215.

30. Corning, P.A. "The Biological Bases of Behaviour and Some Implications for Political Analysis", Worle Politics, Vol. XXIII, April, 1971, pp. 321-370.

31. Stine, G.J. Biosocial Genetics: Human Heredity and Social Issues. New York: Macmillan, 1977.

32. Lappe, M. "The Myth of Genetic Determination." In J. Kegley (Ed.), A New Challenge to the Educational Dream: The Handicapped. Bakersfield, Calif.: California State College, Bakersfield, 1980, p.93.

33. Ibid, p.95.
Kan, Y.W., & Dozy, A.M. "Antenatal Diagnosis of Sickle-cell Anemia by D.N.A. Analysis of

Amniotic Fluid Cells". Lancet, 1978, October 28, Vol. II, pp. 910-912.

34. Ibid.
35. Fadiman, A. "Saving a Baby's Brain," Life, 1983, 6, 44.
36. Bessman, S.P., & Swazey, J.P. "Phenylketonuria: A Study of Biomedical Legislation," In E. Mendersoln, J.P. Swazey, & I. Taviss (Eds.), Human Aspects of Biomedical Innovation. Cambridge, Mass.: Harvard University Press, 1971.
37. Ibid.
38. National Academy of Sciences. Genetic Screening: Programs, Principles and Research. Washington, D.C.: National Academy of Sciences, 1975.
39. Reilly, Op. Cit.
40. Holtzman, N.A., Welcher, D.N., & Mellitis, E.D. "Termination of Restricted Diet in Children with Phenylketonuria: A Randomized Controlled Study, New England Journal of Medicine, YEAR?, 293, 1121-1124.
41. Blank, Op. Cit.
42. Wortis, J. "What is Mental Retardation," In J. Wortis, (Ed.), Mental Retardation: Annual Review II. New York: Grune & Stratton.
43. Gunzberg, H.C. "Pedagogy," In J. Wortis (Ed.), Mental Retardation: Annual Review II. New York: Grune & Stratton, 1970.
44. Ibid, p.118.
45. Sorenson, J.R. "Some Sociological and Psychological Issues in Genetic Screening: Public and Professional Adaptation to Biomedical Innovation," In J. Wortis (Ed.), Mental Retardation: Annual Review II. New York: Grune & Stratton, 1970.
46. Cooperman, E.M. "Meningomyelocele: To Treat or not to Treat?" CMA Journal, 1977, 116, 1340.
47. Powledge, Op. Cit.
48. Sorenson, Op. Cit, p.177.
49. Reilly, Op. Cit, p.127.
50. Ibid, p.131.
51. Ibid.
52. Twiss, Jr., S.B. "Ethical Issues in Genetic Screening," In D. Bergsma (Ed.), Ethical, Social and Legal Dimensions of Screening for Human Genetic Diseases. New York: Stratton Internal Medical Book Corporation, 1974.
53. Murray, R.F. "The Practitioner's View of the Values Involved in Genetic Screening and

Counseling". In D. Bergsma (Ed.), Ethical, Social and Legal Dimensions of Screening for Human Genetic Diseases. New York: Stratton Internal Medical Book Corporation, 1974, p.196.

54. Fletcher, J.C. "Ethical Issues in Genetic Screening and Antenatal Diagnosis." Hastings Center Report. Clinical Obstetrics and Gynechology, December 24, 1981 (4).

Chapter Ten

MENTAL RETARDATION AND GENETIC ENGINEERING

R.S. Laura

We are, I believe, at the crossroads of human history. With the splitting of the atom came the dawn of the Nuclear Age and the potential power in the flick of a finger or two to annihilate the entire human race. While our forefathers once lived in fear of plagues and contagious diseases, we now confront daily the threat of nuclear holocaust. Given the impact of nuclear science upon our lives, it is for most of us unimaginable that recent developments within biology could approximate nuclear technology in respect of the sheer magnitude of its range of actual and possible social transformations. Notwithstanding our incredulity, the discovery in 1973 of recombinant DNA has given rise to genetic technology and an attendant set of social, legal and ethical problems which may well serve to eclipse our wildest fears of neclear destruction. With the advent of recombinant DNA technology, we have within our power the ability to alter and to manipulate every life form on this planet. For the first time in human history we have become the masters of our own evolution, but are we equal to the task? The miracle, if one could call it that, of recombinant DNA technology extends to the creation of new life forms, to the creation of chimeras, of sub-human beings, and of post - or super-human beings. Control over our own evolution is the power to modify and to alter beyond recognition the biological forms of our own and all other species. The biological destiny of all life on this planet is now in our hands and in our test-tubes.

Needless to say, the power to play God in this way carries with it perhaps the greatest challenge and responsibility of our times. Genetic technology, not unlike nuclear technology, can be used for benevolent or malevolent purposes. The uses and possible uses of genetic engineering for benevolent ends have considerable ramifications for those forms of mental retardation whose aetiology is genetically based. Indeed, the total eradication of all genetically caused mental retardaton is part of the benevolent promise of genetic engineering. It is the aim of this chapter to examine the ethical implications logically associated with the realisation of this promise. To achieve tihs goal, I shall begin with a brief account of the biological revolution of which genetic engineering is one expression, highlighting the philosophical assumptions which underpin it. I shall then consider some actual and proposed applications of genetic engineering to the eradication and modification of mental retardation. Particular attention will be paid to genetic screening, genetic transfer, and in vitro fertilization in the service of genetic engineering. Finally, I shall try to show that genetic engineering in the context of mental retardation forces upon us a number of ethical questions for which we have no standard answers. We are not without principles of action, but genetic engineering has so radically altered the framework of their application that our decisions cast one principle against the other. What is in tension is the very foundation of ethics and how we characterize it. Our ethical calculus has always covertly contained a fundamental asymmetry in the adjudication of the respective roles played by considerations of life and death. However, the asymmetry has gone unnoticed, because our system of morality defines its principles of concern in terms of causing deaths of saving lives. Given that we have previously only ever had the power to bring about death, that is to say, the focus of ethics has been largely devoted to the issues of saving lives. Now that we have added to our power to bring about death, the power to bring about life, our ethical calculus must be viewed from a vantage that does not prejudice the one or othe other. To broaden our vision, however, we are obliged to broaden our very system of ethics itself. What is required, I shall argue, is a shift from the ethical reductionism in terms of which we presently deliberate, to an ethical holism which incorporates the biographies of all living things.

THE BIOGENETIC REVOLUTION: THE PHILOSOPHICAL BACKGROUND

To appreciate the full and continuing impact upon society of the Biogenetic Revolution, it is essential to have some understanding of the philosophical assumptions which underpin it. Without making these assumptions explicit, the discussion of genetic engineering will rely implicitly upon certain of the very concepts which serve inevitably to distort it. The Biogenetic Revolution did not just happen serendipitously. it marks the culmination of a long and venerable tradition in science whose thrust has been predominantly reductionist. Biological reductionism reflects the persistent disposition to reduce the biological functions of living organisms to their most fundamental chemical properties and to explain malfunctions of the human organism in terms of malfunctions of these properties. It is against the background of biological reductionism that the Biogenetic Revolution took place.

One of the most significant developments to shape this background was philosophical. The edifice of biological reductionism is built upon mechanist foundations. Reductionism is appropriate to the human organism, it is supposed, because the human body is a machine whose function depends wholly upon the parts of which it is composed. Dependent upon a paradigm in which the human organism is viewed as a machine, reductionism regards illness as a malfunction of the machine's parts. In embracing tihs picture of the body as a machine, the physician comes naturally to be regarded as a kind of mechanic whose job it is to repair the body, by intervening either to restore or to replace its parts. It is, as we shall see in the task that follows, in the extension of this paradigm that genetic engineering is applied to mental retardation. Before proceeding to that task, however, more needs to be said of the philosophical background which makes it comprehensible.

The mechanistic interpretation of the human organism has an ambiguous ancestry in the Ancient Greeks and finds explicit expression in the medical tradition of Hippocrates. It was not until the time of Galileo and Descartes, however, that the link between the mechanist framework and bio-reductionism was finally secured. It was Galileo who held that mathematical laws governed the function of all nature, including the human body. All that was required to comprehend fully the mysteries of the nature of the human body was a mathematical theory of its anatomical workings. The possibility of the mathematical analysis, Galileo averred, depended upon restricting science to the primary or quantifiable properties of the phenomena under investigation.[1] Secondary properties such as colour, taste and smell belonged, he thought, to the domain of subjective experience and therefore had no place in objective science.[2] Nature was to be understood, and in turn controlled, by effecting its reduction to the basic mathematical, or more precisely, the geometrical relations of which it was constituted. Mastery of the human body was simply a result of this reduction.

Contemporary with Galileo was the distinguished philosopher Rene Descartes whose philosophy of science more closely parallelled that of Galileo than has often been appreciated. Not unlike Galileo, Descartes perceived the true structure of nature as reducible to mathematical relations which described its most fundamental constituents. Just as the workings of a watch could be explained purely in terms of its parts, so too the material world could be explained by reducing it to its fundamental constituents.[3] It was Descartes however, not Galileo, who succeeded in wedding reductionism to the mechanist framework in terms that would produce a conceptual lineage sufficient to nurture the Genetic Revolution. For it was Descartes who crystallised the sundry mechanisms of scientific procedure into a monolithic method of analytic enquiry, and it is the analytic method that has come to figure as the instrument of the bio-reductionist orientation of which genetic engineering is the current culmination. The analytic method is in essence the method of divide and conquer, and reductionism is its nature expression. To understand the world requires analysis, and analysis leads to division of the world and all that is in it, to its fundamental parts. The analytic reduction of matter has led to atomic theory and nuclear physics, whereas the analytic reduction of living things has led to molecular biology and genetic engineering. We have in the light of the analytic paradigm been led also to reducing knowledge to ultimate and incorrigible beliefs and ethics to absolute principles of action. The genetic revolution is not a development separate from these developments; it is a part of the biography of human thought of which each development is in its own way a biographical sketch of the same paradigm.

It would, of course, be misleading to suggest that the concept of analysis and the concept of reductionism are co-terminus in extension. Analysis is tantamount to epistemic reductionism, for example, only when it is formalised into a dogma which demands that the complexity of nature can be known <u>exclusively</u> by way of its analysis into its fundamantal parts. On such an interpretation, the theory of knowledge becomes perversely analytic, setting the precedent for scientific investigation solely in reductionist terms, thus transforming the openness of enquiry into the stricture of dogma. This is epistemic reductionism at its worst, and I shall endeavour to show later in this chapter, it has led to a reductionism in ethics that has in the end served to limit the scope of our morality.

Although Descartes may not have intended that analysis be used in this way, it is clear that it has since been so used. The philosophical search for the foundations of knowledge has been parallelled within science by the search for the foundations of biology. Descartes unwillingly assured that bio-reductionism would not stand unsupported, for its analytic 'backing' so to say, was in his own terms given by the reductionist theory of knowledge itself. The aims and values of our social and eductional institutions reflect, then, a philosophical view about the nature of reality and of how we come to know it. What we say about genetic engineering, whether in the cause of eradication of mental illness or in the hope of creating a super-race, must be set against the background of philosophical assumptions which inform what we say.

It is in this light that one final observation should be made about the philosophical heritage of the genetic revolution before turning directly to the matter of its examination. To appreciate the full impact of Descartes' thought upon the assumptions and values implicit in the genetic revolution, it is imperative to couple his epistemic reductionism with his doctrine of dualism. It was the separation of <u>res cogitans</u> from <u>res extensa</u> that made it possible for the first time to describe, without an embarrassing residue, the world of <u>res extensa</u> as a machine whose workings could be reduced to mechanical laws. It was only by taking the mind or spirit out of matter that matter itself ould be characterised in purely mechanical terms without reference to spirit. The ramifications of Descartes' dualism have been far reaching. Not only has it transformed our perception of the world and paved the way for the presentation of Newtonian mechanics, but it has also profoundly altered the attitudes taken to the human body. The decisions we make about the role genetic engineering will play in the future of our species will depend in part upon those attitudes, and it is encumbent upon us to make them explicit. Fritjof Capra has captured this point well when he writes:

> The Cartesian division between mind and matter has had a profound effect on Western thought. It has taught us to be aware of ourselves as isolated egos existing 'inside' our bodies; it has led us to set a higher value on mental and manual work; it has enabled huge industries to sell products - especially to women - that would make us owners of the 'ideal body'; it has kept doctors from seriously considering the psychological dimensions of illness, and psychotherapists from dealing with their patients' bodies.[4]

The transition from the Cartesian to the Newtonian picture of the world followed without philosophical encumbrance. Indeed, it was Newton who provided the systematic mathematical articulation inspired by Descartes' mechanist reduction of nature. Epistemic reductionism was given its most powerful expression in Newton's invention of the differential calculus. By means of its deployment Newtonian mechanics not only set the stage for the future development of the medical sciences for the next three centuries, but it mapped the particular direction that development would take. The degree of development within the medical sciences was proportional to the degree of formalised epistemic reduction within them. Medical knowledge of the nature of the human body and its workings was thus a matter of the progressive revelation of the nature of its fundamental parts. The historical progression of the bio-reductionist orientation led first to an analysis of the human body in terms of its appendages, then its enternal organs, and later to the cells of which those organs are constituted, and now to the DNA components of wihch the cells are made. DNA is the last stage in the reduction, we are told, for it marks the discovery of the ultimate building blocks of all living organisms.

THE POWER OF THE GENE: THE STATE OF
THE TECHNOLOGY

Although the techniques of genetic engineering
were only introduced into molecular biology as
recently as 1973 with the advent of recombinant DNA,
a number of earlier developments in genetics
heralded the possibilities of the diverse
application of these techniques. As is well known,
it was in 1953 in that now celebrated April 25th
edition of the journal Nature that the American,
James Watson, and his British colleague, Francis
Crick, reported the discovery of the twisting double
helix or spiral staircase microscopic structure of
deoxyribonucleic acid, or DNA as it is now commonly
known. The steps of the spiral staircase structure
were constituted of what they called 'base units'.
The base units were made up of a modest sequence of
four chemical nucleotides, capable of assuming an
almost infinite variety of patterns, each of which
expressed a specific genotype. The further
production of the particular protein structures
responsible for the individual characteristics of
all living organisms was said to depend upon the way
in which the genes interact by way of their
collective arrangements. Generally speaking the
fewer the number of genes in concatenation, the
simpler the resulting organism and vice versa.
Depending upon the particular collective arrangement
of genes, the result ranges from the simplest of
life forms at one end of the spectrum to the most
complex of life forms at the other.
The discovery of the structure of the salt of
deoxyribonucleic acid was seen as a great victory
for and confirmation of the reductionist tradition
in science. With the discovery of DNA came both
substantial government support for further research
in genetics and a series of consequent discoveries
that prepared the way for genetic engineering. Four
years subsequent to Watson and Crick's discovery of
DNA, for example, Dr. Arthur Kornberg unravelled the
mystery of the structual replication of DNA. On his
account DKA undergoes a division into two separate
strands, or 'unzipping', as he described the
process, each strand of which in turn utilizes
chemical substances from the immediate cell
environment to reproduce its original structure.
Kornberg's contribution did much to prepare the
context for genetic engineering, as it provided the
basis upon which techniques for the current
synthesization of DNA have been implemented.[5]

The mystery of the genesis of all living organisms was in principle solved in reductionist terms, it was alleged, inasmuch as the fundmental genetic constituents of the simplest organisms were reiterated in the genetic components of the most complex. The secret of life revealed by the discovery of DNA was the blueprint not just for this or that life form, but for all possible life forms on this planet. Hidden within the structure of DNA lay the genetic information, that is, for the determination of all living organisms that there are, of all that there have been, and of all that there could be. The impact of the reductionist revelation is thus staggering. From an understanding of the structure of DNA the biological sciences have progressed to the stage where it is now possible to manufacture and to manipulate life itself. This is the power of genetic engineering. Genetic engineering refers to the techniques whereby DNA from one organism is recombined with the DNA or genetic material from a different and often unrelated organism. The discovery of recombinatory DNA thus permits the incorporation of genetic material from unrelated organisms by splicing DNA segments together in such a way that the grafted gene is established as part of the natural process whereby the engineering organism produces its own DNA. When the germ-line or sex cells are affected, the introduced genes can be transmitted to subsequent generations. 'Pronuclear' or 'zygotic' injection is one such genetic engineering technique which has been used successfully to double the size of mice and their offspring (affectioned dubbed 'supermice') by grafting together the growth hormone gene of a rat with the genetic material of the mice.[6]

For the first time in human history, the human race achieved the potential power to control its own evolutionary future and destiny and thus the destiny of every life form on this planet. There is, when all is said, a mordant irony in the fact that along with Francis Crick, a number of distinquished physicists abandoned their research into nuclear physics because they found it morally repugnant that the research in which they were engaged was potentially destructive of humanity. Little did they know that in their migration to the life sciences, discoveries would be made capable of altering beyond recognition the living face of this planet. What they seemed not to realize is that there is no human activity which constitutes a

GENETIC ENGINEERING

sanctuary from moral responsibility.
We are now in a position to appreciate the full
panoply of ways in which genetic engineering
impinges upon future directions in mental
retardation. There is no doubt that mental
retardation is caused primarily by genetic
disorders, and it is estimated that approximately
80% of all mental retardation is linked to genetic
diseases. Four main categories of genetic disease
are employed in tracing the aetiology of mental
retardation. The largest of these classes is made
up of Constitutional Disorders and these are
estimated to account for 14.8 per 1,000 births.
Diabetes mellitus and idiopathic epilepsy fall
within this category. The next largest class is
characterised by assorted Congenital Malformations
which exhibit an incidence of 14.1 per 1,000 births.
Phenylketonuria or P.K.U., Tay Sacks disease,
galactosaemia and X-linked mental retardation are
examples of what are classed as Single Gene Effects,
occurring in 11.2 affected births per 1,000 births.
Diseases such as Down's Syndrome, Klinefelder's
Syndrome, Turner's Syndrome, and Cri du Chat
Syndrome are included uner the heading of
Chromosomal Abnormalities and account for 5.4 per
1,000 births.·[7]
One obvious application of genetic engineering
to mental retardation can be seen in its service to
genetic screening. At present prenatal diagnosis
may involve collecting genetic data from family
histories in the hope of identifying suspected
carriers of genetic diseases, and where detection is
succussful, to provide genetic counselling as
appropriate. In certain cases, a couple might be
admonished of the complications of marrying, of
having children, and in some cases where pregnancy
has already occurred, of the effects on the future
life of the child if carried to full-term. A
reputedly more effective and relatively recent
development in screening is amniocentesis. In
amniocentesis a sample of fluid containing
desquamated foetal cells is obtained from the
amniotic sac during the early part of the second
trimester of pregnancy. The foetal cell sample is
obtained by passing a long needle into the sac and
drawing off a small amount of the amniotic fluid.
Utilizing recent genetic innovations in chromosome
analysis, it is possible to detect more than sixty
genetic abnormalities. Inasmuch as there are some
1600 human diseases caused by defective genes,
including congenital blindness and deafness.

193

Genetic engineering could be employed to reduce further the incidence not only of genetically based mental retardation, but the incidence of other genetic diseases as well.

Consideration of the sundry applications of the techniques of genetic engineering to mental retardation, even in regard to genetic screening, lead ineluctably, however, to a discussion of in vitro fertilisation or I.V.F. This is an important point, as it shows that the role which I.V.F. plays in genetic engineering is pivotal, not peripheral. One can no longer sensibly regard I.V.F. merely as a technique for overcoming some forms of infertility in those who would otherwise remain childless.[8] It is I.V.F. which itself provides the laboratory context in which various of the techniques of genetic engineering can be tested and introduced. In this sense I.V.F. is a technological presupposition of genetic engineerng and not just one separate expression of it. Thus to talk of the way in which genetic engineering can facilitate genetic screening inevitably involves appealing to I.V.F. for its elucidation. In coming to appreciate this point it is to be hoped that we become less susceptible of failing to perceive the extent to which assumptions of value both inform and are informed by technological development. This is a matter to which I shall later revert.

It is in any case clear that given the ostensible objectives of amniocentesis, genetic engineering can assist in achieving those objectives more efficiently. Using the in vitro fertilisation environment as the screening context, for example, it is possible to extract - presumably without harm - cell sample from the early embryo for recombinant DNA analysis. Normal from abnormal gene variants can be differentiated by the creation of 'gene probes', and it is envisaged that techniques of 'mapping' or 'marking' will soon permit the identification of any gene which exhibits genetic anomalies.

It is conjectured that most of the 1600 genetic anomalies could in principle eventually be tested in this way. If the DNA analysis proved to be satisfactory, the embryo could then be implanted, otherwise not. Since identification of the gender of the embryo can also be readily determined through chromosomal analysis, sex-linked inherited diseases such as the Duchenne type of muscular distrophy and haemophilia could be effectively reduced by ensuring that only zygotes of a certain relevant sex are implanted. In the case of the Duchenne type muscular distrophy, for instance, it is the sons of the heterozygous mother which risk a fifty-fifty chance of being affected. In the case of male haemophiliacs who produce children, it is the sons who are normal and the daughters who are heterozgous carriers. By implanting only female zygotes in the former case and male zygotes in the latter, the incidence of both type of genetic diseases could be considerably diminished. The adoption of in vitro fertilisation, coupled with genetic screening would thus have the putative advantage of reducing the numbers of so-called therapeutic abortions by making them unnecessary.

It is in connection with heterozygous carriers that the impetus to cloning is perhaps at its strongest. Cloning, as is well known, refers to the reproductive process which results from recombinant DNA manipulation utilising a cell sample from the body of only one person. An individual or any number of individuals possessed of identical constitutions with each other and the parent cell source is the consequence of this quite remarkable feat of genetic engineering. Cloning is now a sophisticated engineering technique which has proved extremely successful in its application to amphibians. A female carrier of haemophilia, for example, need not worry about having a son who stands a fifty-fifty chance of being affected. The genetic manipulations which constitute cloning would permit her to have daughter whose genetic constitution would be identical with her own, a carrier of haemophilia, but not a haemophiliac victim. It is worth noting, however, that cloning would do little to overcome the problem which remains even when screening for heterozygotes is successful. For while the restrictions placed on the gender of offspring born to heterozygotes would serve to reduce the number of children born with genetic disorders, these restrictions would do little to diminish the incidence of the recessive gene which heterozygotes carry. Only a prohibition on the reproduction of heterozygotes or comprehensive gene therapy could achieve that aim.

In addition to the proposed benefits then which genetic engineering affords for the screening of genetic disorders responsible for mental retardation, genetic engineering can also be combined with I.V.F. techniques in the service of gene therapy. The possibilities of human genetic manipulation have been markedly increased by the introduction of I.V.F. Besides making the genetic material accessible for manipulation, I.V.F. ensure that it is possible to identify (genetic screening) and to replace (genetic transfer) a defective gene at an early enough stage in embryonic development that the non-defective DNA molecule can be incorporated into the germ-line (sex) cells as part of the normal integrative and developmental process of the zygote. Although genetic transfer is also possible at later stages of development, including adulthood, the ability to direct the non-defective gene for integration into the specific community of cells which manifest the defect is enhanced by I.V.F. The alternative procedure for removing from the body a sample of the defective cell population for recombinatory therapy and then return to the body has thus far been unsuccessful, though considerably research continues to be directed to this end. Once again, it is evident that I.V.F. provides the experimental context in which gene therapy can be most effectively executed. If genetic manipulation of defective DNA is permitted, it then becomes possible to alter the genetic material of an otherwise defective zygote, thereby permitting its implantation, while thus further reducing the alleged necessity of therapeutic abortion. The technique of gene therapy would thereby also overcome the moral objections to withholding certain zygotes from implantation. Enough has now been said, however, about the technique of genetic engineering in the avoidance of mental retardation, and we are now in a position to consider some of the ethical issues which arise therein.

THE ETHICAL ISSUES: HOW BRAVE A NEW WORLD?

The range of ethical issues raised by the foregoing considerations is kaleidoscopic. Scientific concern, for example, expressed resolutely at the Asilomar Conference of 1975, was directed primarily to ethical issues of safety. Inasmuch as recombinant DNA research usually involves the transplantation of genetic material into a bacterial environment for propagation, there have been ethical worries as to whether the resulting bacterial strains could be pathogenic to humans. Escherichia coli, better known as E. coli and used as the common bacillus of recombinant DNA propagation, represents a laboratory strain of the same bacteria normally found in the colon and the human intestinal tract. While the gut strain of E. coli is not pathogenic to humans, it is unknown whether its laboratory counterpart is equally favourably disposed to life in the human intestine.

The anxiety is not simply conjectural in its source. It is known that varient strains of E. coli can be seriously disruptive of the multiplicitous functions of the human organism, causing diarrhoea, infantile meningitis, and bloodstream infections, to name a few of its deleterious effects. A bacterial strain resistant to antibiotics, moreover, could be genuinely inimical to the survival of the human species. As a result of this concern, attempts have been made to produce weaker strains of bacteria, the prime example of which is the bicentennial bug bred in 1976 by Professor Roy Curtis of the University of Alabama Medical School.[9] Nonetheless, the dramatic steps taken to make recombinant DNA research safe betrays - or so it would appear - a measure of just how unsafe it would otherwise be, or indeed in essence is.

Despite efforts to make recombinant DNA research safe, it has often been argued that a total moritorium should be declared on genetic engineering and its research. Given that we cannot predict the consequences of this relatively unexplored technology, it is possible that its negative utility to society is such that continued research constitutes too great a risk to bear. I do not wish to engage here in a protracted debate in these terms as to whether a total ban on genetic engineering is warranted, though I shall later in this section raise this question in a different way and in different terms. In the present terms of argument, however, it does not seem to me that the 'doomsday argument', as the risk objection against recombinant DNA research has come to be called, succeeds.

Although it is undeniable that even precautionary experimental research in genetic engineering could possibly have catastrophic consequences, it does not follow from this possiblity that such research should be banned. I say this for two reasons. First, to have demonstrated the logical possiblity of the catastrophic consequences of genetic engineering is not in itself to have provided any reason whatsoever in support of the likelihood of their actual occurrence. It is simply to have provided a coherent description of some possible event or events. Second, the fact that no assurance can be

given of the non-zero probability of their
occurrence is not an anomaly peculiar to research in
genetic engineering. It is the same problem which
confronts almost all scientific research and many
commonplace activities as well. As Steven Stich
puts it:

> It is, after all, at least logically possible
> that the next new compound synthesized in an
> ongoing chemical research program will turn out
> to be an uncontainable carcinogen many orders
> of magnitude more dangerous than aerosol
> plutonium. And, to vary the example, there is
> a non-zero probability that experiments in
> artificial pollination will produce a weed that
> will, a decade from now, ruin the world's food
> grain harvest.[10]

The point of all this is, of course, that if on the
grounds of <u>possible</u> catastrophe, we invoke a
prohibition on recombinant DNA research, we are
equally committed to a prohibition on all research
in general.

The possible military, terrorist, and other
nefarious applications of the products of
recombinant DNA research is another of the diverse
issues raised, even by that body of research
innocently and benevolently intended to reduce
mental retardation by genetic engineering. the
sinister uses to which malevolent governments,
terrorists or the demented could make of a
debilitating or lethal bacterial strain,
accidentally or otherwise derived, are too heinous
to contemplate. The imaginative but all too
possible and provocative constructions of
recombinant DNA chimeras have also served to
stimulate ethical qualms for professionals and
laymen alike. Is the human form inviolate? Can we
ethically employ genetic engineering not only to
improve the human species, but to transform it? Is
it right, for instance, to exploit cloning to
advance either the commerical or scientific
interests of a society? Is it wrong, as Fletcher
suggests,

> ... to use cloning to produce legless people,
> dwarfs, individuals distorted functionally in
> various ways - for example, to man spaceships
> to Jupiter ... Similar is a proposal to solve
> the fruit picking problem in a future leisure
> society by using a genetically 'designed' and

then cloned submental people with prehensile tails to do the work. It can be countered immediately with 'Why not monkeys?' (which are already being considered by some orchards). [11]

Yet the degree of difficulty in deciding these issues in the terms in which Fletcher decides them is shown by his own ambivalance as to what provides the criteria for the acceptable limits of cloning. Elsewhere in the same work he writes:

There could also be reasons for the social good. Individuals might need to be selectively reproduced by cloning because of their special resistance to radiation, their small body size and weight, because they are impervious to high decibel sound waves; these things could be invaluable for professional flights at high altitudes and space travel, for example. In a stretch of imagaination, a biologist could solve the weight problem by going alone to a distant planet with a supply of different somatic cells, and colonize it for a cloning start. [12]

If the former case of cloning is wrong and the latter case right, as Fletcher suggests, to what could he appeal to justify the difference? Is it that in the former case we design the functional distortion, whereas in the latter case, it is an accident of nature? It is not at all clear why this difference, if it is a genuine difference, should be regarded as morally relevant. After all, why would it be right to clone an already existing legless person to produce many such legless persons to pilot our spaceships to Jupiter, but yet be wrong to design and clone legless persons? In both cases there is, in the name of the social good, a genetic proliferation of legless persons. Either both cases are right, it would appear, or both cases are wrong. Yet there is something awkward in putting the matter in this way, something ethically fullsome in the discussion itself. For in our deliberate efforts to seek the ethical principles by which to guide humanity we have unwittingly contributed to the very conditions which make us less human. I shall in what follows try to give some sense to this presently obscure epigram.

In the first section of this paper I was concerned to show that genetic engineering is the

199

current culmination of a long and venerable tradition in bio-reductionism, in turn underpinned by certain philosophical assumptions about the nature of reality and all that it contains. Genetic engineering is postulated on the assumption that human beings, indeed all living things, are essentially machines, the sum of their genetic parts, perhaps nothing more. The precedent for engineering the environment, including plants and animals, to suit human needs and interest is deeply entrenched in the biography of the human race. Genetic engineering simply extends that precedent one stage further by establishing techniques to engineer the human race itself. The respectability of genetic engineering is thus powerfully expressed by its laudable objectives: the reduction and prevention of genetic disease, the alleviation of suffering associated with these diseases, and the more effective deployment and distribution of our health-care resources. While the standard way of putting the case for genetic engineering is attractive, its attraction is, I submit, at least partly meritricious.

It is true that as a race we have seemingly from the beginning, engineered the world around us. What has also to be admitted, however, is that we have not always engineered it to the better. Our reverance for science and its technological inheritance, in combination with prevailing institutional interests for profit, have all too often engineered the environment for destroying and distorting it. We have treated the world like a machine whose parts can be used up and replaced, and our engineerings have brought about the natural holocaust of lakes and rivers dying from pollution, drinking water unfit for consumption, plant and animal life diseased and ravaged. Now that we have distorted the world so as to make it almost unlivable, genetic engineering provides the prospect of distorting us to allow us to live in it. Moreover, our adjustment to the world is sponsored on the pretense that it is not we but our biological imperfections that will be eliminated.

It is a strange coincidence, if it is a coincidence, that at the very time in our history when so much of the mindless prejudice against persons with genetic defects has finally been rooted out that genetic engineering should engender attitudes which only serve to reinstate it. For the more capable we are of preventing genetic defects, the more difficult it becomes to tolerate them when they exist. Genetic engineering may unfortunately give rise to the potential situation in which those who escape the detection of screening, or who as a result of foetal injury, mutation or accident are born defective, will be regarded as genetic mistakes - as those who need not have been and who, in being, are somehow less human in consequence. That we today sometimes treat those born with defects as second-class humans is symptomatic of this inclination. Consider, for example, actual cases in which children with Down's syndrome, who not infrequently also suffer intestinal blockage, are refused the surgery necessary to correct the condition, a surgery which would otherwise be given unhesitatingly to so-called normal children. Professor Kass makes a similar point when he writes:

> It is ironic that we should acquire the power to detect and eliminate the genetically unequal at a time when we have finally succeeded in removing much of the stigma and disgrace previously attached to victims of congenital illness, in providing them with improved care and support, and in preventing, by means of education, feelings of guilt on the part of their parents. One might even wonder whether the development of amniocentesis and prenatal diagnosis may represent a backlash against the same humanitarian and egalitarian tendencies in the practice of medicine, which, by helping to sustain the age of reproduction . . . has itself contributed to the increasing incidence of genetic disease, and with it, to increased pressures for genetic screening genetic counselling, and genetic abortion.[13]

Kass also recognizes that the language of genetic engineering creates the mistaken impression that the afflicted foetus or person is rather than has a disease.[14] He laments justifiably that we slip far too cavalierly from the language of possession into the language of identity, from "He has haemophilia" to "He is a haemophiliac" or "The foetus has Down's syndrome" to "The foetus is a Down's". Our use of language in this connection reflects an important matter, and I have commented upon its ramifications at greater length elsewhere. [15] Suffice it to say here that inasmuch as the way in which we describe 'things' reflects our concepts of those 'things' it is clear that by identifying the person with the disease, we create the illusion of mitigating ethical responsibility by talking of the elimination of genetic defects or genetic defectives, rather than of the elimination of persons or of human beings <u>with</u> genetic defects. This is particularly interesting in respect of the case of the use of the term 'mental retardation', as its predicative attribution has become embedded grammatically as a nominative structure. It is grammatically proper, that is, to use the reference of identity "He <u>is</u> mentally retarded" in place of the grammatical impropriety "He has mental retardation". The linguistic structure tells us something about the way in which the description "mentally retarded" has come to function conceptually as a substitute for what would otherwise be recognized as a person. Once the humanitarian concepts of description are eroded, we inevitably dehumanize our ethics in no longer being able to reflect the human concerns upon which we pass judgement.

In saying this I am not of course denying the laudibility of the ostensible aims of genetic engineering in the prevention of genetic defects, at least insofar as this is not equated with the elimination of persons afflicted with such defects. This is obviously a crucial difference.[16] It should also be made clear that the concept of 'defect' is not itself a pellucid concept. Since each of us is alleged to have a minimum of between five and ten genetic defects, the objective of eliminating all defects becomes puzzling, if not decidedly disconcerting. The question of what a defect <u>is</u> and of <u>what</u> defects will be eliminated is a matter of <u>who</u> is doing the defining and the eliminating. This raises unavoidably questions of power and control and the misuse of both.

The concept of 'defect' acquires its pejorative connotation when viewed as a condition we have no wish or need to tolerate. Inasmuch as the techniques of genetic engineering would, as I earlier suggested, put us in a position technologically to have to tolerate less, progressively <u>more</u> traits would come to be regarded as defects. An IQ of 100, for example, might plausibly be viewed as a defect if we were able via recombinant DNA procedures, to increase standardly the IQ of all or most children to say, 150. The issue of the defect of the so-called 'supermale karyotype' is pertinent here. It is estimated that one out of every 800 men has an extra Y chromosome, and that although most of those who possess this XYY arrangement are law abiding, there is a better than average probability that those who possess this chromosomal arrangement will display aggressive and antisocial behavior. Could not our blind commitment to the reduction of genetic defects commit us to the foetal elimination of all those with this defect, in spite of the fact that the majority will never exhibit the criminal behavior associated with the having of the defect?

There is another approach to these questions which addresses them by enlarging the conceptual prism through which they are viewed. I earlier intimated that having engineered our world to distortion, we are now relying upon genetic engineering to distort our own being to assist our survival in a distorted world. Let me conclude this chapter by elaborating this charge further. Genetic engineering and the particular bio-ethical questions to which it gives rise are symptomatic of a much deeper social ill than our traditional treatment of the bio-ethical questions has satisfactorily brought to relief. Bio-ethical questions are traditionally articulated as personal or individualistic dilemmas which are resolved by the provision of the right answer to the dilemma, derived from a fundamental principle or principles of action. Our ethical understanding, in other words is reductionist. We reduce the problems of genetic engineering to the specific problems of individuals, and we reduce the problems of ethics to specific principles of decision. Either we act, for example, on utilitarian grounds or we do not. The entire process is encapsulated as a peculiarly ethical problem. There is a weakness in this process, and it has in part blunted our ethical appreciation of the deeper questions of value presupposed by our institutional structures, customs and life styles. In accepting the terms in which genetic engineering casts the problem of ethics, we are encouraged to narrow our focus on the factors which contribute to their immediate or short-term solution. In so doing, our attention is deflected from a consideration of the underlying framework of assumptions which underpin the human activities whose adjudication we seek. This deflection is infelicitous; for it is in the light of these assumptions and their examination that our ethical vision can be re-directed to the long, rather than short term solutions to the human problems we confront. Inasmuch as there is already a presumption in favour of the rightness of

eliminating defective genes, the issue is joined at
the level of conflicts of principle, say, between
individual and community rights.   To what extent,
for example, can the state legislate the genetic
engineering of defective foetuses?   I have no wish
to minimize the gravity of this conflict, but only
to indicate that such questions do not arise in
isolation and cannot thus be answered in isolation.
In this sense there is no such thing as an uniquely
ethical question.   Questions of ethics are also
questions about our emotions, attitudes,
institutions, and customs.   The problems of ethics
are systemic problems, and their resolution is less
a matter of juxtaposing one reductionist principle
of decision against another, as a matter of showing
the way in which conflicts of value arise out of and
are expressed by the web of values we have ourselves
created.   This is why no fundamental ethical
principle contains, or could contain, within itself
the decisional criteria for all its future
applications.   To treat it as such is to treat it
a-historically and in isolation from the web of
beliefs, institutions and customs by which it is
conditioned and defined.   'Holistic ethics', as I
shall call it, is concerned to show that the answers
to the questions of genetic engineering must be
given in terms which are more comprehensive than
those contained in the questions it raises.

In responding to the ethical problems of
genetic engineering our answers must do more than
perpetuate the conditions which gave rise to the
problems in the first place.   To reconstruct one's
genetic heritage at the level of individualized
genetic engineering is not to contribute one iota to
the eradication of the conditions which caused it.
In this sense genetic engineering is tantamount to a
palliative.

> Although the U.S. spends over $100 billion per
> year on health care, it ranks fifteenth among
> the nations of world in infant mortality and
> life expectancy.   Part of the reason for this
> lies in the fact that our health-care system is
> structured for short-term treatment of
> illnesses rather than long-term prevention of
> them.   Despite the fact that hundreds of
> reports and studies have concluded that the
> major causes of death and disease are
> preventable and related to occupation,
> environmental deterioration, nutrition,
> consumer products, and poverty, only limited

government or private funds are put into programs designed to address the problem.[17]

It is the bio-reductionist approach and the values it fosters which require challenging. To regard human beings as machines is to reduce our ethical inhibitions in respect of engineering them to ensure their efficiency and performance. As we earlier observed, it is the mechanist model that also encourages the interventionist disposition. Machines require mechanics, and the king of the mechanics is the engineer. If the problem is exposure to environmental radiation, why not alter the genetic program of humans to be radiation resistant? This is, of course, a caricature of genetic engineering, but it exaggerates only the state of the technology, not its inspiration. Herein lies the rub.

Genetic engineering is a remarkably impressive technological development. Because it is impressive, however, it has the power via the institutions that have sponsored and sustain it, to distract us from the task of making ourselves more rather than less human. By holding out the promise of genetic transformation as the panacea of our humanaity, we lose sight of the myriad ways in which our engineerings of the world have made us less human. We have exploited the lands of the earth, its waters, its plant and animals, and more recently, even its skies. To what extent our genetic defects are themselves, either in their origins or in their manifestations, partly or wholly consequent of these exploitations is a question which is, I believe, fundamental to our humanity. The time is long overdue to turn our attention to the prevention of the genetic conditions for which genetic engineering is one remedy. The laudable aim of eliminating genetic defects must surely be more than a technique for eliminating their appearances. The technoligization of our lives has done much to depersonalize and to de-sensitize our culture. In our endless efforts to reduce things and people to their smallest parts, we have lost the sense of what makes them and us whole. It is perhaps what makes us whole that makes us healthy and in turn minimizes our own defects, as well as those we bequeath in perpetuity. The technology of science may thus have transformed us into giants but little does it avail us, as I have argued elsewhere, if it leaves us as blinded giants.[18] Inasmuch as the promise of genetic reconstruction lures us from the humanistic

task of _social_ reconstruction, it functions
inevitably to dehumanise us even further. In the
end, the task of social reconstruction must be seen
to be less a matter of trying to turn back the hands
of the clock, than a matter of trying to make better
use of our time.

NOTES

1.   Galileo, C., Discoveries and Opinions of
        Galileo, Drake S. (Tr. and Ed.), Anchor, 1957,
        particularly 64ff.
2.   Singer, C. & Underwood, E.A., A Short History
        of Medicine (Oxford: Oxford Univ. Press, 1962)
        pp.113-15; see also Capra, F., The Turning
        Point, London: Flamingo, 1983, pp.39-40.
3.   Descartes, R., Philosophical Works, (Tr. and
        Ed.) Haldance, E.S., & Ross, G.R.T.,
        (Cambridge: C.U.P., 1931) particularly his
        "Discourse on Method".
4.   Capra, The Turning Point, p.45.
5.   Howard, T. & Rifkin, J., Who Should Play God?
        New York: Dell, 1980, p.24.
6.   For a concise and clear account of these
        matters see Bartels, D., "The Uses of in vitro
        Human Embryos: Can the Public Participate in
        Decision Making?", Search, Vol.14, No.9-10,
        October/November 1983, pp.257-62.
7.   Hayes, S.C. & Hayes, R., Mental Retardation:
        Law, Policy and Administration, Sydney: The
        Law Book Company Ltd., 1982, pp.28-29.
8.   Bartels, "The Uses of in vitro Human Embryos:
        Can the Public Participate in Decision
        Making?", p.257.
9.   See Pouledge, T.M., "You Shall Be As Gods -
        Recombinant DNA: The Immediate Issue is
        Safety; The Ultimate Issue is Human Destiny",
        Biomedical Ethics, ed. by T.A. Mappes & J.S.
        Zembaty, New York: McGraw-Hill, p.498.
10.   Stich, S.P. "The Recombinant DNA Debate", In M.
        Cohen, T. Nagel, & T. Scanlon (Eds.), Medicine
        and Moral Philosophy, Princeton: Princeton
        Univ. Press, 1981, p.171.
11.   Fletcher, J. "Wild Talk Warnings Galore, and
        Cloning", in Biomedical Ethics, p.496.
12.   Ibid., p.495.
13.   Kass, L.R. "Implications of Prenatal Diagnosis
        for the Human Right to Life", in Biomedical
        Ethics, p.466.
14.   Ibid, p.467.

206

15. See the Introduction to my anthology, <u>The Impossible Takes a Little Longer</u>, Canberra: Commonwealth Press, 1982.
16. I have elaborated this point in "Do the Mentally Retarded Have a Right to Reproduce?" with A. Gazzard in my anthology <u>Problems of Handicap</u>, Melbourne: Macmillan, 1980, pp.156-66.
17. Howard & Rifkin, <u>Who Should Play God</u>?, p.217.
18. See my "Philosophical Foundations of Science Education", <u>Educational Philosophy and Theory</u>, January 1981, pp.1-13.

Chapter Eleven

RIGHTS, INTERESTS, AND MENTAL HANDICAP

Ronald S. Laura and Adrian F. Ashman

Biomedical science has exerted an enormous
impact upon contemporary society and has, by way of
its development and application, raised a range of
ethical issues for which we have not been prepared.
The advent of highly innovative life-support systems
has made it possible to maintain the lives of
individiuals who, given the gravity of their
defects, would perhaps have otherwise died. We have
in almost every chapter of this book seen that
society has been confounded ethically by
technological achievement and the success it enjoys
in transforming virtually every aspect of our lives.
    The result of technological success is
manifold, and it is no part of our purpose here to
enumerate its diverse manifestations. Suffice to
say that technological achievement has engendered a
cadre of ethical considerations beyond all previous
contemplation. The very concepts of 'life' and
'death' are in turmoil.
    Herein lies the problem. Technology has made
it possible to prolong life, but 'living matter' is
a necessary, not a sufficient condition of 'personhood'. Technological innovation has also made it
possible to overlook this fact. There was a time
when the concept of death was demarcated by the
cessation of life-functions. Now we have mechanical
devices capable of sustaining some functions but not
others. Given that we maintain all life-functions
with the exception of consciousness, for instance,
does it follow that we have saved the life of a
'person'? Or have we simply succeeded in
maintaining 'living matter' embodied in a human
form?
    It is questions such as the foregoing that have
obliged our reflection on the very concepts that
would once have seemed fundamental: 'life',

'death', 'person', 'human being', 'living matter', and so on. The way in which we resolve these questions affects the way in which we resolve our ethical future; whether we destroy humanity or enhance it.

While the profoundly and irreparably retarded are human beings (members of the species <u>homo sapiens</u>), does it follow, for example, that they are 'persons'? Do they have a right to life? If so, do they have a right to whatever medical resources they need to enjoy their right to life? Do they have a right to more of these resources than do so-called 'normal persons'? In this book we have seen philosophers puzzle over these questions, providing a range of different answers for our consideration. If we are to know where we are heading, as a society and as a world, such questions are among the most important questions of our time.

It is only by having a clear idea of the value of life, or perhaps as we have seen, of different kinds of life, that we can give perspective to the Biogenetic Revolution now confronting us. If genetic engineering provides the bio-mechanical means for the elimination of the genetic diseases which lead to mental retardation, why not deploy its techniques to this end? If genetic engineering techniques can be employed to prevent the birth of children with low IQs, why should it not be used to ensure the birth of children with high IQs? Why set up sperm banks to which only Nobel Prize Winners can contribute their genetic heritage, instead of cloning the Nobel Prize Winners themselves? Should the sex, race or height of a child be left to chance, determined by parents, or legislated by governments? Just who should be born? After all, given finite resources or as many would argue, diminishing resources, coupled with rampant population growth, is it not encumbent on the State to deliberate on just such matters? If so, is a cost benefit analysis the form such deliberations should take? Again, we believe that these are among the most important questions and issues of our times, and we have in this book endeavoured to have them aired.

In conclusion, there is one final point we should like to explore. We have been suggesting that the relation between ethics and technology has traditionally been one in which ethics is always trying to catch up, so to say, with technology. Technology poses a morally unreferenced set of social circumstances, and ethics provides a particular way of responding to it. Couched in the terms in which this picture is presented however, is a deeper truth that the picture relies upon but does not directly show. In a sense technology has served not only to transform our environment but in some cases to inure us to the radical nature of its transformations. Consider, for a moment, the role which <u>pain</u> plays in the protection of the human organism. Pain is not something we like to have, but the having of a pain is usually the way in which our body tells us that something is wrong. It is clear that the invention of the aspirin interfered with this process. If we have a headache, we tend to ask ourselves where we can obtain an aspirin, not whether we should eat more wholesome food or exercise more regularly, or change our stressful lives.

Similarly, the range of application of surgical techniques was originally checked by the natural inability of the human organism to suffer the pain of surgery, in addition to the pain or condition of defect the surgery was intended to correct. By its very intrusive nature, the procedures of surgery had to be regarded medically as a last resort. The nature of the human organism thus conditioned the applicability of the procedure, functioning as a control mechanism of the role played by surgery as a therapeutic technique within medicine. It was not long, however, until further technological developments within medicine yielded the means, in the form of anaesthetics, to undermine the natural defences of the body against the intrusion of surgery. We are not, of course, suggesting that surgery is in itself a bad thing, though the extent to which it has become commonplace in our culture may well have little to recommend it. The immediate point is that technology has, by dint of its own intervention, inured us to the fact that it is an intervention.

In respect of the bioethical issues which constitute much of the subject matter of this book, the question of the intervention of technology in the treatment of the mentally retarded is itself a fundamental ethical question. In much the same way that medicine has become technologized, so bioethics has incorporated a presumption in favour of medical technology. In essence, bioethics has covertly been subsumed as part of the technological processes and procedures of medicine to which we have come inured. That is why consent to the technological procedure of amniocentesis is, on the part of the woman

211

involved, construed as tacit consent to abortion, should the foetus be found defective. What has happened is that we have unwittingly recast morality in terms of the technology of medicine, and in so doing, we have exploited the coercive power of medicine in the making of moral decisions. For the medical judgement that a foetus is abnormal is tantamount impliciitly to an ethical judgement regarding the value of its birth.

Indeed, as we have tried to show in several chapters throughout this book, there are legitimate ethical questions to be asked about the propriety of knowingly bringing into this world a child with profound mental disabilities, but these are not questions whose answers are to be expressed simply in the terms of development of interventionist technologies which make it progressively easier to detect and to prevent such births.